e Unfinished Dream

MERCER UNIVERSITY PRE

Endowed by

TOM WATSON BROWN
and
THE WATSON-BROWN FOUNDATION,

Contents

Dedicated to

Reverend Dr. Kelly Miller Smith Sr. (1920–1984)

The Honorable John Lewis (1940–2020)

Reverend Dr. Cordy Tindell (C. T.) Vivian (1924–2020)

Reverend Dr. Julius R. Scruggs (1942–2024)

Dr. James Lawson (1928-2024)

Acknowledgments

My deepest appreciation is extended to all the contributors involved in developing this volume of essays honoring Dr. Forrest E. Harris. As any book editor knows, editing a book is a team effort. It takes players with a collaborative spirit to bring an idea to full fruition—to bring home the victory.

Mary Carpenter, Executive Assistant to the President, was invaluable in managing the many details involved in acquiring author contributions and keeping in touch with all respective authors throughout the development of this publication.

Dr. Forrest E. Harris is president of American Baptist College (formerly known as American Baptist Theological Seminary) and Director of The Kelly Miller Smith Institute on Black Church Studies at Vanderbilt University. Nevertheless, he unselfishly devoted complete cooperation to this project. Working with us at every phase, Dr. Harris demonstrated a spirit of humility and appreciation. He continually hoped that this publication would become more about the College and The Kelly Miller Smith Institute than himself.

I am extremely grateful to Dr. Harris for his invaluable recommendation of Jean Reynolds, a meticulous Nashville author and editor, who edited these essays before final submission to Dr. Marc Jolley at Mercer University Press. Dr. Jolley's crucial expertise and dedication shaped the final version of this publication.

Marc Jolley was receptive to publishing this book of essays honoring Dr. Harris. We appreciate Marc's willingness to ensure the finalization of the publication in time for American Baptist College's Centennial Celebration in October 2024. The editors at Mercer University Press were professionally instrumental in making this publication possible.

We also acknowledge and appreciate the gracious communications assistance provided by Marsha Luttrell, Dr. Marc Jolley's assistant, along with expressions of deep gratitude to Brad Ost and Regina Prude for their editorial readings of the final draft.

I cherish the memories of those Black religious leaders chronicled in the archives of history and laid to rest in the cemeteries within the formerly identified Confederate slave-holding states. Many of these individuals remain anonymous.

I am deeply indebted to my dear wife, Natasha Coby Earl, who supported my work at every turn. I give special thanks to her and our children, Ariane and King, who sacrificially gave space and time for me to devote attention to this volume.

Finally, I take responsibility for whatever errors may appear in the final presentation of this book.

Foreword

Leadership became a "thing" in religious administration circles with the arrival of Ken Blanchard and Spencer Johnson's book *The One Minute Manager* in 1982. Pastors and other church professionals began to translate the three techniques of Blanchard and Johnson—one-minute goals, one-minute praisings, and one-minute reprimands—into church speak. *The One Minute Manager* went on to spark a veritable cottage industry of management books that were read and used in various religious gatherings and eventually led Blanchard to focus on leadership and the spiritual life through the lens of the one-minute manager.

This, I recall, set the stage for the enthusiastic reception of Stephen R. Covey's *The 7 Habits of Highly Effective People* in 1990. Many church professionals, not only preachers, translated Covey's seven habits—be proactive; begin with the end in mind; put first things first; think win-win; seek first to understand, then to be understood; synergize; and sharpen the saw—into sermons, church mission plans, spiritual direction, religious education programs, and more.

These more secular books, with their commonsense approach to managing people and oneself, are still in print and in use. However, they have faded from the enthusiastic and, at one point, overwhelming use they prompted from holy pulpits when they first arrived. There are many reasons for this, I believe, but the chief one, for me, is the very reason that this book highlights the impact of the black leadership tradition on the academy, the church, and the community. When I look at the realities that black life in our communities brings inside black churches, something is missing, and ultimately our churches are not hitting the deep soul notes of the questions these realities prompt. These demands of church leaders require more than a list that must constantly be adapted because of the exigencies of what it means to live one's life, no matter how richly or poorly one may be situated, with the ongoing threat of a demonic oppressive matrix made up of classism, heterosexism, sexism, transphobia, racism, and more, which eventually traps black, brown, beige, and gendered bodies.

That missing something is what I call the spiritual soul of black leadership models and styles. This is the foundation for the ways in which the authors of the essays in this book approach their work. The spiritual soul of leadership helps us realize that we must take responsibility for the ways in which we shape the institutions in our communities. This is wrapped up with our lived experience of faith that is embodied in people and found in the concrete contexts in which people are living out their faith. Thus, it is grounded in the context of struggling for faith and justice and takes on antagonistic dualism—such as sacred or profane, black or white, rich or poor, progressive or conservative—as unhealthy in many places in our faith journeys.

The goal is both individual and communal wholeness through integrating faith and life. It is not so much that the two popular books I began with, when adapted by church folk, do not care about or address this integration; it is more about taking into rigorous account the context that many, if not most, black folk live in. We are constantly having to argue our worth and value in a world—and, unfortunately, in our religious households—that we are made in God's image (that forms the very fabric of our existence—immanent and transcendent) and that God's love for us is unconditional. In short, we matter, and, in this dark mattering, we are called to live our lives out of the possibilities and not our shortcomings as we answer "Yes" to God's "What if?"

This divine/human community is based on love and hope and is pointed toward justice. This book guides the reader into three areas that reflect this justice call and are emblematic of the black leadership tradition: education, religion, and public policy. The spiritual soul of leadership evidenced in this volume listens for and hears the word of God's call for black leaders to answer the need to take on the responsibility of leadership that meets black folks in our everyday human struggle against the structural and systematic racism that is wrapped in plantation capitalism, sexism, heterosexism, transphobia, ableism, ageism, and more in a society that seems determined to denounce its democratic roots in favor of a mean-spirited oligarchy. We are in a time that is demanding that we think with as much faith and precision as possible about what leadership models will set us free and also benefit the rest of society, if not all of creation.

The spiritual soul of leadership must encompass all of life as we seek leadership styles that proclaim the dignity of black lives in the ongoing call to live in a vibrant hope with righteous agency as we step out and guide others on their journeys, even as we are discovering our own. This is an embodied, personal, and communal understanding of leadership that brings together the historic force of black folks' spiritual lives with the demand of the Spirit to contextualize and live one's faith. It is a reflection on the particularity of one's own faith journey that lives and unfolds into communities. It is liberation.

The movement, the passion for liberating leadership, comes in a variety of sounds and textures. Too often we suffer and forfeit our lives through the silences that muzzle and stifle us or through a warped sense of tradition as hegemonic rather than tradition as reminder of the dreams and hopes for a vision of our passages into wholeness. It is, indeed, a terrible thing to lose one's voice to the demons of self-hatred, horizontal violence, and a vision of one—and we are the only one. As the authors show, it is deadly to never find our voices because we model our ministries and our witness after styles that are not who we are or fashions and models that only channel our gifts and abilities into a small and narrow space in our souls. Hence, we lose the vitality and hope we learned in Sunday school, prayer meetings, Wednesday night Bible studies, all those chicken dinners and fish fries, and just sitting in the presence of the Spirit.

So, it is tragic when we fail to recognize this leadership in another tone or perhaps in a different octave. It is important to recognize that, as much as we have good things to provide with vibrant leadership, it is also true that silencing and voicing are deadly marrow for traditions that constrain our growth while proclaiming, what I would term, false orthodoxy. We must listen closely through our expectations and categories to hear *God's* call to us to join the Holy Spirit in creation and to move away from a crabs-in-a-bucket leadership style that cannot see that we exist and have our ministries in the great expanse of creation itself with no limits on where we can be planted to grow ministries that lead folk to a deeper and richer relationship with God and with each other. We must be vigilant because our categories of reflection and mission can run roughshod over the subtleties of the Gospel and the kind of faith-filled witness to which we each are called.

From where I sit as a theological school administrator, minister, and womanist Christian social ethicist, I am heartened that the essays in this book invite us to take up the challenge that our seminaries and divinity schools and our churches need new visions that may be shaped from old dreams—but perhaps these are not the dreams that can lead us into the present and future we are facing. Simply put, we cannot keep doing it the way it has always been done and believe that we are doing the work of God or calling this leadership and that a just and whole kingdom will come.

God's revelation is ongoing—it is relentless in its desire to bring in a new heaven and a new earth. Liberating leadership knows that genuine salvation does not refuse to hear the different voices and tones of God's work in our worlds such that we seek to conform to (in)human simulations of leading. No, we must be engaged in the loud work of a multiplicity of voices in which the keys are *not* meant to blend but the ruckus stands as a sign of movement and hope.

Black leadership must take a whole new look at what it means for any of us to refuse to be cannon fodder for a bureaucracy—ecclesial or secular—that declares its holiness or its scholarliness or its relevance while colleagues engage in mind-numbing, studious, lint-picking from their scholastic navels while some white male academics rail on about how cisgendered white men cannot find jobs and then look at those of us who are not cisgendered white men as if we should dignify such inane chatter. Or while students call out for practical skills for ministry and some of us immediately assume that they are trying to avoid "the real" courses in the curriculum.

The spiritual soul of black leadership models, as represented in this book, dare transformation by challenging us to live into a new vision of what it means to be ministers—lay and ordained, academicians and church-based, agency oriented and denominational—to a word and a grace that is amazing. We ask tough questions of ourselves and our churches and our academic institutions and our ministries about just how faithful we are being when there is a whole laundry list of things that we *cannot* talk about in many of our churches and seminaries, and that list is made up of people's lives and people's questions—their joys, their fears, their hearts and souls—and we somehow deem this as nasty or worldly or evil. We should be ashamed of ourselves and the not-so-sacred spaces we create when we do this.

Truth-filled black leadership styles tell us that love, faith, hope, and justice are found by unpacking the Gospel *into* living. Yes, there are many leadership models out there, but to take them on without asking the basic questions of how we craft in ourselves and others what holy and abiding witness looks like and must be in our lives, now and into the future, is an exercise in obsequious sycophancy at best and an ill-conceived orthodoxy at worst.

The authors (and I join them) do not argue for a style of leadership that simply exchanges one kind of oppression for another while it continues to suppress and oppress all of us and holds the church back from being a living witness to God's work in the world. We must not offer others (and settle for ourselves) a partial Gospel of muffled success, flawed strategies, and a ministry that is dying— if not already dead.

This book invites you, the reader, to stretch into *your* ministry— discover anew what leadership can and must mean when it is grounded in grace rather than solely on the latest business model of success. Instead, heed the call to walk around in the possibilities of a leadership that widens the circle for others to find a place and space that lives into God's grace and then invites others to join us. Sit down and play with the holy sand that God has given each of us, for who you are is a gift and what *your* ministry, *your* sense of being with and guiding others, *your* sense of lifting as you climb, *your* leadership style sits on the rim bones of glory.

The contributors of this volume approach the rich proving ground of the spiritual soul of black leadership models and styles by focusing on identity, situations, and visions. They encourage us to follow them into leadership alternatives and paradigm shifts that break out of the old molds that we have found ourselves in that may have been liberatory in earlier eras but the even more deeply entrenched forms of hatred that color our landscape demand new ways to lead and to follow. The business of God's ongoing revelation demands that we provide new, fresh models of transformation in life and living.

We must join them.

Emilie M. Townes
University Distinguished Professor of
Womanist Ethics and Society and
Gender and Sexuality Studies
Vanderbilt Divinity School
and Vanderbilt University
Nashville, 2024

Introduction

Riggins R. Earl Jr., PhD

What Martin L. King Jr. and John Lewis called the "beloved community" has been, and still is, the unfinished dream of the Black religious leadership tradition (BRLT). That tradition started in the nightmare of slavery. It has been kept alive in Black people by their ancestors' Jesus Spirit of faith, hope, and love.

Several questions arose when we solicited article writers for this publication honoring Forrest Harris's stellar career in theological education. These questions stemmed from our exploration of what constitutes the BRLT and its relationship with the White Protestant Religious Leadership Tradition (WPRLT). Many responses to these queries presume some awareness of the religious narratives of the Black Atlantic world and the intersections between the church and the academy.

During his illustrious career, Forrest Harris pastored in the Black church and taught in the academy. He has stood in the leadership gap that had been trodden by recognized predecessors such as the late Drs. Benjamin E. Mays, Samuel D. Proctor, Mordecai Johnson, and Mary McCleod Bethune. He and William Myers, a contemporary of his who has an article in this collection, have maintained that leadership tradition to some degree in this generation. Harris has stood faithfully in the leadership gap between the Black church and the academy. He continues to pedagogically and administratively symbolize the best of the Black leadership tradition.

Forrest Harris began his professional clergy journey as the pastor at Oak Valley Baptist Church in Oak Ridge, Tennessee, and concluded it at the Pleasant Green Baptist Church in Nashville, Tennessee. Harris resigned his pastorate to assume directorship of the newly launched Kelly Miller Smith Institute on Black Church

Studies at the Vanderbilt University Divinity School in Nashville. As the director of the institute, Harris has been able to focus on the study of the leadership tradition of the Black church—thanks, in part, to his keen understanding of the white Protestant religious leadership tradition. In this administrative role, Harris has drawn upon both the best of the BRLT and the WPRLT of America to teach religious leadership in the academy and the Black church.

Harris assumed the task of academically introducing the Black and the white Protestant religious leadership traditions of students and church leaders to a) America's white Protestant religious leadership tradition and b) America's Black Protestant religious leadership tradition. The descendants of enslavers shaped the first relationship, and the enslaved formed the latter. In some ways, these traditions are distinctly different in creation and mission, yet they are similar in other ways. When explored in the South, these religious leadership traditions provoke several major questions: 1) What is the WPRLT in relationship to race relations? 2) What is the BRLT in relationship to race relations? And 3) what are the similarities and dissimilarities, if any, of each tradition respectively? Harris' professional career of working jointly between Vanderbilt Divinity School and American Baptist College provides a textbook case in theological education and Black religious leadership.

Harris and the White Protestant Religious Leadership Tradition (WPRLT)

The conflicted history of race and the divinity school is best delineated in *Vanderbilt Divinity School: Education, Contest, and Change.*[1] It must be in the foreground of any discussion regarding Harris' major leadership contributions. The two most insightful articles in said source for understanding the context and complexities of Harris' work are by Joseph C. Hough Jr.[2] and Peter Paris[3]. Hough served as the divinity school's dean, and Paris served on the faculty.

Hough's article "Theological Studies in the Context of the University" illuminates the evolution of Vanderbilt University, and its divinity school from a parochial Southern space to a national one. He illustrates how the divinity school rose to national and international visibility by embracing the enlightenment model of theological education. Hough notes how the divinity school's ethic of programmatic cooperation with major Protestant church constituencies reshaped its character from the early days of its founding. That ethic was prophetically expressed by those who challenged its lack of gender and ethnic diversity.

The Kelly Miller Smith Institute was established in 1985 to promote educational opportunities for leaders in the black churches."[4] The Institute honors the legacy of the late Kelly Miller Smith, Sr., who served as assistant dean of the Vanderbilt Divinity School from 1968 until his death in 1984. Under Hough's administrative leadership, endowment funds were acquired to strengthen this project. Forrest Harris was hired as director of the Kelly Miller Smith Institute in 1988.[5]

Less than ten years later, Harris became president of American Baptist College. This assignment of being the leader of both programs empowered Harris in the Black church and academies. Paris reflects in his article that this joint relationship is important because of American Baptist College's stellar history of producing premier leadership for the Black church in the civil rights struggle in Nashville.[6] The core of this same leadership went on to work on Dr. King's staff. Paris rightly notes that Harris had been a student of both Kelly Miller Smith and himself. Of note, Kelly Miller Smith had been a homiletics professor at American Baptist College before joining the divinity school administration part time. Smith taught and bonded with students such as John Lewis, C. T. Vivian, and James Bevel. James Lawson, a pivotal figure in the civil rights movement, trained many of these students in civil disobedience at the church pastored by Kelly Miller Smith, Sr.—First Baptist Church of Nashville. This church, now known as First Baptist Church-Capitol Hill, witnessed the transformation of these students into leaders of the civil rights movement, marking a significant chapter in history.

In the basement of Smith's church, James Lawson became the new moral guru of the young college and seminary generation by providing workshops on Martin Luther King Jr.'s. philosophy of nonviolent protest. Lawson's teachings precipitated a social crisis that forged a new moral frontier of radical Black leadership. Lawson introduced the participating Vanderbilt Divinity School and American Baptist College students to his uncompromising sit-in tactics and a different frontier of high-risk faith and moral practices.

Both groups of students were influenced by Paul's radical proclamation of virtues, which consisted of faith, hope, and love (1 Corinthians 13:13, Revised Standard Version). The protest movement challenged its participants to rethink what voluntary suffering in the name of Jesus Christ meant. Even some white student observers of that era stood to be morally influenced by the lessons of disobedience being taught and practiced in the streets and the jailhouse of Nashville. A new moral frontier of the BRLT was emerging as Black religious leaders extended their hand for cooperation with white ones. This was done in the face of hostile moral spaces.[7]

Hostile Moral Spaces, Nashville's Streets, and Its Jail

Downtown Nashville's streets and its jailhouse, commonly seen by the upper class as the dwelling place for deviants and beggars, were transformed into places of protest for social justice. Young Black religious leaders such as John Lewis and Diane Nash emerged with the Spirit of faith, hope, and love out of the Nashville streets and jailhouse. The BRLT's Jesus' Spirit of faith, hope, and love became flesh in a young generation of Black religious protest leaders. They rocked the streets and jailhouses with these virtues as their mantra.

Nashville's streets and its jail became the places where Black religious leaders taught their ancestors' Spirit of Jesus' mantra of faith, hope, and love. Here they applied new methods of knowing, being, and doing in relationship to the oppressor. From these hostile places a new type of Black leadership emerged. Nashville's streets and its jail provided an alien seminar context for theological education, allowing for a marriage between theory and praxis. Forrest Harris would make the study of theory and praxis of theological education the focus of the Kelly Miller Smith Institute and American Baptist College.

New challenges for Black religious leadership, beginning with enslavement, were born out of encounters that took place in what became strange and hostile public spaces in Nashville. The city's nonviolent sit-ins provided a chance for students of American Baptist College and other Black schools to share with white students' new spaces of knowing, being, and doing. In conjunction with the sit-ins, the Lawson case challenged the Vanderbilt Divinity School to a new theological horizon in race relations. These events produced moral shock therapy for the schools, the city of Nashville, and the nation. These nonviolent actions created a strange tension between elder leaders of the BRLT and young Black students aspiring for leadership. Under the mantra of faith, hope, and love, a youthful generation contributed to transforming a city in race relations. Black preachers—who were masters at dramatizing, from their pulpits, the biblical story of Daniel in the lions' den—often lacked the courage to display nonviolently these principles in the same streets for fear of violent retaliation by the white population.

In the face of violent attacks and threats, this new frontier of the BRLT was born out of the courage of young Black religious leaders and their faithfulness to their ancestors' Spirit of Jesus. They demonstrated the courage to be hopeful in the face of hopelessness and to love in the face of the unlovable. The nonviolent sit-in movement, a hybridization of the Gandhian and Jesus philosophies and method, forged a radically new frontier of the BRLT. During enslavement, the BRLT was transformed by young Black individuals' nonviolent spirit of Jesus that was conjured up by the Black community of faith, hope, and love. We had heard, felt, and seen our elders dramatize the Jesus story via the ritual of sing-

5

ing, praying, and preaching. We publicly displayed in city streets the incarnate Spirit of Jesus' love, hope, and faith in our personage.

Forrest Harris academically engaged the BRLT, making it pedagogically foundational for the growth and development of the Kelly Miller Smith Institute. The mission of the Institute has been that of researching and teaching the BRLT as a normative for understanding the Black church tradition.[8] The student leadership that emerged from the campus of the American Baptist College symbolizes the genesis of the public display of that tradition for the Black church and America.

Harris's leadership ability to waltz between American Baptist College and the Kelly Miller Smith Institute models a new frontier of the BRLT. It brings the Black church, which was less than marginal in the social order, into mainline theological education. This leadership gives Black people a modicum of respect for their own BRLT. Before the Black Church Studies program at Vanderbilt Divinity School, Black social scientists were the only ones to research and write about the Black church.[9]

The Best of Two Religious Leadership Traditions

Forrest Harris deserves credit for working within and between these two educational institutions in Nashville. Both institutions embedded the best of the BRLT and the WPRLT in their narratives. As products of American enslavement and racism, select leaders from both institutions struggled to institutionalize the quest for the common good in race relations.

The white elitist religious leadership tradition was embedded in the making and operating of Vanderbilt University and its divinity school. As noted above, Vanderbilt Divinity School symbolized the institutional making of a rather conservative white Protestant leadership tradition. Richard C. Goode's article "A School for Prophets of the New South" best illuminates this fact. Most instructive is his scholarly treatment of the earlier leaders of the Divinity School in the latter part of the nineteenth century.

Goode notes how the faculty and administrative leaders in that period primarily became victims of the normative South's civilization. Alva Taylor and others found themselves interpreting Christianity for to accommodate the white Southern elite. Taylor has been dubbed the Divinity School's constructive critical thinker of Southern civilization:

> Taylor's version threatened to alienate the School of Religion from the surrounding society—the heart of recruiting and fund raising. Although he lasted only eight years, in some ways Taylor foreshadowed the prophetic understanding that would define the Divinity School's mission in the latter half of the twentieth century. More iconoclastic, more antagonistic, toward the New South, The Divinity School since 1960 has trained ministers and theologians to challenge prophetically southern society's assumptions on matters of race, gender, sexual orientation, and economic class.[10]

James Lawson recognized the invaluable leadership contributions of such students as John Lewis, C. T. Vivian, James Bevel, Julius Scruggs, and Bernard Lafayette from American Baptist College. Lawson made this observation in his eulogy of Lewis at the Ebenezer Baptist Church of Atlanta. American Baptist College was jointly founded by and operated by Black and white Baptist leaders to educate Black church leaders. The common idea was that Black leaders were expected to preach a gospel of respectability to their people. They were expected to preach such a gospel while living with the white man's definition of being "a good Negro." Students at the college, primarily from poor backgrounds, were expected to be priests for his people, binding up the wounds of their broken and bruised souls. Students at this little school dared defy the Southern ethos of segregation when it came to studying the Bible.

Here, students of what was called "the Holy Hill" formed their own ethnic hermeneutic, informed by their Black ancestral folk heritage. This heritage was discernable in chapel services, where some of us heard the difference between the way that the Black preacher interpreted the Scriptures versus the white preacher's interpretation. The Black preacher relied upon the oral canon of the Black folk religious tradition, which required that he/she musicalize the scriptural interpretations handed down from white preachers. The white preacher generally cited commentary sources produced by their own scholars.

An Institutional Symbol of the New BRLT

American Baptist College has stood on the east side of the city of Nashville, opposite Vanderbilt's location in the west end of the city, for a century. American Baptist College was built to educate the pariahs' class of the BRLT. The pariah class, made up of the descendants of former field hands and the children of sharecroppers, were generally called to preach without a formal education. Perched atop the rocky bluff bordering the Cumberland River flowing below, American Baptist College is mounted above the flowing body of water that had been used to transport and trade enslaved Africans. This natural resource was used to create the second largest slave port in the Volunteer State. Selling enslaved Africans was Nashville's first and most lucrative big business.[11]

Less than three generations following slavery, descendants of enslavers and those of the enslaved covenanted to build a school to educate the latter. Many avoided the painful question: was the school built to educate the enslaved descendants in the white man's theological proclamation of salvation only through the blood of Jesus? The language of liberation that came from the mouths of Black people was deemed offensive to white ears. White preachers and teachers taught Black individuals that salvation was, in their theological interpretation of suffering, a presumed salvific virtue. Such theological belief implied that Black people, having been brought from Africa minus Jesus, were victims of their own innate ignorance. Black preachers were expected to believe in this neo-enslavers' view of Christianity. This type of preaching intended to keep the Black population in the muck and mire of poverty and ignorance. It made Blackness synonymous with poverty and sin. It stood antithetical to the sermonic proclamation of the sit-in movement of the BRLT.

The Sit-in Movement and the BRLT

The theological and ethical relationship between the sit-in movement and the Black religious leadership tradition remains a haunting question. More than thirty years following the founding of the college, students like Lewis, Scruggs, Vivian, Bevel, Lafayette, and I all entered the school after hearing the call to preach from different social and geographical locations. These newly located sermonic preachments became an embodied presence of the Spirit of Jesus that Nashville was beginning to see and hear. Nashville was being awakened to a new version of the BRLT. It was a leadership transforming young Black religious leaders from pulpit orators to social catalysts for racial justice.

White churchgoers in Nashville were openly offended by our embodied sermonic intrusion into the city's streets in the name of Jesus' love. Writers of this movement would come to discover in its participants a spiritual energy that transcended white violence. Few understood that a public rebirth of the Black ancestors' Spirit of Jesus was being reborn and displayed in the public square of the city. The Spirit empowered a young generation to be receptive to Lawson's teachings on the method of nonviolence and the movement of the Spirit.

Some white individuals who have written about leaders such as Lewis and Vivian have made it appear that the Black students from American Baptist College were enamored with Lawson because of his pre-dismissal affiliation with Vanderbilt Divinity School. Not enough has been said about the Jesus Spirit of receptivity that they brought to Lawson. The Black community also risked of thinking that the name "Vanderbilt" gave prestige to Lawson's civil disobedience. The question is: was it not the Spirit of Jesus, mediated through their ancestors, that made many Black individuals receptive to Lawson's teachings of nonviolent resistance? The nonviolent sit-in movement introduced the Vanderbilt community and the larger white community to the Spirit of Jesus that was particular to Black ancestors, especially by way of Black students from American Baptist College. It was the Spirit of Jesus that created a longing for the "beloved community."

Harris as a Synergist of the BRLT and WPRLT

As president of American Baptist College and director of the Kelly Miller Smith Institute, Forrest Harris has extracted the best of the principles from these two institutions. In doing so, his contribution has illuminated our understanding of both the BRLT and the WPRLT, helping us to see why both pedagogical communities need each other.

The articles of this publication, by both young and seasoned scholars, better illuminate the importance of the BRLT. Some of these authors have taught, researched, written, and published from the social location of the theological seminary for years. They have seen that the possible fulfillment of the unfinished dream of the BRLT, at times, looks like a nightmare. There is a strand of the WPRLT that continues to support the oppression of the Black community in the name of Jesus. Despite this despairing reality, the study of the work of Forrest Harris's contributions keeps hope alive. As is the case despite the wilting life of both the Black church and the seminary.

I hope that these writings will inspire more Black academics to research, write, and publish on this subject. I also hope that Black church leaders will come and build an institutional bridge between the theological academy, the Black church, its pew, and the pulpit. May this edited volume bring us closer to realizing the beloved community that is foundational to finishing the unfinished dream of the Black religious leadership tradition.

Chapter 1

The Genesis and Making of the Black Preacher: The Betwixt and Between[1]

Riggins R. Earl, Jr.

Introduction

The genesis and the making of the black preacher must be seen in part as the white enslavers' church's troubling legacy to the Black community and the world. It is a complex phenomenon, born out of the polarized religious and ethical needs of both the enslaver and the enslaved. The following types are explicit and implicit in the literature: the parrot-preacher[2], the prophetic-preacher, the folk-preacher, the educator-preacher, and the holistic-preacher. The enslaver's church had no intention of producing the prophetic, folk, educator, or holistic types.

How could the Black preacher simultaneously be a parrot of two masters, his enslaver and his enslaved people? How could he become a liberating voice for his own people while his enslaved self concurrently experienced subjugation to his enslaver's weaponized interpretation of Jesus for the oppressed? As another aspect of the parrot-preacher type, the prophetic-preacher highlights this essential polarization during slavery in America.[3]

The Civil War, for Black America, became God's cataclysmic event for the making of the distinctly separate Black folk-preacher and Black educator-preacher, a later-determined false duality. The Black educator-preacher taught and preached Jesus as enlightener, reconciler, and apocalyptic liberator. The Black folk-preacher preached the mysteries of otherworldliness, of Jesus as healer, sustainer, and apocalyptic liberator. These four types—parrot, prophetic, folk, and educator—must be seen as necessary and ultimately inseparable for understanding the Black preacher as a holistic and complex religious, political, and moral phenomenon.[4]

There is very little literature on the scholarly interpretation of the genesis and making of the Black preacher[5] even though they have long been considered pivotal figures in Black America's religious, social, political, and moral development. She/he[6] stood in the gap between the enslaved and the enslaver, between God and the Devil, between heaven and earth, between slavery and freedom, between time and eternity. The enslaver made the Black preacher a parrot-preacher subject to the white preacher's interpretation of Jesus and the Bible. He was to parrot his enslaver's interpretation of Jesus to the enslaved community. This parroting occurred in the segregated balcony of the enslaver's church.

In contradistinction to the segregated balcony experience, enslaved worshipers secretly called each other to worship in the plantation brush harbors. They expected the parrot-preacher, when in the brush harbor, to be a seer, i.e., a prophet of hope within the veil of darkness, thus allowing for the revelation of the prophetic-preacher in this new time and place. Denied the Bible, the prophetic preacher was to rely on the guidance of the Spirit for interpreting sacred mysteries. Called by her enslaved community, she functioned between the master's segregated balcony worship time and the enslaved community's secret brush harbor worship time.

These different worship times and places produced, in certain Black individuals, a robust appetite for the mysterious.[7] The different views of worship *times* and *places* illuminate the genesis and the making of the Black preacher. How did the Black preacher emerge as a religious and moral leader without becoming enslaved to the enslaver's racist interpretation of Jesus? This is a difficult question. The answers lie between the balcony of the white enslaver's church and the enslaved's secret brush harbor, between chattel slavery in America and Black Reconstruction, between newly built edifices and the streets of a racist America, between Post-Black Reconstruction and the Civil Rights Movement. At best, we must view the Black preacher as a liminal figure, hermeneutically caught in the betwixt and the between.[8]

The Parrot-Preacher, the Prophetic-Preacher: Between the Balcony and the Brush Harbor

Enslavers built balconies and galleries in their churches for the purpose of keeping the Black preacher on the leash of white paternalism. In the church balcony or gallery, enslavers and their pastors made the Black preacher the shadowy moral and spiritual godfather of his people.[9] On Sunday and during weekdays, the Black preacher was expected to maintain moral order among the enslaved and he was expected to receive and pass on the white pastor's quote from Paul: "Slaves, obey your earthly masters with respect and fear, and with sincerity of heart, just as you would obey Christ" (Ephesians 6:5, NIV). The Black preacher was forged out of this racist paternalistic ethos of enslavement and, paradoxically, were the result of both enslavers' and enslaved people's creation of them for different reasons.

Anna Scott tells of how she experienced the Black preacher in this triangular relationship between the white preacher, Black preacher (or deacon), and God in the worship service:

> Those of the slaves who "felt the sperrit" during a service must keep silence until after the service, when they could "tell it to the deacon," a colored man who would listen to the confessions or professions of religion of the slaves until late into the night. The Negro would relay his converts to the white minister of the church, who would meet them in the vestry room at some specified time.

> Some of the questions that would be asked at these meetings in the vestry room would be:

>> "What did you come up here for?"
>> "Because I got religion."
>> "How do you know you got religion?"
>> "Because I know my sins are forgive."

13

"How do you know your sins are for given?"
"Because I love Jesus and I love everybody."
"Do you want to be baptized?"
"Yes sir."
"Why do you want to be baptized?"
"Cause it will make me like Jesus wants me to be."

When several persons were "ready," there would be a baptism in a nearby creek or river. After this, slaves would be permitted to hold occasional services of their own in the log houses that were sometimes used as a school.[10]

Anna's story sheds light on how the Black preacher started in the role sometimes as deacon in the balcony, serving under white authority. Before the Civil War, some of these preachers and deacons, such as Denmark Vesey, Harriet Tubman, and Nat Turner, erupted into the prophetic-preacher type. The Black preacher was the created result of two antithetical forces, the oppressor and the oppressed. For this reason, he and his people produced their own version of what contemporary African scholar Diane B. Stinton called a schizophrenic faith.[11]

A Schizophrenic Faith

The social and ecclesiastical triangular relationship between the Black preacher, the enslaver, and the enslaved community resulted in a schizophrenic faith.[12] The enslaved expected their preachers to assume both the role of liberator in the wilderness and servile servant of Jesus in the enslaver's church balcony. On the one hand, the enslaved expected the Black preacher to model the white man's expectations of servility in the balcony while simultaneously expecting her to model the militancy of Moses and the apocalyptic interpretation of Jesus at the secret brush harbor worship. These conflicting expectations produced a communal schizophrenic faith posture.[13]

In this communal relationship, the enslaved expected the also-enslaved Black preacher to lead them carefully, without being seen as a troublemaker, into the wilderness of spiritual freedom. This required the Black parrot-prophetic-preacher's coexistence between his enslaver and his own enslaved people. Black preachers and the other enslaved people lived daily within the parameters of their schizophrenic expressions of faith, of what became for them, too often, a balcony and brush harbor conflict. It was the period of the making of Black survival religion,[14] where on the balcony side, it required that the Black faithful affirm Jesus as *only* the savior of their souls. Whereas on the brush harbor side, in the making of Black radical religion,[15] it required that they affirm Jesus as the holistic liberator of both their bodies and their souls. The preacher and his people had to forge a secret place and space for their own survival between what they deemed the truth and a lie, between secrecy and revelation.[16] The suffering of slavery often required that the enslaved blur the margins between truth and falsehood. This was necessary for them to work between the segregated worship space of the balcony in the enslaver's church and the worship space of the plantation secret brush harbor.

The enslaver generally chose a Black male to serve as a parrot-preacher to the enslaved in the church balcony, often choosing one of his own biological children whom he had fathered with an enslaved female for the role.[17] In short, these preachers, who were generally closer to the skin color of the enslaver, were often seen by the enslaved as being more authentic in the role of preacher than their darker-skinned brethren. Assigning sacred value to the lighter-skinned preacher in the Black church has haunted the Black psyche since slavery. This made a much darker skin-toned flesh appear more sinful, creating a dichotomy and exacerbation of a flesh-spirit dilemma in the Black mind. Subscribers of this view associated deeper melanated skin tones with a greater propensity for sinfulness, a super-capacity for demonstrative emotionalism, and a deficit in intellectual prowess. The lighter-skinned preacher was believed to be more trustworthy and, therefore, a better parrot of the white preacher's proclamations of the Jesus story. The color issue merely enhanced the theological and ethical conundrum for the enslaved preacher and his people.

A Theological and Ethical Conundrum

The white preacher's question to Anna in the earlier quoted exchange—"How do you know that you have got religion?"—and Anna's response, "Cause it will make me like Jesus wants me to be"—must be thoughtfully contemplated and considered in the context of the making of the Black preacher. This idea of having to serve Jesus through his earthly master presented the Black preacher with an irresolvable theological and ethical conundrum. It forged a world that required her to live between two different and contradictory interpretations of the Bible and the role of Jesus in the lives of the enslaved. Theoretically, this caught the Black preacher in what some cultural anthropologists called the liminal space, the betwixt and between.[18] This liminal reality pushed the enslaved preacher to struggle with and through what really constituted legitimate sacred space, place, and time.

Unavoidable is the fact that the Black preacher of the balcony and brush harbor was expected to and did function both in sacred spaces as legitimated by their perceived owner and creator. In this regard, the created spiritual space of the brush harbor place was made sacred by the enslaved people who selected it in the larger reality of the plantation. The enslaved's brush harbor experience of *space and time* shaped their view of Jesus. In this space and time of experience, they encountered and engaged Jesus as being more than just a savior of their souls. As they expressed his name ritualistically during plantation brush harbor gatherings, they experienced and recreated Jesus as inhabited in their African rhythms and polyrhythms space. In this created space, they knew Jesus as an aesthetic power, as the lord and liberator of their holistic being in the space of enslavement on the plantation. In these specific and translocatable meeting places, the also-enslaved preacher had to be the prophetic-preacher, one who secretly advocated Jesus as their holistic (body, soul, and mind) liberator." This preacher, as a member of the enslaved community on the place of the plantation beyond the brush harbor, still functioned in the collective consciousness of the other enslaved people as the prophetic-preacher in the fields, the master's house, and on the land while stealthily being Moses in a braid pattern or Jesus teaching a parable by leading a call-and-response instructional song. In these sacred places, spaces, and times, the prophetic-preacher had to be the Moses/Jesus type for her people, pointing, if not leading, them to the promised land.

The theological and ethical conundrum born out of the antithetical worship in variations of place, space, and time created a hermeneutical angst[19] for the enslaved and their assigned preacher. It forged the Black preacher into a phenomenally complex agent: he was both a duplicitous pleaser of his master's whims and goals of a presumed good end as well as a suspect for compromised trust to the enslaved community for the sake of his and their intrinsic and utility value. For survival's sake, it required the preacher to be a situation ethicist and sometimes just a barefaced liar. Further, it obligated him and them to serve two white masters, the white enslaver and the enslaver's projected deity.

Interpreting the meaning of Jesus for the enslaved was the Black preacher's great challenge for his and their self-understanding and identity. The tension held in these interpretations of Jesus, from balcony to brush harbor, from light of day to dark of night, aggravated an ongoing inner turmoil while further laying crucial foundations for how Black individuals, and preachers in particular, would live and serve within, and perhaps emerge from, this schizophrenic-producing ethos.

Following the Emancipation Proclamation, establishing boundaries for the role, selection, and identity of the Black preacher became more complicated, especially as the demands of the newly freed people grew. Access to formal education enabled many preachers to become more than a parrot of the white preacher, allowing them to become insightful and constructive social critics of

17

the white preacher and his world. Additionally, the elimination of the need for brush harbor secrecy, along with access to their own places of worship, enabled the Black preacher to more freely use the common parlance, or folk language, of the period to convey the Christian message and to use coded language to offer social critiques of the white preacher and his world. The Civil War, Black Reconstruction,[20] and Post-Black Reconstruction stimulated in the formerly enslaved Black people and their preachers a desire for a new and different type of *free* preacher. This newly liberated preacher would be essential in preparing the Black community for Christian discipleship, citizenship, and social development.

From the Parrot- and Prophetic-Preacher to the Educator- and Folk-Preacher: Between the Civil War and the Civil Rights Movement

Civil War, Black Preachers, and General Sherman. Understanding the subtle nuances in the conflation of the parrot and prophetic Black enslaved preacher is necessary for exploring the genesis of the new *free* preacher as educator-preacher and folk-preacher types. The Civil War, its ending, Black Reconstruction, and Post-Black Reconstruction were definitive historical events and periods of time that informed theological and ethical elements in the genesis and making of the Black preacher. In these periods, the formerly conflated parrot- and prophetic-preacher types were dismantled, separated, and redetermined through education and class status, thereby worsening an already fraught-with-tension schizophrenic faith. These events ushered Black preachers and their people into an era of exercising their political right to speak for themselves just as it ushered them out of the formerly necessary parroting-in-public, prophetic-in-secret tradition. This era is symbolized in the twenty Black preachers who met in 1865 met with General Sherman in Savannah, Georgia, to discuss the future of the many newly freed Black individuals in the country and land ownership.[21] It signaled, symbolically, that God had torn down the wall of separation between those who were Black and those who were white in the temple of the nation.

Metaphors of Place and Time. The segregated balcony space of the white church and the secret brush harbor space of the plantation wilderness serve as metaphors for this study. They provide theological and ethical insight into how Black people struggled with the white man's racist interpretation and appropriation of the story of Jesus Christ for enslavement and post-slavery. The balcony space was the creation of the enslavers and their pastor. But the secret brush harbor space was where it was possible to work out the enslaveds' counterinterpretation of Jesus through their own African sensibilities.

These two antithetical spaces, the balcony and the brush harbor, required the enslaved to forge their own sense of being and belonging. Here, the enslaved heard that the Jesus of their enslaver required that they be born again, i.e., submerged into the white man's faith practices. Giving up everything that symbolized Africa, even their drums, was the first requirement for church membership. These spaces also provoked the teleological question for the enslaved of the enslaver's misinterpretation of Jesus as the savior only of the Black man's soul for heaven. The brush harbor is where the enslaved preacher took scriptural fragments heard from the balcony of the enslaver's church and appropriated them for their use. In doing so, the enslaved preacher redefined the meaning of the Jesus story for their own liberation.

The Civil War and the coming of freedom, a new time, demanded that the formerly enslaved make a mass exit from the balconies of white churches to buildings of their own.[22] The time of the war tragedy and its subsequent ending summoned them to larger liminal spaces that allowed the newly freed Black preachers to struggle with their evolution as religious leaders.

Sherman and the Black Preachers' Meeting. In this new time, the meeting of twenty Black preachers with Union General Sherman in Savannah, Georgia, following the ending of the Civil War

19

speaks volumes about these preachers' understanding of their role as a collective voice for their people. On the evening of January 12, 1865, they met General Sherman and the Union officers. In the meeting, Sherman asked, "In what manner do you think you can take care of yourselves, and how can you best assist the Government in maintaining your freedom?"

Answered the Reverend Frazier:

> The way we can best take care of ourselves is to have land, and turn it, and till it by our own labor—that is by the labor of the women and children and old men; and we can soon maintain ourselves and have something to spare. And to assist the Government, the young men should enlist in the service of the government, and service in such a manner as they are wanted. We want to be placed on land until we are able to buy it and make it our own.

Speaking on behalf of their race, the Black preachers advocated that white America give them land in the South where they might live apart from the white population. This gave birth to Special Field Orders No. 15 by Sherman, which instructed the government to provide freedmen with forty acres and a mule.[23] The Reverend Mr. Lynch was the only preacher of the twenty who contested the idea of members of the Black community living physically apart from white people.[24]

This is an early example of educator-preachers and folk-preachers seeking to negotiate and navigate new free terrain in the face of a landless nightmare. "Forty acres and a mule" turned out to be a failed promissory note of the United States government from which Black America has never recovered. In lieu of the government's failing to aid the group of African-descended humans who had been enslaved for hundreds of years, Black preachers were compelled to keep this newly freed population hoping in their freedom. The folk-preacher sometimes did this by overly investing in biblical religion, frequently by running the danger of making a virtue out of suffering and being poor. The educator-preacher sometimes did this by extolling the virtue of education and hard work as salvific freedom in the face of suffering. These most often separated differences made new by freedom remained haunted by the lingering underpinnings that created and conflated the parrot and prophetic enslaved preacher.[25]

The Black Educator-Preacher and Black Folk-Preacher: Between Black Reconstruction and Post-Black Reconstruction

The educator-preacher type and the political birth of a newly freed Black people characterized the arrival of Black Reconstruction. White racist backlash shortened this season of hope, creating the Post-Black Reconstruction. The Black educator-preacher fought for the nation's passing of US Constitutional Amendments Thirteen, Fourteen, and Fifteen during Black Reconstruction.[26] Black preacher leaders of this type ran for and won public office throughout the South. They led in building their own churches and schools for the holistic liberation of their people. Educator-preachers took on the responsibility of trying to reconcile two hard-to-conceive, if not impossible, interpretations of Jesus: the white pastor's interpretation of Jesus as the enslaver-savior of the souls of the enslaved and the brush harbor worshipers' interpretation of Jesus as holistic liberator of their bodies, minds, and souls.

Peeking from behind the shadows of the parrot-preacher, Black educator-preachers desiring to liberate their congregations from the white church balcony frequently shared platitudes that suggested "white folks are all right, because we're all God's children," while on another extreme, they, seeking to liberate their people from the brush harbor enslaved worship styles, overreached to eliminate any Africanisms, rhythms, tones, and drums from their new balcony-free religious experience. The Black educator-preacher dared try to liberate Jesus from the white man's racist interpretation of him. Nonetheless, this type of preacher left and led many to acquiesce to a fragmented folk message from other Black

21

preachers who spoke of spiritual and moral liberative salvation while "struggling" in a newly bourgeoning politically and socially correct way, as determined by white conscription, for how to respond to new and lingering oppressions by white people, thus attempting to save their Black bodies. White backlash made it difficult for the educator-preacher and the folk-preacher to reach the Black masses, moving many to settle for otherworldly compensation or complete removal of themselves and their families from the Black Christian experience and Black church life.[27]

The Black folk-preacher,[28] with white church-balcony antecedents and lacking in education, found it easy to draw on the parroting role when confronting white authority. He chose to go along to get along. Black folk-preachers often tried to explain to their people that suffering was a virtue, the means to heaven. They laced their sermons with the biblical metaphors of the "great by and by." The folk-preacher's ability to dramatize the biblical stories of God rewarding those who suffer was an indication that he was God-called and sent. The authenticity of the real Black preacher was located in his testimony of having been made a witness of his own encounter with God. Such phrases as "God struck me dead!" and "I saw my old self looking down upon my new self" dominated his testimony. The hearers believed that this was proof that God had called him/her to preach the Gospel.[29]

Conversely, the Black educator-preacher was called through formal education to prepare to do God's work. Faced in the biblical text with emulating both the Moses and Jesus type, the educator-preacher was yet bound to use the religious discourse of white people to teach the people self-uplift.[30] Churches and schools built and led by this type of preacher reflected the religious ideals and values of the former enslavers. This symbolized Black preachers' desire to be makers and creators of their new social world and to be practitioners of faith, hope, and love *of* and *for* each other. For the educator-preacher, Black churches became venues for teaching a downtrodden race how to read and adopt the white man's Bible and his Constitution.[31]

Post-Black Reconstruction and white racist backlash created a demand for both the educator-preacher and the folk-preacher. Both types were inevitably faced with either assimilating to or adapting beyond the white man's Christian values of *worship time and style*.[32] Black worshipers had to rethink the distinctions that had been made between what was then called heathen African worship and Christian worship. In varying ways, Black educator- and folk-preacher types sought, to assimilate and adapt white people's teachings of what it meant to be in Christian worship. This included addressing what it meant to be on time for Sunday services and following specific dress codes as well as using or abstaining from the use of drums, especially African drums.[33]

For the Black educator-preacher and folk-preacher, assimilations and adaptations came in varying degrees, depending on their focus on a given element of worship. While the educator-preacher might have sought a greater degree of assimilation in music and preaching styles, along with accommodating a shorter time frame for the worship service, the folk-preacher might have sought a degree of assimilation to the day of the week for worship and style of dress. Neither sought wholly to institutionalize the white man's notion and values of worship time and style into the Black church.

Further, the Post-Black Reconstruction preacher pursued varying and distinct adaptations to the white community's valuation of worship time and style. The educator-preacher might necessarily question their need or ability to exorcize aspiring upwardly mobile Black individuals of their aesthetic desire for African musical sounds. Former enslavers, antagonistic people from the white community, and some newly educated Black people frowned upon African rhythmic and polyrhythmic sounds made on African drums. African drums were described as the devil's instruments. The Black educator-preacher type, such as Richard Allen, was expected to preach and teach against the use of such African musical instruments in worship.[34]

However, the folk-preacher—with his brush harbor prophetic-preacher antecedents—and his people freely communicated with

God via drums, washpots, and shouts. They gathered to wait for Jesus, *for* each other, and *with* each other. All night, if necessary! In these worship times and spaces, they eagerly embraced their open musical style adaptations in the worship service, experiencing Jesus as their felt and heard rhythmic host.

The ecstasy of freedom of choice in assimilating or adapting their Christian worship and their fluid status in social, political, and economic freedoms, motivated Black community members to build their own churches, schools, and denominations. Isaac P. Brockenton and Mary McCleod Bethune,[35] both educator-preacher types with studies and degrees from existing white seminaries, are among the earliest examples of this directed motivation.[36] McCleod Bethune, the founder of Bethune Cookman College, and Brockenton, the founder of Morris College, were both committed to inspiring, educating, and developing the soul and intellect of Black people. McCleod Bethune, Brockenton—and other later educator-preacher types that include Edward M. Brawley and Nannie Helen Burroughs[37]—pioneered the way for oncoming leaders like Benjamin E. Mays[38], the heralded president of Morehouse College, and Mordecai Johnson,[39] president of Howard University. These leaders represent some of the early stages of the synergistic merging of the folk-preacher and educator-preacher types, ultimately leading Black citizens into larger religious, social, and political spaces while confusing and infuriating the white community.

In their hate-laden confusion, white people in America amplified their oppressive regimes against the Black community from the Post-Black Reconstruction era into an unforgettable, despairing Jim Crow era. Jim Crowisms[40] experienced by Black people undergirded the continued synergistic merging of the educator-preacher and folk-preacher types. Many, though not all, Black preachers representing further the synergistic merging of these types were now bound to share in sacred spaces, most often devoid of white sentiments and values for and toward Black individuals, to work toward fully realizing their mutual desire for full and holistic freedoms. This would herald the entrance, the birthing, of the Black holistic-preacher type in the Civil Rights Movement (CRM) through today.

Black Holistic-Preacher: Jim Crow and the Civil Rights Movement Era to Now

The Civil Rights Movement and the Black Holistic-Preacher Type. Black preachers are rightly credited with leading the Civil Rights Movement that shook the nation in the decades of the 1950s and 1960s. The CRM contributed to the development of Martin L. King Jr. and a supporting cast of known and unknown Black preachers locally and nationally. Few studies of King, if any, have drawn a correlation between him and the making of Black preachers in America. The thousands of us who stood on the Mall of the Washington Monument likely failed to identify and hear the medley of Black preacher types in King's brilliant speech at the 1963 historic march. King was an iconic mixture of all of them from enslavement to that historic moment—the exemplar of the holistic Black preacher.

Although formally academically trained by white America's standards, King, erudite and scholarly, was more than a modern orator who captured and held the attention of thousands. In the tradition of Black prophet-preachers like Tubman and Turner, King framed his speech in visions and dreams. Heard in his speech, in the similitude of the Black folk-preacher, were embodied jazzy rhythms. In echoes of the parrot-preacher type of the enslavement era and through the later educator-preacher, he could be heard reciting "we hold these truths..." from the nation's founding documents as passed on to the Black community by the nation's white and slave-owning founders. King had risen on the nation's and the world's stage to epitomize the Black holistic preacher.

While the CRM's spotlight was primarily on the leadership of Martin L. King Jr., we often missed what was happening in the making of the Black preacher-at-large in America during this time.

This movement would invite and, in some cases, demand that the Black preacher transport the created space of Black church experience to the space of white racist America—into the streets with nonviolent marches guided by spirituals and movement songs, bus boycotts, and lunch counter sit-ins. Removing the barriers between the created space and place of the Black church and exposing it to those outside within the larger social milieu, the Black holistic preacher turned some of his local churches into venues for holding mass meetings, bringing all people—Black, white, churched, and unchurched—into a kind of brush harbor phenomenon.

More than one hundred years after the need for the brush harbor context, the CRM challenged the traditional, racist American understanding of public space and time. The CRM's aims would thus help more fully realize the synergistically derived remaking of Black preachers as it attempted to remake America. King and other leaders in the movement prophetically challenged the authenticity of the prescribed separations indicated for white and Black people. While churches typically had neither a Black entrance sign at the back door nor a "whites only" sign on the front door, Sunday at 11:00 A.M., as known and stated by many of the period, was still the most segregated hour in America.

Redefining the Black holistic-preacher's place in racist America widened the space of uniquely Black institutional leadership, social and political engagement, community development, and business and entrepreneurial endeavors while beginning to make room for them in integrated spaces. While a central question maintained regular circulation about the role of the Black preacher during the CRM, the shifts and changes associated with educational integration and slow movements toward wider social integration led to further theological and ethical questions about the Black preacher, which people continue to grapple with today. Historians and other scholars have accurately pointed out the central role of Black preachers during the CRM, Black people, the non-monolithic Black church, white people, the whole of America, and other nations of people, silently and out loud, question the necessity and viability of having Black holistic-preacher types as central leaders for anything other than their specific churches.

Conclusion

Questions and Considerations:
For This Present Age and Beyond

As the Black holistic-preachers move seamlessly within the multipolarity of being Black preachers, we contemporarily celebrate them within the sacred walls of churches across America, in the halls of Congress, at the helm of HBCUs and Ivy League universities, as community organizers and leaders, as attorneys and judges, as K-12 educators, and as servant leaders in all pockets of society. Our celebration also challenges us with many questions and thoughts for consideration as we step into the future.

- Must those who celebrate the Black holistic preacher accept the surfacing of one aspect more than the other to the detriment of what has historically defined the Black church?

- Should there be a challenge to any Black holistic-preacher who leans too heartily into the parrot-preacher tradition, owing to the impact of white evangelical Christianity and their leadership and/or their supportive financial resources to Black churches?

- How does an awareness of the Black individual's acquisition of Jesus during enslavement, boarding ships and while enslaved in America, along with the changes of spiritual and artistic renderings of Jesus, affect current understandings about the function of Jesus in the Black Christian life and worship?

- Are Black churchgoing Christians who attend white preacher-led churches defaulting to a desire for the pseudo-authenticating of the preacher role by a white person?

• Does an individual need to be African descended to be a Black preacher?

• How, if at all, should Black Christian churchgoers respond to white and other racial or ethnic groups co-opting what was established in the prototypes of the Black preacher?

• Is there a media trend in portrayals of the Black preacher, with any preference to a particular aspect?

• In this current time of heightened and reemergent overt racist practices and hostilities toward people of African descent in America and abroad, are we doing an ethical, theological, social, and political disservice and harm to ourselves and our future by failing to engage difficult and, for some more than others, uncomfortable questions about the genesis and making of the Black preacher?

• When the history of Black people in America is summarily being removed from the public education sector, do Black preachers have an ethical obligation consistent with their making to educate church members and the community?

• Is it the prerogative of the Black preacher to serve only himself, or does she have a theological mandate to serve the least of these among us, as privileging us, while still supporting the non-Black other among us?

• Can the Black preacher be reproduced in any variety through artificial intelligence?

A committed willingness to engage reflectively and reflexively with who and what it is we think we are witnessing in the Black preacher can help us and future generations flourish as holistic-preacher servants of God and as people. Glimpsing the rich heritage in the inception and creation of Black preachers through these typologies ought now to push us toward reinforcing HBCUs and Black seminaries or divinity schools to the benefit of the development of the Black preacher and Black communities. Encouraging a robust communal consciousness that supports and actively engages socially and politically what we need to sustain our hard-fought-for-and-won freedoms should be our mutual and abiding concern.

Chapter 2

Contour of American Public Theology[1]

Victor Anderson

Introduction

Public theology mobilizes religious languages, discourses, and commitments to influence substantive public discourse and debate.[2] Public theology, I argue, is a mode of religious criticism. I describe religious criticism as a form of cultural critique, and so, *discursively iconoclastic* and *emancipatory praxis*.[3] It is *discursively iconoclastic*, exposing and rejecting totalities that deny persons' cultural and moral fulfillment and moral democratic societies on the grounds of actual or perceived differences—whether ethnicity, social status, biological determinants, sexual orientation, religion, or political theology is also *emancipatory advocacy praxis*, defending aspects of individuality that every person has a right to expect of human fulfillment in Western democratic societies. It thus sees beyond the critique of debilitating and oppressive sociopolitical structures toward programmatically envisioning or imagining liberatory possibilities inherent in democratic culture formations for furthering human flourishing.

However, public theology is always *religiously situated*. It is articulated in an American public culture, iconoclastically described by the African American philosopher Cornel West as "the American empire" and characterized by three *fundamental dogmas*: *free market fundamentalism, aggressive militarism*, and *escalating authoritarianism*. West's religious criticism of these *dogmas* signify our religious situation as embracing a political, fundamentalist religiosity that is snuffing out the democratic impulses that are so vital for the deepening and spread of democracy in the world. In short, we are experiencing the sad American imperial devouring of American democracy. This historic devouring in our time constitutes an unprecedented gangsterization of America—an unbridled grasp at power, wealth, and status. And when the most powerful forces in a society—and an empire—promote a suffocation of democratic energies, the very future of genuine democracy is jeopardized.[4]

Our sociopolitical situation is overdetermined by economic disparities. Neoliberal, multinational, globalized expansionism explodes the worldwide wealth gap between the poor and the rich. Neoliberal globalization champions political party deadlock, legislative and judicial trust mistrust, and it exhibits undeterred collective violence perpetuated by law enforcement agents, white citizens standing their ground, right-wing militia regimes, gang violence, and devotion to uncontrolled gun restrictions that perpetuates mass shootings targeting people of color, LGBTQ+ communities, mosques and temples, and school-age children. Although expanding in scope, these sociopolitical conditions characterize enough of our *religious situation* to warrant an American public theology as a mode of religious criticism.

Public Theology, Leadership, and the Religious Situation

I have referred above to public theology in relation our *religious situation*. Let me make this relation explicit. The religious situation was introduced into public theology in 1933 by the German theologian Paul Tillich in a book by the same title. It signifies sociocultural forces, whether nationalism, fascism, or capitalism, that Tillich addressed. He examined how these sociocultural forces and shifts were overdetermining the public significance of German faith communities, consciously or unconsciously, and so were producing a crisis of public legitimacy and religious faith throughout modern societies. This religious situation was felt throughout the cultural expressive and political spheres: artistic, ethical, religious, and political.[5] How religious thinkers attuned themselves to these sociocultural shifts constituted the religious situation. German theological responses cumulated into a variety of *crisis theologies*. H. Richard Niebuhr, the German American theologian and translator of Tillich's book, aptly comments: "The developments of our times have accentuated doubts about the rationality of science and technology. Politics and religious forces, their alignment, and their hopes, remain astonishingly similar."[6]

In its contestations with our contemporary religious situation in the US, described above, public theology requires a theologically informed intervention of religious criticism. It critiques how religious thinkers attune to contemporary shifting sociocultural forces and shifts that debilitate human flourishing by discursively and iconoclastically robbing every mode of discourse, including its own, of any essentialized totality, thereby "exposing the demonic present even in those forms of criticism that parade as liberating and revolutionary projects."[7] But an adequate American public theology also requires emancipatory or liberatory advocacy of sociopolitical discourses theologically supporting social and cultural forces that advance human flourishing.

Such a public theology, I argue, is in service of the aims of religious criticism. It exhibits two traits worth isolating for understanding and responding to the religious situation of the public theologian: (1) *It involves academic theologians developing critical principles that correct the moral conscience of the political community when public life is governed by social policies that violate the democratic fulfillment of the political community* (this is its iconoclastic or prophetic aim), and (2) *public theology involves the academic theologian in understanding, transmitting, and constructing theological critical principles that sustain the political community in practices oriented toward the moral fulfillment of the political community* (this is its emancipatory or priestly aim).[8]

However, we will not get very far in understanding or marshalling such a public theology, specifically from an academic point of view,[9] if we maintain an academy-versus-the-real-world rhetoric. We would do well to eliminate this kind of talk altogether, as if the academy (one of the West's most permanent and, at times, insidious mediating institutions) were not participating in the real-world formations of power. Academic theologians are not aliens to this world (although we sometimes give that impression) but inhabit shared social realities, a world in common, and participate in a shared collective life. We belong not only to various publics (the church, the academy, society, and various associations) but also hold memberships throughout the generalizable political community of democratic citizenship.

The languages of theology also have cultural significance for their impacts and influences on the perceptions, perspectives, orientations, engagements, and participation of faith communities on public life. Academic theologians are not isolated or detached from public realities that impact the loyalties and trusts of faith communities within the generalizable public. But the public theologian holds stock in the religious languages and traditions of faith communities and is responsible for intervening into the needs, interests, and goods required for the flourishing of the generalizable public. Public theology provides symbolic expressions and meanings to public life, transacting to bring fulfillment to public interests in health, safety, labor, education, public administration, and so much more. It is discursively burdened with interpreting and deploying critical principles theologically derived from faith communities and traditions to critique American public life.

A central question confronting public theology today is, Is the language of Christian theology (*God, Christ, Spirit, redemption, creation, sin, grace, reconciliation, atonement, judgment,* for example) adequate for communicating meanings beyond the narrow borders of the theologian's or church leader's religious community? Can public theology adequately embrace the concerns and hopes of the public at large without alienating and rendering the academic theologian religiously insignificant? So, what would be tests of adequacy? Let me propose four: it is recognized by (1) its descriptive and interpretative contributions to public discourse, (2) the moral agreements it shares with various public discourses, (3) the claims it makes on public life, and (4) the symbolic integration and impact of its claims on public life.[10] The adequacy of public theology depends on its capacities to render public life spiritually meaningful, morally livable, and culturally flourishing.[11] An adequate public theology does this by deploying religious resources for participating in and substantively influencing public debate and social policies that advance moral and social discourse on public life. Theologically derived critical principles such as *sin* and *transgression* become interpretative filters for the critique of public life. But an adequate public theology also discerns, in our life together, signs of *transcendence*, Signs of transcendence show in human encounters where redemption, atonement, and grace may be well manifested.

Every generation of academic theologians and religious leaders constructively confronts their religious situation in their interventions in public life (some for the better and others for the worse). But for better or worse, should their critical principles prove unrecognizable to constituencies, either by the generalizable public or ordinary believers, they will also show themselves doubly irrelevant. Put emphatically: Should contemporary public theologians seek to gain a footing in public discourses, discourse but no one recognizes anything theological about their interventions in their efforts, they will be irrelevant to both so-called secular and religious constituencies in public discourse where they are expected to say something theological! The principle of publicity requires that the public theologian be multilingual, exhibiting competencies to speak relevantly to the generalizable public in ways that are publicly understood not only within their narrow constituencies but also by everyday people, and that they be competent interpreters of the internal languages of faith communities, saying something theological in their interventions into in public discourse.

An American Public Theology
and Pragmatic Theology

My pragmatic theology offers rich possibilities for interpreting and criticizing our religious situation.[12] Among them are finitude, transcendence, God, and grace. Finitude and transcendence can be rendered theological when they circumscribe primordial features of the world and our human experience of it. Following American empirical theologians representing two theological schools of thought that include G. B. Foster, G. Birney Smith, Henry Nelson Wieman, the Chicago school, and D. C. Macintosh, H. Richard Niebuhr, and James M. Gustafson, the Yale school, I have sought to understand the adequacy of theological utterances by their capacity to interpret those features of human life that enlighten and enliven our participation in the world processes and patterns that promote human and planetary flourishing.[13]

Finitude prevails. Despite all of our imaginative powers toward overcoming limits, finitude limits our aims and purposes. Our powers of willing are thwarted by the push and pull of nature, environmental conditions, our bodies, disease, mortality, and the realization that we are not omnipotent. In politics, public policy, moral commitments for advancing human happiness, and interventions into the ecological ordering of life, even in our endeavors to create healthy, prosperous societies where peace and justice prevail, we are met with limits. This fact is not recognition of a human fault (i.e., original sin or fall) but simply the way things are.

Finitude is primordial. It marks a basic quality of human experience of and in the world inhabited by all. Any public theology must simply deal with finitude to human endeavors. But this does not mean that we are fated.

Simultaneous with finitude is transcendence. It too is primordial. Transcendence is evident in small and great ways we get about and act in a world where limits abound. Sometimes we adapt environmental conditions to cooperate toward meeting our deepest aims and purposes. Other times, when faced with powers and patterns of the world indifferent to our aims, purposes, and efforts, we accommodate so as not to be overcome by a sense of futility and cynicism.

For the increase of human life, we muster resources to create safe, healthy spaces where children are provided with the best chances for advancing their flourishing. But sadly, we also know, all too well, that not all will survive, despite the hopes, dreams, and endeavors of families and communities. Some will die at birth, others from disease, and still innumerable others from neglect and violence surrounding them at every turn. For the increase of knowledge, we provide generations with a generous stock of practical wisdom in the community's stored skills, languages, and practices that have proven to be effective at sustaining of human communities through stages of cultivation, years of distress and war, and centuries of famine and disease. We pass on lessons and life-sustaining wisdom mined and learned from ancestors in the hope that we contemporaries will never undergo the precariousness of life suffered by them.

In our religious situation, we are no more fated by finitude than ancestors who survived the transatlantic slave trade to be transplanted into the hostile world of chattel slavery, which sought to destroy in them that realm of human personality in which all are most free, their willing. Delivered by that dogged strength of will, African peoples in America hoped against the limits and brought forth new communities, new peoples, and new possibilities of flourishing despite the criminal history of American Christianity. They brought forth a new creation, Black religion, in a plenitude of being. As much as finitude meets us at every step, so transcendence breaks through in possibilities of freedom, openness, and creativity, all conspiring with the will to adapt and accommodate to our religious situation for the sake of human flourishing.

In my pragmatic theology, finitude and transcendence are not vacuous abstractions but regulative boundaries. They are *felt qualities of the world* and its processes that adequately describe our experience of the world. Their ontological parity can be grasped theologically in a conception of God that entails a fullness of being, a plenitude of being, not reducible to human acts but relates human life and practices to ever-enlarging wholes. The adequacy of public theology depends on imaginative constructions of principles to help people to creatively interact with one another in the processes and patterns of the world. This is exactly what the empirical theologian Henry Nelson Wieman meant when he described God as "that interaction between individuals, groups, and ages, which generates and promotes the greatest possible mutuality of good.

Only such an interaction can carry us to the greatest good...because it is the only way that the accumulated good gathered by all can become the heritage of each."[14] Finitude and transcendence are critical principles of public theology that not only present limiting conditions but also present possibilities of openness and novelty that make world processes and patterns vulnerable to interdependence and interaction. As a metaphysical orientation for public theology, the world is processive, open, and relational, and so our religious situation is but a microcosm.

The African American public theologian Howard Thurman and Martin Luther King Jr. envisioned this as *the Beloved Community*, human and nonhumans. Thurman put it this way:

> It is possible for the individual to move out beyond the particular context by which his [*sic*] life is defined and relate to other forms of life from inside their context. This means that there is a boundless realm of which all particular life is but a manifestation. This center is the living thing in human beings and animal. If a person or animal can function out of that center, then the boundaries that limit and define can be transcended.[15]

I, too, understand this unification of the self and others theologically interpreted in the idea of God. The God symbol conceptually enacts the unification of every reality, reality being the undifferentiated totality of world experience. God signifies the union of all life in its concrete actuality and ideal potentiality. Therefore, God symbolically designates the fullness of world meaning and value. The God symbol signifies "an unrestricted field of value whose harmony involves an ever-enlarging process synthesis of the widest range and deepest contrast of relational data," says religious philosopher Nancy Frankenberry.[16] The God symbol "[enables] individuals (and cultures) to move from narrower, constricted patterns of perception and feeling to wider and deeper modes of sympathetic inclusiveness."[17] In a world where collective violence appears normative of interhuman associations, the God symbol elicits sympathy to see, perceive, and attend to the care of others beyond the immediacy of one's self-interest, racial and ethnic identities, families, neighborhoods, and statehoods. The God symbol expands moral sympathy toward seeking the flourishing of all who suffer from malicious forms of prejudice and violence in our religious situation.

When he argued that theology is a way of construing the world, the Christian ethicist James M. Gustafson gave a compelling interpretation. For him, God is the power(s) bearing down on us, sustaining us, and ordering human life within the nexus of natural and social processes and patterns.[18] God designates powers and patterns of the world that establish possibilities for human capacities for creative interaction and interdependence with planetary life. Gustafson reminds us that God also establishes limits to human well-being and endeavors toward sustaining themselves against the world patterns and processes.[19] Our failure to acknowledge this fact has led human communities and planetary life toward unfathomable destruction.

I have argued that that God symbolizes the union of life in its concrete actuality (finitude) and its ideal potentiality (transcendence). The God symbol illuminates the world in its dark and light dimensions and human experience in its tragic and ironic manifestations. This recognition evokes the theological symbols of redemption, atonement, and grace as critical principles of public theology. For instance, the American public theologian Paul Lehmann made the theological symbol of *grace* central to his public theology, arguing that Christian ethics is not wholly determined by what God is doing in the church but what God is doing in the world.[20] Evoking Lehmann is not meant to reinscribe, on our religious situation, a conception of divine action overlaid by anthropomorphisms. Nevertheless, for him, Christian engagements in politics, public policy, human misery, suffering, and the mass alienation of persons from goods that all require for fulfilling life are related to our estimations of God's ordering of all things to each other and the integration of all particular interests to the whole.

God is the condition for the possibility of rightness (goodness, faith, justice, trust, loyalty, and human fulfillment and flourishing) in our religious situation beset with limited politics, social action, and moral endeavors. Recognizing this potentiality of public theology is to recognize signs of redemption, atonement, and grace. As one philosopher notes:

> The dialectical movement between finitude and transcendence marks the human process during all stages of growth and decline. Neither dimension can assume priority in all respects, so that finitude is never bereft of those fitful moments of transcendence that move the self beyond the opacity of origins. Hope assures us that the destructive powers of origin will never completely overwhelm the human process, and that our radical expectations are secured against the forces of closure and death.[21]

Notwithstanding how our lives are structured by choices, actions, and policies that we did not choose for ourselves but tacitly accept, where great expectations exist for increasing social freedom, moral capacity, and just social policies, we are met with signs of redemption, atonement, and grace.

Redemption, atonement, and grace attend to our moral and spiritual aspirations and actions. But this is no invitation to quietism. If hope of a morally just political order is to be realizable in the present (better housing, better health care, better educational policies, better living conditions for the poor, and better democratic participation), the gracious potentialities of the world must be seized with urgency. Every potentiality of redemption, atonement, and grace is met with tragic-demonic threats of closure. It is one thing to acknowledge how finitude or limits curtail our individual and collective endeavors and another to acknowledge how selfish, private desires, interests, and propensities toward closure and totality also thwart emancipatory or liberating potentials of redemption, atonement, and grace. Traditional Christian public theology names this SIN.

Notwithstanding how, in our religious situation, moral lives seem overdetermined by finitude, limits, sin, and transgression, Howard Thurman pondered the mystery of human transcendence within the ebb and flow of the world processes and patterns. Transcendence and grace were perhaps the most controlling critical principles of his public theology, which is accentuated below in the last stanza of the poem.

> "Knowledge...Shall Vanish Away."
> There is some wholeness at the core of man
> That must abound in all he does;
> That marks with reverence his ev'ry step;
> That has its sway when all else fails;
> That wearies out all evil things;
> That warms the depth of frozen fears
> Making friend of foe,
> Making love of hate,
> And lasts beyond the living and the dead,
> Beyond the goals of peace, the ends of war!
> This man seek through all his years:
> To be complete and of one piece, within, without.[22]

The theological symbols, as critical principles of an American public theology, may adequately be inclusive of finitude, transcendence, God, and grace, redemption, atonement, reconciliation, and judgment, and more that *empirically, concretely show up in interhuman interactions* if only we have eyes to see their powers.

Thurman's public theology took the rich vocabularies of the Christian faith and traditions and constructed them so that they pushed beyond narrow meanings particular to the inner life of the faith community. For him, they were theological concepts fitting religious criticism of our religious situation.

Conclusion

Our religious situation imposes renewed participation of America's academic theologians and religious leaders in the construction of viable, critical principles for public theology. What intellectual and moral anguish comes with hearing church and parachurch theologians and leaders disseminate interpretations of America's public life in languages that offend the spiritual, ethical, and intellectual seriousness of the Christian faith and traditions. In our religious situation, the preponderance of unreflective, uncritical public theologies—uncompassionate indifference to the misery of the poor while privileging the wealthy; legitimating and acquiescing to prevailing cultural drives toward collective violence; malicious social, criminal, economic, and immigration public policies characteristic of our religious situation—are scandalous, blasphemous, and grievous. Critique alone is not enough for an adequate academic public theology. Surely, the public theologian is responsible not only to offer the generalizable public, beyond their small scholarly societies, discursive iconoclastic interventions into the public and its problems, but also to articulate the best emancipatory critical principles, conceivably derived from their faith communities and traditions, toward advancing ultimate goods and ends required of all for their human and planetary wholeness.

> What, then, is the word of the religion of Jesus to those who stand with their backs against the wall? There must be the clearest possible understanding of the anatomy of the issues facing them. They must recognize fear, deception, hatred, each for what it is. Once having done this, they will become increasingly clear that the contradictions of life are not ultimate. The

41

disinherited will know for themselves that there is a Sprit at work in life and in the hearts of human beings which is committed to overcoming the world.... For the privileged and underprivileged alike, if the individual puts at the disposal of the Sprit the needful dedication and discipline, he and she can live effectively in the chaos of the present the high destiny of a child of God.[23]

An adequate academic public theology acknowledges the precariousness of human actions while also acknowledging that "people are warranted in maintaining hope against destructive closures, openness toward a wider vision of human potentialities, expectation that the creative processes of human life will lead towards moral fulfillment, and recognition that the realization of human [and planetary] flourishing [are] signs of divine grace."[24] Such are the limits of public theology. Such are its possibilities.

Chapter 3

Nehemiah's Model of Leadership and Justice: Black Church Praxis, Leadership, and Theological Imagination

Herbert R. Marbury

Introduction:
Reading Nehemiah with the "Hub on the Hill"

In 2018, Dr. Forrest Harris and a design team at American Baptist College established the "Hub on the Hill." Conceived as a think tank, the Hub was designed to equip the Black church to reimagine itself and its work in Black communities as these communities faced new and more complex challenges stemming from their long experience with injustice. An incubator for expanding theological imagination and shaping ministry praxis, the Hub was designed to catalyze pockets of community resistance that would inevitably transform life in Black Nashville and perhaps beyond. In the same year, the Hub launched Called to Lives of Meaning and Purpose (CLMP), and in 2021, it launched Empowering Congregations (EC), two bold initiatives intended to shift the threshold for ministry in Black churches toward justice, resistance, and healing.

In a climate in which evangelicalism and white Christian nationalism increasingly overlapped as the latter gained greater visibility and acceptance in public discourse, these initiatives faced two major challenges.[1] First, society's preference for charity and social services over longer-term, sustainable strategies for empowerment, such as building a community's capacity for resistance and engaging social justice, is evident in the abundance of resources made available for charity initiatives relative to those available for social justice work. While the charity sector's public benefits are commonly accepted, its unintended consequences have proven deleterious for marginalized groups.[2] In their opening statement, Empowering Congregations the proposals explicitly reject charity in favor of social justice as the theological framing for initiatives' work:[3] "to engage congregations in ways Christian activism can come alive when it is not just charitable ministry 'to' but 'ministry by;' marginalized groups seeking justice,"[4] Second, the initiatives' theological vision, although grounded in the tradition of the Black church's heritage, stretches far beyond the theologies of most contemporary Black congregations.

Meeting the first challenge required the design team's skill in crafting a proposal acceptable to the Lilly Endowment, Inc., the external funding source. The second challenge required fashioning a curriculum that challenged the Black church to interrogate the limits of its theological imagination so that it might resummon a fuller manifestation its prophetic voice. In their proposals, the initiatives invoke the biblical story of Nehemiah. They read about Nehemiah's work securing funding from the Persian Empire and building a wall for Jerusalem as a warrant "for" their work in meeting both challenges.[5] However, using Nehemiah loses the meaning that are particular to Nehemiah's world. More importantly, such a reading risks reducing meanings in the life world of the Black church to only those evident in Nehemiah's story. Might reading the story of Nehemiah as a dialog partner in conversation "with" the two proposals offer insight into the biblical story and our understanding of the proposals' visions? Read this way, Nehemiah's story is not a warrant: it is Nehemiah's testimony of his response to God's call. As such, it comes into conversation alongside the proposals' visions of *theological imagination, ministry praxis*, and *adaptive leadership*. Positioning the biblical story this way, the church makes room for both the meanings that are unique to Nehemiah's world and those that are particular to God's work with the Black church. What follows is such a reading. It deeply grounds Nehemiah's work within Jerusalem's history of repression for more than a century under Babylon and Persia to show how those meanings

THE BLACK LEADERSHIP TRADITION IN AMERICA

arise from Nehemiah's context. The reading then takes up a contemporary parallel: Black Nashville's history of repression for more than a century as the context for the Hub's intervention to show this history raises meaning particular to the initiatives' contexts. Finally, it considers the two in dialog and asks, what lessons might we take from such a reading?

Millennia and the geography of half the globe separate Nehemiah's work and the financial resources he brought from the Persian imperial treasury to the Temple in Jerusalem from the initiatives of the Hub on the Hill and the economic investments it brought to Black churches in North Nashville. Nonetheless, the confluences between the stories are obvious: Both Forrest Harris and Nehemiah secured economic resources for their respective communities. With those resources, both turned to their community's religious institutions to organize sites of renewal, healing, and resistance. Further, both communities shared an experience of marginalization. Jerusalem and Black Nashville faced repression in the form of physical upheaval and economic depletion, and both responded with strategies of resistance and resilience. Jerusalem had seen its Temple and surrounding community razed by Babylonian soldiers; Persian economic repression followed. Black Nashville had seen Jefferson Street, its commercial and cultural center, upended to pave the way for an interstate highway. During the same period, it watched much of the rest of its community systematically impoverished by fiscal policies that encouraged divestment and withheld public funding that flowed to white Nashville. While the reach of the Hub's initiatives affected Black communities beyond Nashville, this study focuses on the work of these initiatives within the context and history of injustice, resistance, and resilience in Black Nashville.

Jerusalem:
Physical Destruction and Community Resilience

By the time Nehemiah arrived with imperial funds to revitalize Jerusalem, the city had languished under harsh economic repression for generations. Its infrastructure remained in ruins from the Babylonian devastation of 587 BCE. The writer of 2 Kings describes the horror: "In the fifth month, on the seventh day of the month—which was the nineteenth year of King Nebuchadnezzar, king of Babylon—Nebuzaradan, the captain of the bodyguard, a servant of the king of Babylon, came to Jerusalem. He burned the house of the LORD, the king's house, and all the houses of Jerusalem; every great house he burned down" (2 Kings 25:8–9, NRSV). The destruction of the Temple, the center of the city's life and the symbol of the people's cultural life, did more than physical damage. It ignited a crisis in the community's identity. Who were they now? Are a people without a king actually a people? Where was Yahweh, their God, if the Babylonian army could so easily destroy the Temple, Yahweh's house? Their crisis in identity was compounded by Babylon's harsh economic policies. Decade after decade, imperial policies depleted the city and its surrounding area. Lamentations evokes the community's deep emotional angst as it articulates the people's suffering.

> We have become orphans, fatherless;
>> our mothers are like widows.
> We must pay for the water we drink,
>> the wood we get must be bought.
> With a yoke on our necks we are hard driven;
>> we are weary, we are given no rest.
> We have made a pact with Egypt and Assyria,
>> to get enough bread.
> Our ancestors sinned; they are no more,
>> and we bear their iniquities.
> Slaves rule over us;
>> there is no one to deliver us from their hand.

> We get our bread at the peril of our lives,
>   because of the sword in the wilderness
>   (Lamentations 5:3–9, NRSV)

Babylon destroyed not only the city but also the community's ability to sustain its members. Those who survived found only destitution as they faced disease's blight and starvation's ravage.

Babylonia's conquest was only one in a long history of imperial repression for Jerusalem. Prior to Babylon, Assyrian power subdued King Hezekiah and forced Jerusalem's citizens to pay burdensome taxes as tribute to Sennacherib, their king. Later, Egypt asserted domination and installed puppet kings on Jerusalem's throne. The kings ensured Egypt's control and the people's taxation.

Economic Repression in Jerusalem

When the Persian army wrested Jerusalem from Babylonian control in 539 BCE, forty-eight years after the Temple's destruction, there was hope that conditions would change. Cyrus, the Persian king, initially dealt with Jerusalem generously. He freed the descendants of its former inhabitants who had been held captive in Babylon since the devastation. Darius, a later king, even funded the rebuilding of the Temple that Babylon had destroyed.[6] But soon Persia's imperial policies turned harsh. As Persia escalated its war with the Greeks, they squeezed local communities, and particularly their temples, for more resources. All over the empire, the Persians required communities to contribute to their local temples. From these contributions, Persian kings required temples to pay taxes in the form of barley, beer, wine, livestock, spices, butter, milk, and other provisions for Persian officials.[7] Jerusalem, a small community set in dry, arid land, produced few resources, and its people suffered more. Nehemiah articulated the people's life under Persia: "Here we are, slaves to this day—slaves in the land that you gave to our ancestors to enjoy its fruit and its good gifts. Its rich yield goes to the kings whom you have set over us because of our sins; they have power also over our bodies and over our livestock at their pleasure, and we are in great distress" (Nehemiah 9:36–37, NRSV). These taxes imposed severe economic hardship on local temples and their communities and forced them into debt. Such was the world that Nehemiah found when he arrived years later in 445 BCE.

Black Nashville's Historical Context

Similar to Nehemiah's Jerusalem community, Black Nashville faced its own ongoing repression. No differently than most US cities, the end of Reconstruction meant the resurgence of a virulent white supremacy whose history marked Nashville with violence, economic disparity, and always the exploitation of subjected groups to elevate whiteness.

When Chester Arthur became the twenty-first president of the United States in 1881, four years after the end of Reconstruction, the South was home to a still-bitter Confederacy. Arthur's refusal to speak out against white racial hostility gave silent affirmation to a generation anxious to reinvigorate a more robust white supremacy.[8] Taking Arthur's stance as license, Tennessee passed the first Jim Crow laws in the South that same year.[9] Nashville segregated its railroad cars, forcing Negroes to sit in second class. The railroad cars were only one example of the resurgence of the old Confederate order. Losing the power to vote was far more devastating. Poll taxes, first enacted by the Tennessee Constitutional Convention in 1870 and affirmed by the Tennessee legislature in 1891, effectively deterred Black Nashville from exercising the franchise. From 1868 to 1890, Nashville's Black voter rolls dropped from about 6,000 to just over 600.[10] To ensure Black disenfranchisement, the city expanded the number of wards from to ten to twenty.[11]

> While the city strategized to decrease Black political influence, Nashville's Black community continued its economic and cul-

tural growth. By 1929, the start of the Great Depression, Black Nashville boasted robust commercial activity. According to the *Nashville Negro City Directory*, there were:...52 doctors, 9 undertakers, 35 grocery stores, 5 meat markets, 11 drug stores, 48 barber shops, two hospitals, 26 restaurants, 7 realtors, 3 taxi companies, 9 public meeting halls, one shoemaker, 12 shoe repair shops, 34 hairdressers, 5 barbering colleges, 29 cleaning establishments, 7 masons, 13 postal clerks, 4 orchestras, 6 auto repair shops, 1 amusement park, two banks, and 14 public schools, along with several food caterers, blacksmiths, coal dealers, bakers, architects, candy makers, and electrical contractors.[12]

By the end of the Great Depression, the Jefferson Street district emerged as Black Nashville's cultural and business center. Retail, restaurants, pharmacies, funeral homes, and churches were opening on the popular thoroughfare. "Prominent businesses along the street were K. Gardner's Funeral Home, Isom's Beauty Shop, William Hawkins North Side Ice Cream Company, William Hemphill's Press, Terrance Restaurant, Jefferson Street Pharmacy, Menefee and Bauer Tire and Battery Service, I. E. Green Grocery Company, Terry's Pharmacy, and Frank White's Cleaners."[13]

While economic growth in the Black commercial district proceeded relatively unchecked, the city sabotaged commercial endeavors that might reduce Black dependence upon white-owned businesses. In July 1905, Preston Taylor, along with thirteen other Negro investors, convened to comprise the Union Transportation Board (UTB). The company provided transportation for Negroes without imposing the second-class status that white-owned streetcar companies forced upon its Negro patrons. The company offered service on major routes to and from Black commercial and residential districts. Black Nashville patronized *their* new streetcar company enthusiastically and made it a success in short order. The successful, brazen display of Black independence and self-determination was an affront to the city's white business and political elite. Less than a year after the company began operations, the city council passed a privileged tax of $42.00 per car, forcing the UTB into bankruptcy.[14]

Economic Repression: The FHA and Black Nashville

Despite these and other assaults, Black Nashville flourished as it composed multiple narratives of economic ascent. As Jim Crow forced a more insular economy, commerce and culture continued to develop *within* Black enclaves. Nonetheless, North Nashville's economy was not protected from the broader economic devastation of the Great Depression. Two major policy decisions subsequent to the Depression dealt a devastating blow to the community and set the context for the Hub on the Hill initiatives. The first was the Home Owners Loan Commission's (HOLC) "residential security map" that directed government funding away from North Nashville to build white suburbs. The second was President Dwight D. Eisenhower's National Interstate and Defense Highways Act.

The Great Depression of the 1930s ravaged both Black and white communities. Unemployment rose to 31 percent for white communities while Black unemployment rose to 52 percent. In 1932, 273,000 mortgage foreclosures took place, and in 1933 there were one thousand foreclosures per day. Almost 50 percent of mortgages went into default, and new home construction dropped by 80 percent.[15] To counter the housing shortage, the federal government pursued two policies. First, it began constructing housing projects for displaced white people.[16] James A. Cayce Homes was the first of such public housing projects in Nashville. Finished in 1941, it included a clinic for mothers, a library, and activities for youth. The J. C. Napier Homes, a housing project constructed for Black residents, had no such amenities.

To move white families from public housing into home ownership, the Federal Housing Administration backed mortgages so that banks could securely extend credit and restart the dead housing market. HOLC developed maps of major cities and designated where federally backed mortgages could be extended. The maps had four designations: A (green), B (blue), C (yellow), D (red). Designation *A* was most desirable while designation *D* was "hazardous." The maps rated all of North Nashville and Black neighborhoods across the city as "hazardous." From 1935 to 1972, more than eleven million home mortgages were backed by the FHA, but only 2 percent went to African Americans.[17] Thus, the policy in effect barred North Nashvillians from benefits from the subsidies that uplifted white families from poverty into the middle class. Moreover, segregation laws prevented Black families from moving into blue or green areas. Where the laws might not have been tightly enforced, the FHA ensured segregation by refusing to fund mortgages in integrated neighborhoods.[18] Black families were left to choose between perpetual residency in public housing or renting private homes from white landlords.

Compounding the injury of FHA redlining was the fact that its funds were raised from public taxation. In other words, as Black families in North Nashville paid rent and taxes, their payments covered the property taxes that were used to subsidize areas like Forest Hills, Brentwood, and Green Hills. By 1968, when the Fair Housing Act passed, the policy officially ended but the damage had been done. The disparities between North Nashville and other parts of the city were evident. "As of 2020, in Nashville, a home in a formerly 'hazardous' neighborhood was worth on average $281,000 while a home in a 'best' neighborhood was worth $648,000. And, white Nashvillians have a 40 percent edge on people of color in making up the best neighborhoods."[19] This wealth disparity affected Black Nashvillians for generations. The mortgages backed by the FHA for white families were used to purchase homes that became the basis of intergenerational wealth. Over the course of the sixty years between 1940 and 2000, white families, on one hand, were able to extract equity from those homes to fund college education for their children, care for parents as they aged, and provide for their own care in retirement. On the other hand, Black families, who could not purchase homes, were relegated to rental markets and enjoyed none of these advantages. In general, they were not able to build wealth, their children graduated from college burdened by loans, and they often became financially dependent upon those children in retirement.

Physical Upheaval: Destroying Jefferson Street

Jerusalem faced destruction from a foreign power, but Black Nashville's physical upheaval came when the city determined the route of the Eisenhower Interstate System. On June 29, 1956, President Dwight D. Eisenhower signed the National Interstate and Defense Highways Act (the Highway Act).[20] He had been impressed by the German Autobahn's utility in efficiently transporting military personnel and matériel and believed that such a highway system would be essential to the nation's defense in the case of an invasion. State and local leaders had long wanted an east-west thoroughfare through the state capital of Nashville. Soon after the act was signed, federal, state, and municipal policies, determined in large part by antiBlack racism, conspired to dismantle Black Nashville's center. "Within a year of the I-40's completion, most businesses in the neighborhoods surrounding the expressway experienced severe financial difficulty and some ceased operations. Additionally, property values declined by nearly a third. More than 620 Black homes, twenty-seven apartment houses, and six Black churches were demolished, and fifty local streets were closed by dead-ends."[21] Jefferson Street's music scene, one of the most robust in the US, counted Ella Fitzgerald, Cab Calloway, Count Basie, Jimi Hendrix, Little Richard, Ray Charles, Duke Ellington, and others as regular visitors. They performed at thriving venues like the Silver Streak Ballroom and the Blue Room at Del Marco. Not lost on Black Nashville is the irony that the interstate destroyed a Black "music city" while investing in a white one just over a mile away at the Grand Ole Opry.

Long before the Highway Act was signed, Nashville began planning for the highway. A 1946 study proposed a west-to-east route along Highway 70, then between Charlotte Avenue and Broadway and along the Louisville and Nashville rail line. While the route would have been the most expedient, it encroached too closely upon white businesses and institutions, such as Vanderbilt University, Baptist Hospital, and Nashville's most exclusive white community, Belle Meade. In the early 1950s, the Tennessee State Highway Department commissioned the firm of Clarke and Rupino to offer an alternate route parallel to Charlotte Avenue, effectively bisecting the city between north and south, Black and white, reinforcing the city's segregated structure.[22]

Once Eisenhower signed the act, the state waited almost a year before quietly holding the one required public meeting, on May 15, 1957. State officials only advertised the meeting in white neighborhoods where it was not safe for Black residents to venture. As an extra measure to ensure no Black participation, the state posted the wrong dates on the notices.[23] With no opposition at the meeting, the Federal Highway Administration approved the plan in 1958. Again, the state engaged in subterfuge as it acquired land for the project. It waited six years, until 1965, to begin purchasing land for the right-of-way. In the interim, planners gave white speculators time to purchase land. Planners repeatedly misled and misdirected North Nashville Black residents and their leaders. When Black community leaders inquired about the planning, city officials told them the highway plans were incomplete or that routes were undecided. Even the state highway commission refused to release information. The conspiracy to keep North Nashville uninformed went so far as to include the surveyors, who told the residents that that there was "no cause for alarm" even as they staked the route.[24] By the time North Nashvillians could assemble enough information to mount a legal counter, it was essentially too late.[25] In defeat and reasonable anger, one North Nashville resident concluded the decision was "wretched, inhumane, illogical and an act of persecution."[26]

Initially, the planners sought to route I-40 down Jefferson Street. This route directly displaced businesses and would have made them eligible for federal highway funds as compensation. However, once construction began, the state chose a route just a few yards north of Jefferson Street. By routing the interstate just to the rear of Jefferson Street's businesses, they cut businesses off from their customers and community and were not legally required to fairly compensate Black business owners.[27] Jefferson Street itself was largely left intact, but as the Reverend Kelly Miller Smith lamented with palpable anger, "I-40 was a bitter thing which tore the community apart. Destroyed it."[28]

Black Nashville's Church and Jerusalem's Temple

When Nehemiah went to Jerusalem with funds to rebuild the life of the community, he took those funds to the Temple. In Jerusalem, as it was throughout the ancient world, temples were the center of community life, economy, and culture. In many ancient communities, the temple and the palace were the only two permanent structures. Both the civic and the religious life of the community took place at the Temple. As a center of the community, Black churches have been the site of the social (church picnics), the civic (voter registration drives), and the political life (organizing meetings during the Civil Rights Movement) of the Black community. In that regard, they held a significance similar to that of temples in the ancient world.

For Nehemiah, the Temple was the most enduring institution in the life of the Jerusalem community from the Israelite monarchy until the Romans destroyed it in 70 CE. So important was the Temple as an institution that even after the Babylonians destroyed the building, the community rebuilt it as soon as it was able. The Temple also symbolized an identity that transcended various political factions in Jerusalem: they were the people of Yahweh. By strengthening the Temple, Nehemiah reinforced the community's identity and its resolve to stand firm and unified in the face of Persian repression. Unified as the people of Yahweh, they completed the building project.

From the hush harbors of the eighteenth and nineteenth centuries, the Black church arose as the Invisible Institution[29] and created a religion of freedom out of the slavers' Christianity. It endured the slave regime and Jim Crow. Centuries of white supremacy's assaults through church burning or surreptitious acts to confiscate land could not prevent African American communities from rebuilding its structures. As Nehemiah believed about the Temple in Jerusalem, Harris claimed about the Black church in Nashville: if the people were to be unified to resist evil, then the Black church would be the central and catalyzing institution. Such was the context in which Harris led American Baptist College's "Hub on the Hill."

Called to Lives of Meaning and Purpose (CLMP)

The first initiative, CLMP, called together seventeen congregations divided into two cohorts to work together over five years. It invested $1.5 million in the work of resistance led by Black church communities. In its purpose statement, Harris structured the vision: "To facilitate Black theologically centered congregations as centers and leading facilitators of justice and healing within their communities and cities."[30] Three components constitute CLMP's vision of calling: theological imagination, healing and justice, and calling as communal.

For CLMP, calling demands a theological imagination that resists the God of evangelical spiritualism and seeks diligently the God who liberates. The two are diametrically opposed. The God who spiritualizes suffering and injustice cannot be the God who liberates the exploited from injustice. White evangelicalism has a tradition of imagining a different God than the one who affirms Black life. It affirms theologian James Cone's opening declaration in his classic work:

Christian theology is a theology of liberation. It is a rational study of the being of God in the world in light of the existential situation of an oppressed community, relating the forces of liberation to the essence of the gospel, which is Jesus Christ.... There can be no Christian theology that is not identified unreservedly with those who are humiliated and abused. In fact, theology ceases to be theology of the gospel when it fails to arise out of the community of the oppressed. [31]

In other words, the God to whom those on the decks of the slave ship prayed was not the God to whom those below prayed. Conceived in this way, CLMP worked to fashion a theological imagination that is antithetical to that of mainstream evangelical Christianity.

CLMP's proposal also links calling to healing and justice. For CLMP, calling requires a direct response to suffering and injustice with activity that leads toward justice. This recognition activated Nehemiah when his brother first alerted him to the suffering of his people in Jerusalem.

While I was in Susa the capital, one of my brothers, Hanani, came with certain men from Judah; and I asked them about the Jews that survived, those who had escaped the captivity, and about Jerusalem. They replied, "The survivors there in the province who escaped captivity are in great trouble and shame; the wall of Jerusalem is broken down, and its gates have been destroyed by fire." When I heard these words, I sat down and wept, and mourned for days, fasting and praying before the God of heaven. (Nehemiah 1:1–4, NRSV)

Connecting calling to the work of healing and justice makes discerning God's call political because it is oriented toward repairing the damage of injustice. New Testament scholar Obery Hendricks warns those whose would divorce the political from their understandings of religion: "The nonpolitical Jesus presented by mainstream Christianity ultimately serves the very forces he opposed by foisting upon oppressed peoples a model of Jesus that, tragically, is devoid of the power of Jesus's social witness. As a result, oppressive institutional structures are left essentially unchallenged by the considerable spiritual and material resources of the church."[32] The CLMP model requires understanding God as invested in the real activity of the systems that act upon Black communities with oppressive force. Such a claim calls Black churches to interrogate the long history of injustice faced by Black communities as the central focus of ministry.

Finally, CLMP envisions calling as communal. As a revelatory presence, God speaks to the entire community. God's revelation is democratized and comes to pulpit and pew together. Thus, calling is not singular, static, or hierarchical. By nature, such a concept of calling intends to flatten hierarchies, particularly those structured by social class and gender. Because discernment is communal also, the model holds the church accountable for convening the whole community to hear, value, and respond to all the stories of injury and to conceive together a vision where justice and healing are as widely distributed as is God's calling toward it. Together these concepts construct calling as God's communal call to resistance against evil in its myriad forms.

For the participants in CLMP, responding to God's call to the work of ministry is the process of being conscientized to recognize the needs of the community, to accept responsibility for one's capacity to respond to those needs, and to acknowledge that the legitimacy of both comes by divine authority because it is God who calls.

Empowering Congregations (EC)

The second initiative, EC, launched in 2021, continues the CLMP curriculum. The proposal connected a theology of inclusive justice grounded in a ministry praxis, focusing on the "lived experiences of black life" as it is informed by the teachings and ministry of Jesus Christ. It intends "to empower congregations facing intersecting social crisis and justice adjacent issues by helping them reflect sociologically and theologically on stratagems for effective mission and ministry decision-making."[33]

Its rationale builds upon CLMP's expanded understanding of calling and directs Black theological imagination toward the work of empowering Black churches and communities. As with CLMP, this initiative focused on three concepts: theological imagination, ministry praxis, and adaptive leadership. The three correspond to the three foci of the earlier CLMP initiative (theological imagination, healing and justice, and communal calling), but EC develops each further as the work transitions from "Calling" in the first initiative to "Empowerment." As with CLMP, the initiative finds its warrant in the work that Nehemiah did to empower the fractious Jerusalem community he encountered, "It takes communal bonding to the community and the political savvy of Nehemiah to rally impoverished Jews to vigorously hurry the work of rebuilding the walls of Jerusalem."[34] Once Nehemiah and those few members of the community who assist him complete the wall, the accomplishment raises Jerusalem's esteem among the surrounding communities and intimidates its enemies (Nehemiah 6:16). Rival communities recognized the wall as evidence of Jerusalem's new unity and strength. They began to see the inhabitants of Jerusalem as a formidable people.

Most dramatic is the change in the people's self-perception. During construction, the members of the community who assisted Nehemiah stood in resistance to those who thwarted their efforts. "With lanterns (enlightened consciousness and imagination), swords (armed with defiant self-determined fortitude) and an ancient masonry trowel (praxis tools) in their hands, Nehemiah rallied the people to fight for the heritage and future of their families."[35] Nehemiah rallied them to accomplish a feat that would have appeared impossible before. Their success raised their self-esteem. After completing the wall, the tone of the narrative changed. The people enthusiastically gather en masse to support and to claim membership in this community. Beyond the intangible goods that accrued to the people as a result of completing the wall, there were real benefits. For example, as a fortified city, the Jerusalem community could now protect itself and its members. This union of theological imagination and praxis oriented to a people's achievement echoes the visions of Marcus Garvey and others who rallied people of African descent to both imagine and accomplish their own rise from subjugation.[36] This is the work to which EC calls the Black church.

Theological Imagination

Theological imagination in EC evolves from the conceiving of a God whose primary concern is injustice to conceiving of the ways that God empowers the Black church to confront injustice and create security and healing for its community. For Harlem Renaissance intellectual Zora Neale Hurston, the need for such a perspective was obvious. In her autobiography, she expresses frustration with the congregants who were moved by her father's preaching but not empowered to change their world:

> Come love feast some of the congregation told of getting close
> enough to peep into God's sitting-room windows. Some went
> further. They had been inside the place and looked all around.
> They spoke of sights and scenes around God's throne.... They
> should have looked and acted differently from other people af-
> ter experiences like that. But these people looked and acted like
> everybody else—or so it seemed to me. They plowed, chopped
> wood, went possum-hunting, washed clothes, raked up back
> yards and cooked collard greens like anybody else. No more or-
> naments and nothing. It mystified me. There were so many
> things they neglected to look after while they were right up
> there in the presence of All-Power.[37]

Hurston wondered how people could come into the presence of the "All-Powerful" sacred on Sunday morning and return to the mundane without critique. For the initiative, such a theological imagination requires "re-engaging all forms of oppression and dominant interpretations of reality through a congregation's exercise of critical consciousness and human agency."[38] The EC summary points to Black congregational life and ministry as a contemporary illustration of Hurston's critique: "Black congregations historically and contemporaneously have been locked in the suffocating realities of oppression and locked out of the full exercise and enjoyment of all the rights and privileges of equitable flourishing."[39] The initiative identifies the issue as a crisis of theological imagination. It notes how Nashville has popularly been given the moniker the "It City" for its thriving economy and robust development. However, as tourist dollars inundate commercial districts and the increasing competition for affordable housing fueled by ongoing influx of transplants, gentrification rehearses the script of sacrificing Black communities for white economic convenience. Legacies of white supremacy's redlining and housing policies persist, and "Black congregations are located in communities where social disparities and inequities severely limit the life chances of children and families." In fact, the Brookings Institute found that the 37208 zip code, which encompasses North Nashville, has the highest incarceration rate in the country.[40] Without a theological imagination equal to the challenges faced by the Black community, the church is of little efficacy. EC intends to summon within the Black church such an imagination.

Ministry Praxis

Both CLMP and EC take up justice and healing, but the latter makes them the focus of ministry praxis rather than calling. EC intends to focus Black church "reflection and action upon forms of prophetic communal care to transform the way congregations address social domains of injustice." Central to its action-reflection hermeneutical circle is a turn to the real lived experiences of all members of the Black community. These stories are worthy and essential sources for understanding Black life and for theorizing models of effective justice-making work and community healing. When the body of stories that make up the stock of communal knowledge is circumscribed by socioeconomic standing, age, gender, sexuality, or even political or theological orientation, the community risks replicating unjust structures. Because the stories themselves direct the praxis model, its work toward justice and healing distribute both goods as widely as the real lived experiences that the stories articulate. Omitting this critical dimension of the action-reflection model can be disastrous, as Nehemiah's community experienced.[41]

Nehemiah's work here is at odds with vision-ministry praxis. Placing Nehemiah's testimony of his experience with God alongside the vision given to the Hub creates hermeneutical space to appreciate Nehemiah's circumstance and the decisions he made without accepting them as a mandate. Thus, the interpretation leaves room for the church to hear from God in a different way. Given the opposition he faced from various factions within the Jerusalem community, Nehemiah attempted to structure a homogeneous collective. Unfortunately for Nehemiah, the people in Jerusalem had already married within other groups who were also subjugated by the Persian Empire. Marriages in the ancient world were, by and large, not based on romance but on economic expediency. Marriage was too important a decision in the life of any kinship group to be left to the whims of individual choice. These unions took place among Judahites of various religious persuasions. They shared the experience of oppression by Persian imperial rule. Strategically chosen, these marriages were political alliances that enabled kinship groups to resist Persian dominion.[42]

These alliances did not comport with Nehemiah's vision for the community. He "curses," "contends with," and "pulls the hair" from those who disagree with him (Nehemiah 13:23–27). Rather than hearing their stories, he forced them to swear against their marriages.[43] Nehemiah's choice destroyed scores of families. Such an administrative decision runs counter to the ministry praxis model articulated by the empowering initiative. By acting without considering the stories of these families and their experiences of survival and resistance under Persia, Nehemiah deprived the community of important, invaluable knowledge for the entire community survival under Persia. Here, Nehemiah's story offers the Black church a cautionary example. When enclaves within the church, circumscribed by gender, class, or sexuality, hold privilege, the church reproduces the injustice it seeks to rectify.

Adaptive Leadership

Finally, EC takes up adaptive leadership as the work inspired by CLMP's "Communal Calling." "It re-envisions Black Church leadership toward emancipatory models of non-hierarchical, gender equitable and intergenerational leadership to humanize systems through profound love for people and the community."[44] Adaptive leadership in this model recognizes the rapidly changing social issues that Black communities face, such as gentrifying neighborhoods, hyper-incarceration, police brutality, underfunded neighborhood schools, etc. Responding to most of these issues requires skill sets beyond those developed within seminary courses of study for standard theological degrees. In a focus group leading the initiative, pastors admitted "that seminaries trained them to lead 'churches that do not exist anymore' and deal with contextual realities requiring continuous theological reflection. Admittedly, their congregations are overly vested in hierarchical-male leadership institutional cultures which limit and thwart the creative gifts, particularly of women."[45]

While Nehemiah's leadership proved effective for galvanizing the community to construct the wall, the limits of his leadership became clear as he instituted the reforms that dissolved marriages. Nehemiah's leadership model was shaped by his proximity to the Persian throne and by his position as a Persian governor of the province.[46] Both limited his ability to lead "with" the people. From the Persian throne room, Nehemiah imagined rehabilitating and strengthening a homogeneous group that perhaps fit the image he knew from hearing stories of the Jerusalem community under the monarchy. However, the community in Jerusalem had evolved in the century between the beginning of Persia's rule and Nehemiah's arrival. To survive Babylonian and Persian rule, marginalized groups had made alliances with each other to resist dominion. Marriage was one form of alliance between families. Had Nehemiah taken up an adaptive leadership model, he might have developed a critical consciousness about the limits of his ability and trusted that the gifts for leadership in this situation already existed within the community.

Finally, this study, grounded by the histories of Nehemiah's and Black Nashville's worlds, shows how meanings are not so readily transferable from one to the other but are understood in context. By reading Nehemiah as a dialogue partner "with" rather than a warrant "for" the Black church's theology, Nehemiah's story, his decisions, and his discernment, do not restrict the Black church's theological imagination. In dialog with the Bible, Black church can create the hermeneutical distance necessary to hear from God in the unique ways God speaks to the Black community's particular circumstance. In the instance of CLMP and EC, such a reading strategy makes room to expand the concepts of theological imagination, ministry praxis, and adaptive learning and invites the church to value its own revelation from God with a vision of justice that includes the entire community.

Chapter 4

African American Presidents of Colleges and Seminaries: A Little-Known Legacy of Leadership

Marvin A. McMickle

I began thinking about the notion of African American clergy who have served as presidents of colleges, universities, and seminaries while reflecting on the amazing career of Dr. Forrest Harris of American Baptist College in Nashville, Tennessee. Dr. Harris has served for more than twenty-five years as president of American Baptist College. However, captured within that singular achievement of longevity and success is something far more subtle but just as deserving of recognition in this collection. Forrest Harris is part of a more than 150-year legacy of African American clergy who have served as presidents of academic institutions. That is the legacy that will be examined in this essay.

This legacy began with AME Bishop Daniel Alexander Payne, who served as president of Wilberforce University in Ohio from 1863 to 1876, thus making him the first African American college president in the United States of America. At the time of his installation as president, Payne wrote, "My work henceforth was to lie in two channels, and my whole heart, soul, and body were to need strength from on high to perform it wisely."[1]

This legacy continued with Father Patrick Healy, a Roman Catholic Jesuit priest who served as president of Georgetown University in Washington, DC, from 1873 to 1882. However, since Georgetown was not admitting African American students at that time, it is unlikely that they "knowingly" had an African American president of the university. It is likely that Healy, born of an Irish immigrant father and a slave mother, was able to "pass" as a white person.[2] For that reason, his name features an asterisk in the list of

African American clergy who have served as presidents of colleges, universities, and seminaries, found later in this chapter.

Many Notable African American College Presidents

Much has been written and is widely known about many distinguished African American college presidents. One thinks at once about Mary McLeod Bethune, who founded Bethune Cookman College in Daytona Beach, Florida, and served as president from 1923 to 1942, and again from 1946 to 1947. One would also think about Booker T. Washington, who was president of Tuskegee Institute (now university) in Tuskegee, Alabama, from 1881 to 1915.

However, the list is far longer and more recent than those two names and eras reflect. Graduates of Spelman College in Atlanta remember with pride the years of 1987 to 1997 when Johnetta Coleman served as president of that college. Following that, she served as president of Bennett College in North Carolina from 2002 to 2007. History was made when Ruth Simmons became president of Smith College in 1995 and then Brown University in the Ivy League in 2001 prior to her becoming president of Prairie View A&M University in Texas in 2017. Clifton Wharton became president of Michigan State University in East Lansing in 1969, and in 1978 he became chancellor (president) of the sixty-four-campus State University of New York system. There is a long and distinguished list of African Americans who have served as presidents of colleges and universities. Rather than examining all the people of any profession who have served as college, university, or seminary presidents, this essay will focus on those African American clergy who have filled this significant role.

Presidents versus Academic Deans

This study does not include anyone who served or is currently serving primarily or exclusively in the position of academic dean. Many African American preachers have served very successfully as academic deans. Those who come to mind include Henry Mitchell and John Kinney of the Samuel DeWitt Proctor School of Theology at Virginia Union University in Richmond, Virginia; Valerie Bridgeman of Methodist Theological School in Delaware, Ohio; Renita Weems at American Baptist College in Nashville, Tennessee; Leah Francis Gunning of Christian Theological Seminary in Indianapolis, Indiana; David Forbes of Shaw University Divinity School in Raleigh, North Carolina; Deborah Mullen of Columbia Theological Seminary in Decatur, Georgia; Lawrence N. Jones and Yolanda Pierce of Howard University Divinity School in Washington, DC; Joseph Evans of Morehouse School of Religion, in Atlanta; and Emilie Townes of Vanderbilt University Divinity School in Nashville. Each of these persons functioned not only within an academic setting but also in local church pulpits and on the platforms at national church gatherings.

However, those persons and that position will not receive any further attention in this essay largely because this essay is devoted to the work preacher/presidents. Contrary to what some outside observers might think, the title of *dean* and the title of *president* are not synonymous. Typically, an academic dean focuses on matters of curriculum development and faculty mentoring and concentrates on matters going on within the life of the school. In most instances, deans are not the primary face of the institution to the broader public when it comes to articulating the school's mission, fundraising, and interfacing with various off-campus constituencies. That job is most often assigned to the president.

Second, and as a matter of organization and accountability, the dean reports to the president and, thus, does not hold the primary CEO position. This distinction is easiest to discern with free-standing, independent schools like Union Theological Seminary in New York City, Princeton Theological Seminary (NJ), Colgate Rochester Crozer Divinity School (NY), Chicago Theological Seminary, and dozens more across the country, where the dean's assignment is primarily academic and focused on the internal workings of the school. Meanwhile, the president is focused on the multiple constituencies that affect an academic institution, such as alumni, financial donors, public relations, and the non-classroom employees who keep the school fully operational.

The distinction becomes even more apparent for those seminaries and graduate schools that are embedded within larger universities. For historically Black schools that have seminaries or divinity schools, such as Howard, Shaw, and Virginia Union, the seminary is a school of theology within the larger university structure. The divinity school operates alongside other graduate or professional schools, such as law, medicine, education, nursing, pharmacy, or any other specialized graduate division. Each of those graduate schools may have their own dean, but there is only one president. This is also the model at work for the Interdenominational Theological Center (ITC) in Atlanta. Each of the member schools at ITC has its own dean, but a different person serves as president.

Forrest E. Harris Sr.
and the Preacher/President

This contribution is not meant simply to celebrate Forrest Harris's twenty-five-year career as a college president. In truth, Dr. Harris is not unique or singular in that accomplishment. Many African American presidents of academic institutions have served lengthy tenures at their respective schools. Booker T. Washington served as president of Tuskegee Institute for thirty-four years. In 2016, I spoke for the South Carolina Missionary Baptist Convention on the campus of Morris College in Sumter, South Carolina, where Dr. Luns C. Richardson served as president for forty-three years (1974 to 2017). Thus, it is not simply Dr. Harris's tenure in office that is the objective of this essay. What is lifted and celebrated here is the fact that Forrest Harris is both an ordained Christian preacher as well as a college president. For the past twenty-five years he has stood in the gap between the Black church and the college campus, using his status to help local church congregants,

Baptist convention leaders, and college students navigate the most controversial issues facing American society in the twenty-first century. He is what shall be referred to hereafter as a *preacher/president*.

There have been scores, if not hundreds, of African Americans of various other professional groups who have served as college and university presidents. They have come from disciplines as diverse as science, law, economics, history, politics, teaching and research, the military, business and industry, finance, medicine, and many other fields. A distinguished legacy has been established dating back to the mid-nineteenth century of African Americans who served both the church and the academy, filled pulpits and classrooms, and attained prominence both within denominational gatherings and academic guilds and learned societies. They were preacher/presidents.

Samuel DeWitt Proctor
and the Preacher/President

Forrest Harris was not my first introduction to the preacher/president. My first exposure to this combination of qualities and responsibilities was with Samuel DeWitt Proctor, for whom I worked when I was still a student. In the fall of 1972, I was invited to interview for a staff position at Abyssinian Baptist Church of New York City. That church was home to Adam Clayton Powell Sr., who served as senior pastor from 1908 to 1937, and Adam Clayton Powell Jr., who served as senior pastor from 1937 to 1972.[3] I was being considered for a position under the leadership of Dr. Samuel DeWitt Proctor, who had recently assumed the role of senior pastor. I was invited to work with Dr. Proctor and did so from 1972 to 1976. I will forever remember the time Dr. Proctor sent me to LaGuardia Airport to pick up Dr. Benjamin Elijah Mays. Dr. Mays was himself a preacher/president who had served as president of Morehouse College from 1940 to 1967. He came to New York to participate in a months-long series of events that served as Dr. Proctor's installation as senior pastor at Abyssinian. Along with the Reverend Dr. John Ellison, who had preceded Proctor at Virginia Union University, Benjamin Mays was a primary mentor of Dr. Proctor.

During those years, I got a close-up view of a person who was a central part of an important legacy within the African American community: a clergyperson who had also been the president of two accredited academic institutions, Virginia Union University and North Carolina Agricultural and Technical College (later North Carolina A&T State University). Many of my peers had gone to schools where the president was an African American clergyperson, but this was the first time in my life that I had been personally exposed to a person who was both a seasoned pastor and preacher and a successful college president and professor. In writing an endorsement for Dr. Proctor's memoir, *The Substance of Things Hoped For*, Cornel West wrote, "Samuel Proctor is the towering figure of our time, of intellectual teachers who preach, and intellectual preachers who teach."[4]

Proctor as a President. Samuel Proctor earned his Doctor of Theology degree (Th.D.) from Boston University in 1949. He became president of his undergraduate alma mater, Virginia Union University of Richmond in 1955. In 1960 he became president of North Carolina A&T University in Greensboro, North Carolina.[5] From those vantage points, Proctor was eyewitness to some of the most important moments in recent American history. While serving at Virginia Union, he was deeply involved as an advisor to Martin Luther King Jr. and the Montgomery bus boycott. Proctor's move to North Carolina A&T corresponded with the beginning of the sit-in movement led by students from Greensboro and from Fisk and American Baptist College in Nashville, Tennessee. In 1961, while Proctor was president of the college, Jesse Jackson Sr. was president of the A&T student body. While speaking at the funeral for Dr. Proctor in 1997, Jackson acknowledged that Samuel Proctor, his college president, was the first person he consulted about his 1984 campaign for president of the United States.

Proctor as a Preacher. With every passing day, I learned something new and valuable from this African American preacher/president. How do you preside over business meetings? How do you plan and oversee a budget? How do you address sensitive and confidential personnel matters? How do you plan a preaching schedule when you are expected to speak to the same congregation over the same annual cycle of special days and seasonal celebrations over the course of nearly two decades and not simply repeat yourself year after year? How do you lead a congregation through the changing social and moral questions of the day so they consider them from a faith perspective? This was the preacher/pastor side of Samuel Proctor. This is why he was named by *Ebony* magazine as one of the top fifteen Black preachers in the United States in 1993.[6] This is also why he was invited to deliver the Lyman Beecher Lectures on Preaching at Yale University Divinity School in 1990.[7] As Adam Bond states in his important study of the life of this preacher/president, Samuel DeWitt Proctor was an "Imposing Preacher."[8]

Proctor as Preacher/Professor. By the time he arrived at Abyssinian Baptist Church in 1972, Proctor was no longer a college president. He was serving as the Martin Luther King Jr. distinguished professor of education at the Graduate School of Education at Rutgers University in New Brunswick, New Jersey. He decided to retain his faculty and university status and to serve the church on a half-time basis. He used half of his salary to hire three assistant ministers. Along with William S. Epps and Calvin O. Butts, I was one of those three original staff ministers.[9]

While Proctor brought his amazing preaching gifts to the Abyssinian congregation, he was simultaneously directing the Doctor of Education degree program (Ed.D.) for scores of teachers and school administrators still serving at the secondary or college level in schools across the country. He was also mentoring young seminary students for careers in some form of Christian ministry. After his retirement from Rutgers and from Abyssinian, Proctor continued to teach and to mentor young preachers. He was the director of the Doctor of Ministry program at United Theological Seminary in Dayton, Ohio, and also taught at Vanderbilt University and Duke University.

Following in the Footsteps of Samuel D. Proctor. Two of the three original staff ministers who worked with Samuel Proctor went on to become preacher/presidents themselves. Calvin O. Butts III not only succeeded Dr. Proctor as senior pastor of Abyssinian Baptist Church in 1989, he also served for more than twenty years as president of the State University of New York (SUNY) at Old Westbury in Long Island, New York.[10] In terms of my own journey, after spending thirty-four years as a senior pastor at St. Paul Baptist Church in Montclair, New Jersey, and at Antioch Baptist Church in Cleveland, I served as president of Colgate Rochester Crozer Divinity School in Rochester, New York, from 2011 to 2019.

Whatever success I have had in my career is as much a result of my four years of association with Dr. Proctor as my years of formal academic preparation. Early in my career, the prospect of becoming president of an academic institution was being presented to me as a viable vocational option. However, because of my early exposure to Samuel Proctor, I have never thought about pursuing an academic career that was not linked to service to the local church and the broader Christian and interfaith communities. Early in my ministry, I was captured by the connection between the pulpit and the classroom.

In 1985, I was offered a tenure-track position in homiletics at Princeton Theological Seminary, where I had been teaching on an adjunct basis for some time. The sole condition, though, was that I resign as senior pastor at St. Paul Baptist Church. It made no sense to me to resign from the task of pastoral preaching on a weekly basis to teach preaching courses. I turned down that initial invitation because it made no sense to me to leave the act and artistry of something I loved to engage in the theory and teaching of that same field. I was committed to the model of the pastor/professor.

Fortunately, when I assumed the role of senior pastor at Antioch Baptist Church in Cleveland, I was invited to teach on a part-time basis. I was then invited to join the full-time faculty at Ashland Theological Seminary in Ashland, Ohio, while being able to retain my pastoral position. Thus, from 1995 to 2011, I was engaged in the model of pastor/professor I had first observed in Samuel Proctor.

While serving in that model, I was invited to become president of Colgate Rochester Crozer Divinity School in Rochester, New York. At that point, I made the decision to retire from pastoral ministry, which is how I moved beyond the role of preacher/professor and joined the ranks of the preacher/president. I could not have imagined in 1972 that I would become the president of the school from which Samuel Proctor had earned his theological degree in 1945. That is what happened when Crozer Theological Seminary in Chester, Pennsylvania, closed in 1970 and merged with Colgate Rochester Divinity School, thus creating Colgate Rochester Crozer Divinity School.

Howard Thurman, Mordecai Johnson, Joseph H. Jackson, Martin Luther King Jr., William A. Jones Jr., Wyatt Tee Walker, John Bryant, Harold Carter, H. Beecher Hicks Jr., and many other notable African American clergy leaders are alumni of the school where I served as president. None of this would have been possible without the example and encouragement of an African American preacher/president named Samuel DeWitt Proctor.

Who Is Part of the Legacy of Preacher/Presidents?

Consider the following African America clergypersons who have served in the capacity of preacher/presidents of colleges and seminaries. They have served in undergraduate college settings, as heads of universities, and as presidents of seminaries and divinity schools. Some of them have served in secular institutions where there was no clear connection to any church body. Some of them served at stand-alone or independent seminaries that were only loosely affiliated with any church body. Others served within church-affiliated schools where issues of accountability included not only the board of trustees or the president of the university but also the claims and interests of the church body and denominational leaders with whom the schools were associated.

The list that follows does not presume to be exhaustive. There may well be other African American preacher/presidents, especially at some of the Historically Black Colleges and Universities (HBCU) whose names do not appear here. Every effort was made to identify as many candidates for this list as possible. Names came to me from dozens of sources beyond the persons of whom I was already aware. Therefore, I offer the following listing only as a representative sampling of African American preacher/presidents. Asterisks will appear behind two names, Patrick Healy and Lawrence Jones. Healy is listed with an asterisk because, as stated earlier, he was likely passing as white when he served at Georgetown University in the nineteenth century. Lawrence N. Jones is listed with an asterisk because he served as acting president at Union Theological Seminary in New York City.

1. Estrelda Y. Alexander: William Seymour College (MD): Pentecostal

2. Albert Aymer: Hood Theological Seminary (NC): African Methodist Episcopal Zion

3. Michael Battle: Interdenominational Theological Center (GA)

4. Lee Butler: Iliff School of Theology (CO): Methodist

5. James Alvin Bacote: Leland College (LA): Baptist

6. Brian Blount: Union Presbyterian Seminary (VA): Presbyterian

7. Gwendolyn Boyd: Alabama State University

8. Marsha Foster Boyd: Ecumenical Theological Seminary (MI)

9. Michael Brown: Payne Theological Seminary (OH): African Methodist Episcopal

10. Calvin O. Butts III: SUNY at Old Westbury (NY)

11 James Cheek: Howard University (DC)

12. Kevin Cosby: Simmons College (KY): Baptist

13. James Costen: Interdenominational Theological Center (GA)

14. Michael Curry: Bishop College (TX): Baptist

15. Karl E. Downs: Samuel Huston College (TX): United Methodist Church

16. James Echols: Lutheran Theological Seminary (PA)

17. John M. Ellison: Virginia Union University: Baptist

18. James Evans: Colgate Rochester Crozer Divinity School (NY)

19. James Farmer Sr.: Wiley College (TX): Methodist Episcopal

20. Leah Gaskin Fitchue: Payne Theological Seminary (OH): African Methodist Episcopal

21. Floyd Flake: Wilberforce University (OH): African Methodist Episcopal

22. Marla Frederick: Dean: Harvard Divinity School: Harvard (MA)

23. Robert Michael Franklin: Morehouse College (GA)

24. Charisse Gillette: Lexington Theological Seminary (KY): Disciples of Christ

25. David Goatley: Fuller Theological Seminary (CA)

26. Mark Harden: Ashland Theological Seminary (OH): Brethren

27. Forrest E. Harris Sr.: American Baptist College (TN): Baptist

28. Kenneth Harris: Ecumenical Theological Seminary (MI)

29. Earl Harrison: Bishop College (TX): Baptist

30. Robert E. Hayes: Wiley College (TX): Methodist Episcopal

31. Patrick Healy:* Georgetown University (DC): Roman Catholic

32. Obery Hendricks: Payne Theological Seminary (OH): African Methodist Episcopal

33. M. William Howard: New York Theological Seminary

34. Allix B. James: Virginia Union University: Baptist

35. Mordecai Johnson: Howard University (DC)

36. Lawrence N. Jones:* Union Theological Seminary (NY)

37. W. Thomas Keaton: Arkansas Baptist College

38. Vergel Lattimore: Hood Theological Seminary (NC): African Methodist Episcopal Zion

39. Paul Martin: American Baptist Seminary of the West (CA)

40. Benjamin E. Mays: Morehouse College (GA)

41. Myron McCoy: St. Paul School of Theology (MO): United Methodist Church

42. Lester A. McCorn: Clinton College (SC): African Methodist Episcopal Zion

43. Micah McCreary: New Brunswick Theological Seminary (NJ): Reformed

44. Marvin A. McMickle: Colgate Rochester Crozer Divinity School (NY)

45. Rosemary B. McNatt: Starr King School of Ministry (CA): Unitarian Universalist

46. Garland Millet: Oakwood University (AL): Seventh Day Adventist

47. Clarence Newsome: Shaw University (NC): Baptist

48. Daniel Alexander Payne: Payne Theological Seminary (OH): African Methodist Episcopal

49. Benjamin Payton: Tuskegee University (AL)

50. Alton Pollard: Louisville Presbyterian Theological Seminary (KY)

51. Yolanda Pierce: Dean: Vanderbilt Divinity School (TN)

52. Samuel D. Proctor: (1) Virginia Union University: Baptist and (2) North Carolina Agricultural and Technical College

53. Stephen Ray: Chicago Theological Seminary (IL): United Church of Christ

54. J. Deotis Roberts: Interdenominational Theological Center (GA)

55. C. Shelby Rooks Jr.: Chicago Theological Seminary (IL): United Church of Christ

56. David T. Shannon: Andover Newton Theological Seminary (MA): ABC

57. Talbert O. Shaw: Shaw University (NC): Baptist

58. Emma Jordan Simpson: Auburn Theological Seminary (NY): Baptist

59. Angela Sims: Colgate Rochester Crozer Divinity School (NY): Baptist

60. Kenneth Smith: Chicago Theological Seminary (IL): United Church of Christ

61. Reembert Stokes: Wilberforce University (OH)

62. Wallace Charles Smith: Palmer Theological Seminary (PA): American Baptist

63. Emilie Townes: Dean: Vanderbilt Divinity School (TN)

64. LaKeesha Walrond: New York Theological Seminary (NY): Baptist

65. Jonathan Walton: Princeton Theological Seminary (NJ): Presbyterian Church (USA)

66. Daryl Ward: United Theological Seminary (OH): United Methodist Church

67. William Watley: Paul Quinn College (TX): African Methodist Episcopal

68. Charles H. Wesley: Central State University (OH)

69. Edward Wheeler: Christian Theological Seminary (IN): Disciples of Christ; Interdenominational Theological Center (GA)

70. John Wilson: Morehouse College (GA)

71. Harry Wright: Bishop College (TX)

Forrest Harris: A Preacher/President at a Critical Time

If one of the challenges of the preacher/president is to bridge the values of the church and the mission of an academic institution while being faithful to both aspects of that person's identity. That challenge was on full display in the life of Forrest Harris and American Baptist College beginning in 2015. Bishop Yvette Flunder, who is a preacher and leader within the LGBTQ+ community and who is in a same-gender marriage, was invited by Harris and American Baptist College to speak during the annual Garnett-Nabrit Lecture Series held on campus.[11]

Flunder's appearance was vehemently opposed by, and openly condemned by, several ministers of the National Baptist Convention USA, Inc., a group that claims both ownership and oversight of American Baptist College. Those African American clergy demanded that Flunder either cancel her appearance at the college or that the college rescind its invitation. Yvette Flunder refused to cancel her appearance, and the college refused to rescind its invitation.[12]

What resulted was a very public tug-of-war between a national church body and an academic institution. At stake was nothing less than academic freedom, freedom of speech, and the role of an academic institution to invite public dialogue on its campus for the intellectual formation of its students. At stake in that stand-off was the distinction between what some in the church were condemning as sinful and inappropriate for a college chapel (in this case, an academic lecture by a person who was part of a same-gender marriage) and what leaders of an academic institution considered as part of the school's mission of further empowering their students to function, and even offer leadership, in a world that is increasingly secular, theologically and socially diverse, and increasingly unpersuaded and even disinterested in what preachers have to say on matters of human sexuality.

This latter is the case because so many preachers have been caught up in sexual indiscretions of their own or have chosen to be self-selective about which forms of sexual conduct should be allowed or overlooked and which should be vigorously opposed and condemned. Should a free and open discussion about sexual orientation, same-sex marriage, and the broader issues affecting the LGBTQ+ community be shut down by the angry voices of a small but vocal group of socially conservative clergy?

The clergy who were so outspoken in their use of biblical materials about the presence of a lesbian woman giving a lecture on the campus of American Baptist College would do well to read and consider Paul's writings in 1 Corinthians 6. The opening verses of that chapter deal with a biblical mandate just as clear as anything that is said about sexual practices: namely, that Christians should not seek to resolve disputes by going to the secular courts and using legal maneuvers before they have exhausted every avenue for resolution through discussions among themselves.

How much time and money did American Baptist College spend between 2015 and 2018 in court filings, depositions, and resisting an attempted takeover of the school's governance by elements within the National Baptist Convention? How odd that 1

Corinthians 6, a chapter that involves language about same-gender relations, can be embraced by the critics of American Baptist College while the language about legal actions among believers that appears in the same chapter is conspicuously overlooked.

The persons leading the charge against the appearance of Bishop Flunder, and all preachers who seek to determine what behaviors are and are not acceptable in our society, would do well to consider the words of President Abraham Lincoln in an address he delivered in 1842 on abstinence from alcoholic beverages (*temperance*, in nineteenth-century terminology). Lincoln argued, "When men's conduct is designed to be influenced, persuasion—kind, unassuming persuasion, should ever be adopted."[13] Attempts to shame people, using press conferences to condemn people, and employing legal action to prevent people from doing things you could not prevent them from doing by persuasion are seldom a successful, long-term solution. Lincoln continued by saying, "Assume to dictate to his judgment, or to command his action, or to mark him as one to be shunned and despised, and he will retreat within himself, close all the avenues to his head and his heart."[14] It is unfortunate that people who cannot win the day through persuasion try to achieve by intimidation what they could not achieve through argument.

True enough, there have been major national issues, such as slavery, segregation, and voting rights for all, regardless of ethnicity or gender, where legal action was needed since persuasion proved unsuccessful. However, when it comes to LGBTQ+-related issues, persuasion seems to have worked to the advantage of that community on the national level. Same-sex marriage is legal in the United States. Federal law exists to prohibit any form of discrimination against persons based upon sexual orientation. Persons who may be opposed to these outcomes made their case, but their arguments were ultimately unpersuasive.

Since 1 Corinthians 6 is one of the chapters many people use to justify their condemnation of same-gender marriage or sexual relations, it may be useful to consider that passage more carefully.

It deals with a matter that is as hotly contested in the twenty-first century in the United States as it was in Corinth in the first-century CE: what constitutes sexual immorality? Paul was troubled by the sexual practices he observed in Corinth, most notably prostitution and other acts that were driven less by human love and more by human lust. Paul viewed these acts as sins that prevented or disrupted one's relationship with God. Sexual immorality was, according to Paul, incompatible with the new life in Christ that he was urging the people of Corinth to embrace. Paul was stating that membership in the church included having the indwelling presence of Christ in one's life. Paul viewed the body of a believer as the holy temple in which the Spirit of Christ resided. That led Paul to the conclusion that sexual immorality was not just the sex act itself, but a failure to realize that the immoral act corrupted the body that had been made holy by the indwelling presence of Christ.

Paul was resting his case about a sexual code of conduct that was shaped by his exposure to the tenth-century BCE Holiness Code found in chapters 17 to 26 of the Book of Leviticus. The challenge was what to do with that code of conduct as far as the people of Corinth were concerned since they were Gentiles who were completely unfamiliar with ancient Jewish religious law.

This effort by Paul is part of the challenge for those who stand between the pulpit and the classroom or between the church and the seminary. The challenge for Paul was not just sharing the Gospel of Jesus Christ with the Gentile nations. The greater challenge was associated with the existing religious and cultural practices of those who were spreading the message about Jesus to the Gentiles and the existing religious and cultural practices of those to whom they preached in cities like Corinth, Ephesus, Galatia, Philippi, Thessalonica, and Rome, where sexual norms and mores were entirely different.

Those religious and cultural differences included such things as dietary restrictions, monotheism versus polytheism, the physical act of circumcision, and what actions constituted sexual immorality. These and other differences were matters of agreement at the

THE BLACK LEADERSHIP TRADITION IN AMERICA

Jerusalem Conference recorded in Acts 15, where Jewish Christian leaders reached consensus on what would be required of Gentile converts. The things agreed upon were abstaining from food offered to idols, sexual immorality, food where the blood of the animal was still present and eating the meat of strangled animals (Acts 15:20–29). However, agreement among the apostles who preached to the Gentiles was one thing; getting agreement from the Gentiles to embrace these religious and cultural differences was another matter altogether.

What Is Appropriate Sexual Conduct in the Twenty-first Century?

This challenge is no easier for preachers in the twenty-first century. The challenge begins with the fact that there is no single definition in the wider American society about what constitutes sexual immorality. In truth, there is no collective agreement among all Christians in this country or in the global Christian community about what specific actions constitute sexual immorality. For some people, the issue involves condemning any sexual activity that occurs outside of marriage between one man and one woman. Under this definition, behaviors like adultery, fornication, pedophilia, pornography, self-gratification, or any other heterosexual forms of sexual activity would be the focus. Not surprisingly, one seldom hears a sermon that touches on any of those topics other than homosexuality.

Other people are likely to bring the full force of divine judgment primarily on anyone who engages in any form of homosexuality. For persons who embrace this definition of sexual immorality, the operative texts would be Leviticus 18:22, Romans 1:24–27, and this passage in 1 Corinthians 6. This approach poses several problems for those who use them in their assault on sexual immorality. There are many behaviors set forth in the Book of Leviticus beyond homosexual activity, and it is odd to observe people who condemn homosexuality who also eat rare steak with blood still

81

present (Leviticus 17:11–12), who eat shellfish and rabbit (Leviticus 11:6–11), who call for harsh treatment of immigrants and migrant workers (Leviticus 19:9–15), who wear clothing made of two different fabrics, or who plant two different kinds of crops in the same soil (Leviticus 19:19). Some people seem comfortable enforcing some biblical passages, even some parts of the same passage, while ignoring or disobeying others.

Things do not get better for those who rush to Romans 1:26–27 to condemn same-sex relationships but completely ignore the behaviors listed in verses 1:29–30 that include greed, envy, slander, arrogance, gossip, malice, murder, and boasting. How many sermons on these topics have been preached by those who opposed the appearance of Yvette Flunder at American Baptist College? Add to this list the behaviors listed in 1 Corinthians 6:9–10, which includes drunkards, swindlers, thieves, and idolaters. All these things are far more prevalent in twenty-first-century church life than the appearance of a lesbian woman on a Black college campus. Must these preachers vet all invited guests to American Baptist College from the National Baptist Convention to see if they pass the moral purity test they were trying to impose on Yvette Flunder?

Ministry in the Age of the #MeToo Movement

Our society is awash in examples of sexual assault and violence. Iconic figures in the worlds of entertainment, politics, journalism, government, and the military have been removed from their positions of power because of their immoral sexual behaviors. The nation watched as the United States Senate confirmed two Supreme Court associate justices to lifetime appointments after they faced credible charges of sexual assault. The #MeToo movement emerged as an indicator that sexual assault is not an odd and occasional occurrence in our society. It is a cruelly common occurrence that many people still refuse to acknowledge.[15]

We are talking about sexual immorality at a time when a former president of the United States is known for multiple marriages, a string of adulterous affairs, and arranging hush money payments to former mistresses to keep them from reporting their affairs just ahead of the big election. Why should society take seriously what the church says about sexual immorality when this person won the election with overwhelming support from so-called evangelical Christians even after he was caught on tape bragging about what sexual behaviors women allow celebrities to perform?[16]

Even more intriguing is the confession of some that they voted for the former "groper-in-chief" because they could not bring themselves to vote for a woman to be president of the United States. This leads me to the observation that the focus on Yvette Flunder and the question about human sexuality by those Baptist preachers who focused on American Baptist College and sought to challenge the judgment of Forrest Harris is subject to a second critique.

In many Black Baptist churches and in most Black Baptist conventions across the country, there is equal resistance to the notion of women serving in any ordained role in ministry whether those women are heterosexual or homosexual. Women have been pushing back against the notion of male-centric ministry for years. This issue is the focus of an informative article by David Crary of the Associated Press entitled "Placing Their Faith in Gender Equality."[17] This observation is important in this context because the entire group of Black Baptist preachers that led the attack against Yvette Flunder and who continued in their attempts to take control of American Baptist College are male.

The Twenty-first Century Church
and Sexual Indiscretions

The challenge of preaching about any kind of requirements or restraints regarding sexual misconduct is made greater by the fact that the authority and influence of the church itself is undercut by the behavior of some male church leaders. The church has serious credibility issues when it comes to preaching about sexual immorality. Charges of pedophilia are regularly being launched against many Roman Catholic priests. Bishops have come under fire for not taking swifter action to address that practice. Charges of inappropriate sexual practices have also been lodged against some of the highest profile Protestant preachers in the country, many of them on record condemning the very actions they engaged in themselves. The church has lost much of its authority for speaking about sexual immorality. None have been more prominent within the context of the African American church than Bishop Eddie Long, a harsh critic of homosexuality who was accused by several young men in his church of inappropriate sexual contact.[18]

Ida B. Wells Barnett is most closely associated with efforts to report on and end lynch-mob justice in the South through her newspaper, *The Memphis Free Speech and Headlight*. While noting that many acts of lynch mob justice involved false claims of Black men attacking white women, she did report on the actual sexual misconduct of many of the Black preachers in Memphis.[19] When she reported on one such instance, the Baptist Clergy Alliance threatened to boycott her newspaper. They were more protective of the reputation of the sexual assaulter than they were in holding that person accountable. In response, Wells Barnett wrote: "We answered this threat by publishing the names of every minister who belonged to the alliance in the next issue of the Free Speech, and told the community that these men upheld the immoral conduct of one of their number and asked if they were willing to support preachers who would sneak into their homes when their backs were turned and debauched their wives."[20]

84

Of course, hypocrisy when it comes to sexual conduct is in no sense limited to Black preachers. Consider the case of Donnie Romero of the Stedfast Baptist Church of Fort Worth, Texas, who was recently forced to leave his church after acknowledging that he had paid for sex with prostitutes. The irony of this situation is that Romero is part of a group of independent Baptist churches that have been outspoken critics of homosexuality. Romero offered praise to the gunman who killed forty-nine people at a gay nightclub in Orlando, Florida. Not only that, but Romero went on record as praying for the death of Barack Obama so that he would not be able to appoint any more persons to the US Supreme Court who might vote to uphold *Roe v. Wade* and a woman's right to choose in matters of abortion and reproduction.[21]

The pastors who took it upon themselves to condemn American Baptist College and Bishop Yvette Flunder on the issue of homosexuality owe it to their own churches, to the congregations of the National Baptist Convention, and to the Christian community at large to tell us where they stand and what they have said publicly about the other behaviors, heterosexual and otherwise, that Scripture may reference but concerning which they have remained conspicuously silent. What Forrest Harris has had to navigate since 2015 is the selective self-righteousness of pastors who have targeted homosexuality as their sin of choice without offering equal public critiques of other behaviors that appear in the same chapters and verses from which they have been quoting on matters of homosexuality.

A Classroom Is Not a Congregation

The broader issue Forrest Harris stood firm on was that the role of an educational institution is different from the work of a congregation or a denomination. I repeatedly argued from my own position as president of a divinity school that "the seminary is not a church." Some of the people we train may pursue careers in parish ministry, but whether they do or not, our role as a school is not indoctrination into a particular way of thinking about issues. Our job is to encourage and equip students to engage in critical thinking skills so they can hear and learn about various points of view regarding any topic or social construct. Once exposed to various points of view, these students are in a better position to understand their world and to find their place in that world. That is exactly what Forrest Harris and American Baptist College did with the issue of homosexuality beginning in 2015 and continuing to this day.

Preachers and denominational leaders have every right to express their own views on any matter that seems to fall within their sphere of interest and influence. Sermons and calls to Christian discipleship that take place in a church, from the pulpit, or inside a sanctuary, and that are conducted by persons who have been ordained or designated for that task are not in dispute. The right of preachers to challenge the society in which they live on matters of sexual immorality as understood by and agreed to by their church body is not being questioned or challenged. The issue is whether representatives of an ecclesiastical body should seek to impose their theological views on what occurs within the life of an academic institution whose mission is not primarily about making disciples but about forming persons as critical thinkers through coursework, readings, lectures, writing assignments, and grappling with one's own prejudices and personal practices in dialogue with those who think and believe differently.

Consider the State of the
Southern Baptist Convention

Some schools have failed to see the distinction between being a church and an academic institution. At both the undergraduate and graduate levels, some schools adhere to the views of certain conservative church leaders on matters like human sexuality, abortion, national politics, international relations with the state of Israel (Christian Zionism), and the appropriate use of Scripture in discussing each of those issues. This was the problem for Southern

Baptist Theological Seminary and other Southern Baptist Convention-related schools. In many instances, both faculty and students must sign a covenant statement that binds them to the teachings and values of the convention. Moderate voices within the Southern Baptist Convention were silenced as a conservative wing took over the leadership of that group beginning in 1979 in what came to be known as the "fundamentalist takeover."[22]

Perhaps this is the understanding of the relationship between the church and the academic institutions that informed the actions of those pastors who have sought to impose their views on American Baptist College through protests, legal action, and media coverage about who should and should not appear at that school. It should be instructive for them to note that in 2016, the Southern Baptist Convention repudiated that part of its recent history. They voted out those who were leaders of the fundamentalist takeover and elected a new slate of officers who are younger and no longer defined by the social agenda of their SBC predecessors.[23] Recently, the SBC adopted a policy of the exclusion of women in positions of pastoral leadership. This followed the fundamentalist tradition of Southern Baptist Christian doctrine that Black churches struggled to incorporate yet struggled against it to honor the dignity and liberation of all persons. The discrimination and exclusion of women based on gender is in opposition to a true understanding of Jesus' truth.

Some of the leaders of the fundamentalist takeover of the SBC were forced to resign because they were caught saying or doing things that were inconsistent with what they had been preaching or because they were contrary to the ways in which society has evolved on certain matters. In 2018, Frank Page, who had been president of the Southern Baptist Convention from 2006 to 2008, was removed as the SBC's chief executive officer for undisclosed sexual abuses.[24] In the same year, Paige Patterson, president of Southwestern Baptist Theological Seminary in Fort Worth, Texas, and former president of the Southern Baptist Convention, was forced to resign after more than 3,200 Southern Baptist women protested following his advice that women should return to their physically abusive husbands.[25]

The Black Baptist Church in the Twenty-first Century

Perhaps it is time for the National Baptist Convention and the Southern Baptist Convention to promote into leadership at both the local and national level persons whose views more faithfully reflect the teachings of the Gospel and who have taken the time to consider the Gospel and the ministry of the church in the context of a twenty-first-century, secular society. Failure to look to the future and to ignore the shifts in both the cultural and political contexts of the twenty-first century is already proving to be catastrophic for the church. The title of Walter Fluker's recent book cannot be ignored: *The Ground Has Shifted*.[26]

Does it make sense to impose a tenth-century-BCE moral code, shaped within a theocratic form of governance inside a patriarchal culture, upon twenty-first-century CE, secular American society? We can see where such a thing could lead when we see that the Taliban in Afghanistan has reestablished the mandate that women who appear in public must conform to the eighteenth-century CE practice of wearing a burqa, a head-to-toe body covering.[27] We see the same attempt to turn back the clock on women's reproductive rights as conservative white Christians and their hand-picked US Supreme Court seek to accomplish by coercion what they could not achieve by force of argument.[28]

Leaders within the church must find ways to navigate the fact that while ancient Israelites were bound to their collective covenant with God as a matter of national life, twenty-first-century life in the United States is rooted in individual adherence to the laws of the state and to personal conviction on matters of morality. That is the context within which we must contend for the Gospel and to defend the faith. That is the context in which Abraham Lincoln's advice about the use of persuasion in pursuit of particular policies and/or practices is most useful. That is the context in which Forrest Harris and many other Black preacher/presidents have been working for years.

Chapter 5

A Pentecostal Justice Preacher

Yvette A. Flunder, D.Min.

I am a desperate preacher who knows personally how theologies are fluid and that new ones are born at friction points. My voice is rooted in the African American, Southern-influenced Pentecostal church where passion for God in Jesus is heard and seen in the songs, preaching, dancing, and daily at-home meditations. I have struggled with the history of the church and the interpretation of the Bible but not with the freestyle celebratory worship of the Pentecostal church. My struggle has been with the Christian church's changing position regarding the treatment of women, same gender loving persons, war, immigrants, people of color, and slaves. (My grandmother, Bessie Hamilton, born 1895, was the daughter of Stella Wyatt, who was born a slave.). I am an avowed womanist and a reconciling liberation theologian who dances in the Spirit and speaks in tongues. Holding on to Jesus despite the church and the tortured interpretations of Scripture that have been used to mortally wound my people and my faith has been a lifelong journey. Finding my way, following the Light, refusing to believe God didn't love me/us—this is the foundation of my preaching. Mine is a voice that passionately preaches justice and freedom with responsibility; however, not to the exclusion of Jesus. Justice and Jesus along with Justice for Jesus works for me.

I preach to a desperate people who are struggling to make sense of their lives on the margins of society. They are my beloveds.

In the communities where I serve, we must find God in the struggle for equality, parity, and justice; the struggle is the long, strong, deep, resonant base of all I preach, sing, and pray about.

"Through many dangers, toils, and snares" is foundational to our worship and the locus of our passion. If we cannot see God in the struggle and believe day after day that God will make it all right, we cannot see God at all. The seeing by faith is the starting point.

I preach faith-based sermons to build self-worth and self-value in the lives of people who have often been stripped of all that is right and good. I strive to see peace and a sense of security present in the lives of those I pastor, preach to, and serve. Emil Thomas said, "Our slave ancestors had a basis for calm: a special inner peace born of a profound conviction that their self-worth had been well established already and was guaranteed by the Ruler of the universe."[1] This is a peace born from the assurance that God will come through for us, that God is on our side. This is what I believe; this is what I preach.

Preaching Influences

I identify with Fred Craddock in his book *Preaching*[2] because his approach to preaching/teaching is very Bible, Jesus, and God centered. I've seen the methods he recommends for sermon structure used both in the United Church of Christ, where I presently serve, and in the churches of my youth; what flows out of Craddock's center is Scripture-based preaching with other sources used to support the Scripture. While I am not in total agreement with the extent to which Craddock lifts up the authority of the Bible, I do appreciate and believe strongly in Scripture-based, Christ-centered preaching for liberation. This kind of preaching requires study with an eye to taking Jesus back from the fundamentalists, and it is the most effective kind of preaching for my community. I, like David Buttrick, would argue "for a church animated by the Gospel, rather than a church heavily under the rule of an imposed scriptural authority"[3]; people who have for generations been abused by the preaching of the Bible need to hear the Bible preached in ways that affirm and validate them.

Preaching in my tradition uses life experience, or what I call *personal transparency*, to identify with the experiences of the listener. There is a need for the preacher to be sensitive to the needs of the listener: sermons should speak *for* as well as *to* the congregation, the Gospel is *from* the community as well as *to* it. This is the beautiful Circle dance. There is also a need for honesty and intimacy, and it is important to preach using themes, hymns, and stories that are familiar to the listener.

I believe that in order to genuinely be a blessing to the congregation, the preacher must seek to know and understand who she/he is preaching to. Lenora Tubbs Tisdale, in *Preaching as Local Theology and Folk Art*,[4] calls this "exegeting the congregation." Tisdale says, "If we as preachers are going to proclaim the Gospel in ways capable of transforming congregational identity, we first need to become better acquainted with the ways our people already imagine God and the world. If we are going to aid in the extension of myopic vision or the correction of astigmatic values then we must first strive to 'see' God and the world as our people do." Through this synergistic relationship, the preacher and the congregation become one organism, worshiping God together. The preaching and the response are then filled with faith, passion, and power. This is preaching as I understand it. New and difficult truths should be packaged in a familiar wrapping so a common relationship of trust based on collective experience can be established. Preaching that is outside of the theological, intellectual, or cultural reach of the listener is an insult to the life experience the listener brings to the preaching moment. It is not enough for me to simply be profound; I seek to be a profound blessing by hearing from God and paying close attention to voice of the listening congregation.

My preaching is greatly influenced by my grandfather, my stepfather, my uncles, my mother, and my grandmother, all of whom were preachers. I spent my youth as a pastor's kid in the Church of God in Christ, a predominately Black Pentecostal denomination. My style of preaching echoes the preachers who surrounded me, both in my family and throughout the organization.

Most of the preachers I knew were blue-collar folk who came to their role as preacher or pastor without the benefit of formal training. There were not many African Americans in college, and those who were in school were seeking a way to make themselves more eligible for jobs. The call to preach was not often planned as a vocation. It seemed to sort of run up behind them and tackle them while they were trying to get ahead in life. Authorization for ministry came from the church at such time as it was determined one was ready. *Ready* meant having demonstrated faithfulness and an ability to preach. The Church of God in Christ believed that no matter how educated or filled with deep knowledge a person was, that knowledge had to be evidenced by good preaching for a preacher to gain affirmation from the church. Good preaching meant good performance, which included choosing a good text, a good reading of the text, good entertainment, believability/authority, identification, food for thought, power, humor, passion, and a super closing celebration. I know that Craddock's statement that "listeners tend to lean into narratives which have emotional force, but which are presented with emotional restraint"[5] is an indication that we come from different cultures. Emotional restraint was not exercised particularly at the close or celebration time in the sermon. I tend to agree with Frank A. Thomas regarding celebration and emotion. Thomas writes, "It is precisely because so much of Western preaching has ignored emotional context and process, and focused on cerebral process and words, that homileticians most recently have struggled for new methods to effectively communicate the Gospel."[6] The preaching was central to the worship experience; it was the highlight. All things lead up to it and out from it. It was a word from the Lord.

I am fascinated when I read books like *Speaking from the Heart*[7] that detail the performance model often present in Black Pentecostal preaching and lift up that method as an example of how good preaching is accomplished. I find myself often wishing that my Grandpa Eugene (Bishop Eugene E. Hamilton) and my Uncle Rudolph (Bishop S. Rudolph Martin) could have lived long enough for me to share with them the fact that a science is being taught that captures what they did among us for many years. They did not adhere to any particular preaching calendar or use many sermon helps written by others, but the power of their sermons lives on.

Of particular interest is the science and skill I now recognized in the preaching I grew up around. I know most of those folk did not realize what masters they were in the art of using illustrations, simile, or hyperbole, but all these things were part of their preaching process and, by inheritance, part of mine.

Storytelling and speaking in hieroglyphics and word pictures were methods employed to leave a lasting impression on the hearer. You could see it, taste it, and feel it while they preached. My grandpa lived his sermons, so his ethos and personal conviction came through with great passion, energy, and emotion.

The Pentecostal preaching style is one where the language is ordered, the lines are metrical and poetic, and the sermon is *sung* in places with the help of the congregation and the musicians. This form of performance art entertained the congregation while driving home the truths in the sermon. Engaging the audience in a call-and-response to both the meter and the message encouraged the congregation to not only participate but also signaled that the sermon was successful. Preaching as performance art was and is an essential part of the African American Pentecostal worship experience.

How I Come to the Preaching Moment

Reading is a passion for me. I read history, literature, Scripture, magazines, web articles, newspapers, and anything else I can get my hands on. In my reading, I listen for themes of freedom with responsibility, hope, perseverance, culture, and real people. I look deeply into the characters in Scripture for their humanity and how they identify with us. I want to demystify the saints while not losing respect for their struggle. I seek to know by revelation and through literature contemporary with the text what things the writers and interpreters did not tell us. We all keep secrets, so what would they rather we did not know? What is it they assumed we would understand? What meanings have been lost or changed with time? What is the truth under the writings? I seek to bring those things to the preaching moment.

Incarnational Interpretation

I seek a fresh method to interpret Scripture. I know there must be a new, more faithful way to handle the text that can move me to a method that seeks to embody the feelings, message, and spirit of the original creator. I would go further and suggest that it is the faithful embodiment of the text *and* the writer that enables incarnational preaching. It is a work of the Holy Spirit in harmony with humanity. With all our study and faithful attention to the text, we struggle seeing what is truly there: What we see is often not what is historically accurate and may not translate to our time. What we see and read is often what the text has come to mean, synthesized through lenses fashioned from our experiences. The Holy Spirit must help us grasp the form to melt into. The interpreter and the originator must connect spirit to spirit, heart to heart, sometimes over centuries—a long-distance love relationship. This would be extremely difficult unless there were some mutual and similar experience between the interpreter and the character being embodied. This is the work of the Spirit—to see and feel humanity in the Scriptures.

In the history of Black music is a type of music referred to as Negro Spirituals. These songs, filled with eschatological metaphors, could be taken at face value for the original art form that they are. The words could be embraced, and the appropriate interpreter could seek to embody the form or the experience of the slave authors and sing with the passion of the hope and the dream of the slave: "Soon Ah Will Be Don Wid De Trubbles Ob De Worl" or "Swing Low, Sweet Chariot" or "Saint Peter Open Dem Gates."

95

However, if that someone did not know the code in the language of the songs and relate to the necessity of the oppressed to create a form of communication not understood by the oppressor, they might well come away having faithfully and lovingly connected to an assumption. Years and years of lacquering over both the text and our perceptions of it beg the question, is seeing believing? I think not, in many cases, and we can only connect Spirit to spirit.

Additionally, there is the lens of culture and time that makes the intention of the originator of the poem, the song, or the text quite different from that of the interpreter. I am reminded of a cartoon I once saw that described how people excavating ruins 5,000 years in the future might interpret our domiciles. Of particular note was the beautiful porcelain work of art created by someone named *Toilet*. Can the translated and revised language faithfully communicate the values, stance, posture, and physical attitude intended by the originator without some analysis of the originator and their environment and culture *and* some work of the Spirit? Essentially, the meaning of words and all artistic expressions is relative to the culture it proceeds from. When the text says *tree*, is it the *tree* I relate to that I envision or is there something totally different that would never enter my mind as *tree*, but the meaning of which would drastically change my understanding of the text?

I love the Scripture and constantly seek a faithful, loving way to hold and embody the text, informed by the Holy Spirit, with an eye to the culture and the changes in perception that speak to how the text comes to us.

I seldom know what I am going to preach from one Sunday to the next. The sermon subject matter comes through a song I hear or a Scripture or a book I read or an experience I share with someone. Some word or principle comes to my attention, and my spirit says, *Ah-hah, that will preach*. I tend to write the thought down on anything I can find because I know it is preaching fodder. I experience great joy when a fresh word comes to me for my people because I know God is communicating with my spirit. I often don't do anything with the thought for a time; I just let it sit and simmer in my spirit while I think and pray about the scriptural and human context for the sermon. There are often two or three sermon pots simmering simultaneously, and the last one may be first and the first one may be last. Other things come to witness to the truth that has already been deposited in me. The Scriptures, examples, parables, illustrations, and stories that bring the thought to life come in waves when I am bathing or driving or working on something else. I keep something handy to write with all the time. I have little notes everywhere that I accumulate when I come to my computer to pull the sermon together.

When the sermon is ready to be preached, it is often brief on paper because I know I will get the rest of it in the pulpit. I anticipate the Circle dance with the people and the Holy Spirit working in the preaching moment to finish the sermon. I have often taken the same notes with me on different occasions and preached totally different sermons each time.

Preaching on the Edge

As to the content of my sermons, I often preach to raise the consciousness of those who feel they have exclusive rights to Jesus and to empower oppressed people to take their place at God's welcome table. I preach to build faith and to demystify success for oppressed people. I do not consider preaching adversarial or divisive when it speaks truth to power. I call myself a reconciling, liberation theologian, and my desire is to see harmony in the body of Christ, but it is important to challenge bad religion that constantly wounds, diminishes, and destroys.

Empowerment and liberation are consistent themes in my preaching. Marginalized people often ask, "Is God for us?" Incarnational liberating preaching is vital in these communities, as preaching has often been used to push more and more oppressed people to the margin. Preaching in the community evidences the extent to which the community is welcoming. After a natural disaster, people come to church in record numbers asking, "Is God for us?" and they listen for the assurance from the pulpit. In marginalized communities, crises are a way of life, and incarnational preaching is essential.

Preaching to people who are on the edge of society and the mainline church must have good content *and* good form. Preaching to marginalized people must be believable, powerful, and passionate. Marginalized people frequently have a memory of strong words from the pulpit used to destroy. They need stronger words of affirmation and inclusion. Our sermons should carry a message that counters the teaching of those who support a theology that calls anyone unclean or claims to have exclusive "truth."

Toward a Transforming Moment

I believe there must be a relationship between loving and knowing *God*, the *text*, and the *people* the text is shared with. When the interpreter of the text begins by incorporating integrity, relatedness, and faithfulness to a relationship with God and to the text, a more honest relationship to the congregation/listeners develops. Additionally, preachers must be secure in their relationship with the God of their understanding and witnesses of the truth of the Gospel. Oppressed people seem to be particularly aware when there is disparity between what the preacher says and what she/he really believes. Ward asserts, "If you do not have a secure sense of self and conviction about your right to address your people, then it will be nearly impossible to engage them."[8]

Marginalized people are people who need to hear from God. How can they hear without a preacher? And the preacher must love God, faithfully handle the text, and identify with the people in order to be authentic.

When these things come together, I believe we achieve the moment of transformational preaching. I constantly seek this moment. I have no greater joy than to embody a liberating truth and to participate in the Circle dance as the Holy Spirit brings life to me and to those who hear and receive the Word—God in Christ through the Holy Spirit empowering the preacher and the congregation through the embodied Word. The circle is complete, and the kingdom ("kindom") is revealed. It is a glimpse of heaven!

Conclusion

Many more groups and individuals could have been used as examples of people we serve on the visible margin. However, I felt compelled to write about some of the more difficult issues facing the communities where I have served and continue to serve. The locus of my experience is primarily among African Americans in the inner city, but there are margins surrounding every community, and there is an overwhelming need to take the heart of the church to the edge rather than seeking to bring the margin to the center. The edge is where Jesus did His best work, but most mainstream Christians fear it deeply. In 1901, James Bryce, the British historian, wrote about the United States during the time when African Americans were thought to epitomize the edge. Fear of the other speaks through his words:

> The presence of the blacks is the greatest evil that threatens the United States. They increase, in the Gulf States, faster than do the whites. They cannot be kept forever in slavery, since the tendencies of the modern world run strongly the other way. They cannot be absorbed into the white population, for the whites will not intermarry with them, not even in the North where they have been free for two generations. Once freed, they would be more dangerous than now, because they would not long submit to be debarred from political rights. A terrible struggle would ensue.[9]

Sadly, this kind of misplaced apprehension and fear still exists.

Africans were taken from their homes and brought to the Americas by force. In relationship to the effect of slavery on the African, Noel Erskine writes, "Tremendous damage was done to the personality of the Black person when he or she was forced to live outside the indigenous community. Existence-in-relation sums up the pattern of the African way of life."[10] African slaves were from one continent but many tribes, speaking many languages and representing many cultures. Yet, in spite of their diversity, their common bondage and need for a healing community encouraged them to create common bonds, communities on the margin. After a while, the many tribes became the African American community. There is a quote from the slave narratives that epitomizes how community was created on the margins of slavery and what they did when they grew tired of oppressive theology:

> The preacher came and.... He'd just say, "Serve your masters. Don't steal your master's turkey. Don't steal your master's chickens. Don't steal your master's hawgs"...same ole thing all the time. My father would have church in the dwelling houses and they had to whisper...that would be when they wanted to have a real meeting with some real preaching...they used to sing their songs in a whisper and pray in a whisper. That was a prayer meeting from house to house—once or twice a week.[11]

These people were separated from their communities of origin, enslaved, and oppressed by those who feared those they did not understand. Their common oppression created common bonds, a common need for affirmation, and a common need for community

All humans need community. According to Paris, "African Americans have always known that persons cannot flourish apart from a community of belonging."[12] However, it is extremely important that community be created among marginalized people due to the real distance between people on the edge and their communities of origin. Paris states, African Americans "have also known that any community that oppresses its members is no community at all but, rather, a seething cauldron of dissention, distrust, and bitterness."[13]

People who are oppressed by the church must be empowered to develop communities separate from the mainstream or their faith in a God of justice will be severely damaged by the continual attack of their oppressor. One cannot thrive in an atmosphere of moral contradictions where the love of God and hatred of the *other* or the stranger are preached simultaneously. Where these moral contradictions exist, there remains the potential of the victim becoming the victimizer just to survive, as this oppressive theology is contagious. Racism is wrong. Homophobia is wrong. The people who have been victimized by prejudice must decry it and establish communities that labor to love. The preaching moment is vitally important to the marginalized!

I have attempted to identify some groups truly marginalized by church and society and to suggest some methods and theology for creating sustaining and celebrating community on the margin. Additionally, I have shared my thoughts, experience, and passion regarding preaching on the edge because my heart is committed to the mission of seeing the radically inclusive love of Jesus Christ visibly, tangibly, and palpably demonstrated in this world.

When I think of creating, sustaining, and celebrating Christian community on the margin, I am reminded of a documentary on volcanoes that showed the power that exists just below the surface of this planet. Volcanoes have shaped this planet and have given us our island paradises, warm springs, and geysers. However, they also have the power and potential to erupt, disturb, and reshape everything as we know it. Such is the passion and power of a group of people in crisis grouped together with no pretenses and an earthshaking faith in God. Although there exists the potential for destruction if the passion is not channeled, if care is taken, the power can be harnessed for the good of the community.

This is a story without a conclusion as it is still being written and celebrated through the lives of people who thought they could never have a seat at the table. "It does not yet appear what we shall be" or what new, prophetic, and powerful results will come from the next eruption. Just as new land emerges from the mouth of a volcano creating fresh possibilities, so emerging Faith communities are rising with power and purpose. "What shall we then say to these things? If God be for us, who can be against us?" (Romans 8:31, KJV).

Chapter 6

On Being Black and Christian:
Reengaging and Reframing the Conversation

Lewis V. Baldwin and *DeWayne Stallworth*

Forrest E. Harris Sr.'s life and work in the academy and the church testify to the power of not only the personal and interpersonal but also the public and prophetic aspects of the Christian faith. With the publication of his first book in 1993, Harris highlighted the nexus between the structures of liberation theology and sociopolitical and prophetic praxis in the Black church tradition.[1] He later joined other pastors and theologians in a deep and provocative conversation around the question What does it mean to be Black and Christian?[2] This question should perhaps be raised and answered with an even greater sense of urgency in this third decade of the twenty-first century. While devoting some attention to how Harris and his colleagues approached this question in the mid- to late 1990s, this essay focuses more on the pressing need to reengage and reframe the conversation about what it means to be an African American and a Christian today—at a time increasingly defined by the nation's changing demographics; the public resurgence of the most powerful and vulgar streams of white supremacy and white nationalism; the renewed and growing threats to multiracial, participatory, and representative democracy; the breakdown of shared standards of what constitutes truth and untruth; the decline of the neighborhood church; and the mounting questions and challenges confronting the megachurch phenomenon.

There is a sense in which the question of meaning, and/or definition, relative to Black Christian identity extends back to the earliest slave missions, when the enslaved confronted the glaring paradox of being African while converting to the religion professed and propagated by their oppressors. The question was inescapable for Richard Allen, Andrew Bryan, Peter Spencer, James Varick, and countless others who, in the eighteenth and nineteenth centuries, walked out of white, segregated churches in search of their own separate and independent houses of worship. The question is implied throughout the writings and speeches of generations of Black leaders and thinkers, from David Walker and Martin R. Delany to Henry McNeil Turner and W. E B. Du Bois down to Benjamin E. Mays, Howard W. Thurman, Martin Luther King Jr., Ella Baker, Fannie Lou Hamer, and others who seriously engaged the meaning of the Christian faith in the context of the crusade for freedom, justice, human dignity, and peace. Also, the Black Christian identity question was foundational for the liberation theology of James H. Cone, Albert B. Cleage, Major J. Jones, J. Deotis Roberts, Sr. and others, who were inspired by the modern Civil Rights and Black Power movements. In this context, and with the larger history of the African American struggle in mind, Forrest E. Harris Sr. and others were compelled to begin "a national dialogue" around what it means "to be Black and Christian."[3]

Harris was heavily involved in the publication of two volumes on this subject in the 1990s, but the extent to which "the identity question" of being Black and Christian was answered remains open to serious debate. Judging from the content of the two volumes, it appears that generating an ongoing national dialogue between church leaders and professional Black theologians was considered more important at that time than providing a set of specific answers to the question. The essays included suggest that the contributors generally agreed that the significance of what it means to be Black and Christian rests at the core of the African American struggle for liberation and empowerment. It is imperative that the academy and the church engage in more serious dialogue relative to issues of Black faith, theology, and ministry. That is a formidable challenge to Black churchpersons of various denominations to equip their communities—psychologically, spiritually, theologically, and materially—to not only speak prophetically against racism, classism, sexism, and homophobia but also to address, in practical ways, the needs of the poor, the breakdown of the family structure, the homeless, substance abusers, the criminally inclined, the incarcerated, and pregnant teens.[4] Undoubtedly, such cultural and sociopolitical concerns will continue to drive much of the conversation about being Black and Christian, and necessarily so, but major attention should also be devoted to how the conversation is affected by the changing state of the contemporary American society, culture, and institutions. The discussion that follows provides clues about how the conversation might move in this direction.

In the second volume of *What Does It Mean to Be Black and Christian?*, Gayraud S. Wilmore, the widely known Black theologian and ethicist, contributed a short piece entitled "Educating the African American Church for the Twenty-First Century." Wilmore wrote poignantly about the need for the African American church to educate its constituents, reminding them of their ancient roots in Africa, of "the Black presence in the Bible," and of the lessons we must learn from the history of slavery and racism.[5] We feel that such an approach to education is clearly foundational for establishing what it means to be Black and Christian. We also think that African American churches today face an equally important, and perhaps more challenging, educational responsibility in that they must find creative ways of being vital sources of enlightenment for Black people as they seek to live and function in a society and world quite unlike what they have known in the past. A case in point is the nation's changing demographics, or what scholars call "the browning of America,"[6] as America is rapidly becoming less white and Black, and instead browner in population. Black, Hispanic, Asian, and multiracial Americans are increasing and the numbers of white Americans are decreasing.

There are different opinions in the media, the academy, political and religious circles, and the larger public square about what the ultimate impact of this shift from a predominantly white to a predominantly nonwhite nation, or this "remaking of America," will mean culturally, socially, politically, and otherwise.[7] We are already witnessing how this rapidly emerging demographic trend is increasing white racial fears, fracturing the nation's political life, creating vastly diverse and ever-changing religious constituencies, and sparking mounting cultural wars.[8] The question here is what this potentially means for Black Christians and especially the Black church, which has long been the epicenter and core organizing unit of Black communal life. The racial composition and identity of the Black church will undoubtedly undergo some changes, as is already the case with the megachurches. Black Christians will be compelled to rethink and redefine who they are and what constitutes their mission priorities and outreach, especially if they wish to remain meaningful and relevant as agents of positive and constructive change in an increasingly racially and ethnically diverse society. Their traditional interest in issues like education, matters of personal ethics, benevolence, and missions will have to be thoroughly evaluated and prioritized. The task could not be more challenging, and perhaps even daunting, at a time when Black churches are already facing a titanic ideological struggle to reach and reclaim the loyalty and support of Black youth.

Racist extremism is another challenge confronting Black Christians as we address who we are and what we should be about, in terms of ministry and mission, in this third decade of the twenty-first century. The election of Donald John Trump as president in 2016 not only "ushered a white nationalist agenda into the White House"[9] but also put the lie to the claim that we live in a post-racial society and frustrated any notion that "the browning of America" is "one of the greatest hopes in the fight against white supremacy and oppression."[10] Fueled largely by the "raging national debate over immigration," the "ugly racism and violence of the growing white nationalist movement," as the Southern Poverty Law Center (SPLC) describes it, "exploded into view in Charlottesville" in 2017 when Mr. Trump claimed that there were "'very fine people' among the neo-Nazis and other white supremacists" who marched while chanting "Jews will not replace us."[11]

The continuing explosive increase of hate groups is in itself a challenge to Black Christians to join the search for "new initiatives" to counter all forms of right-wing extremism, including online hatred, conspiracy theories, and misinformation. Much of this effort might occur through the kind of financial and moral support Black churches can give to the SPLC and its headquarters in Montgomery, Alabama, especially since the SPLC has done more than any other agency or institution in this country to monitor and fight hate groups.[12] The fact that all too many African Americans, including Christians, know little or nothing about the activities of the SPLC is inexcusable. Thus, as part of its teaching function, the Black church would also do well to become a vehicle for the dissemination of information about the Southern Poverty Law Center, its messaging strategy, its legal fight against hate groups, and its recurring efforts to secure the rights of people of color through the judicial process.[13] The Christian faith demands as much and more in these times. Also, this would be very much in line with the demands of the Gospel of Jesus Christ, which envisions a Kingdom of God defined by love and community, not hatred and tribalism.

The need for the Black church to reclaim its rich tradition of civil and human rights activism could not be more important in this period of racist and white nationalist extremism. The Black church has an unbroken tradition of crusading for freedom—a tradition that extends from the likes of Richard Allen, Frederick Douglass, and Sojourner Truth, in the abolitionist crusade of eighteenth and nineteenth centuries, to Rosa Parks, Martin Luther King Jr., and the modern Civil Rights Movement of the 1950s and '60s, to Bishop William J. Barber II's current, "renewed version" of King's "campaign to lift poor people."[14] This tradition is a critical part of what it means to be Black and Christian. Civil rights activism did not die with King—it simply moved from the streets to the voting booths and the halls of government. In other words, Black churches that had been centers of mass meetings and rallying points for demonstrators in the 1950s and '60s became arenas for voting clinics and proving grounds for Black political leadership in the decades that followed, even as many of them retreated into zones of conservative, Bible-based Christianity.[15]

Being Black and Christian today means telling the story of the long, historic quest for civil rights while advancing the freedom cause to another level. We cannot afford to succumb to what Carlyle F. Stewart calls "the disillusionment of a post-civil rights malaise,"[16] especially since the spirit of no-surrender still lingers in vital ways deep within the souls of so many Black clergy and laity. The social witness and activism of Bishop Barber[17] and Black Lives Matter can serve as models for how the contemporary Black church might strengthen its moral leadership while reestablishing its credibility as a prophetic force not only in the struggle against white supremacy and white nationalism but also in that larger crusade to eliminate sexism, classism, homophobia, and other forms of bigotry, intolerance, and injustice.

The need for a revitalized and socio-politically engaged Black church cannot be overstated in view of renewed and growing threats to multiracial, participatory, and representative democracy. Democracy, as described in the Constitution and the Declaration of Independence, rests on certain self-evident truths about human equality and God-given, inalienable rights of life, liberty, and the pursuit of happiness. Black Christians have always assumed a pivotal role in the shaping of a culture of inclusive democracy, the type of democracy that encourages the mobilization and empowerment of local communities, participative leadership, mass mobilization and movement, and possibilities for the expansion of rights and human enlargement. The emphasis has always been on democracy that serves "the least of these" and not merely the elites. Moreover, Black churches have long afforded lessons on how to reconcile faith with the values of modern, pluralistic democracy.[18]

What we are observing in these times is actually a vicious and sustained attack on democracy by the forces of untruth, anti-democracy, and authoritarianism. The injection of the extreme right-wing Christian view of Bible-based church values into

American civic and political life has increasingly led to an erosion of constitutional protections for everyone, especially women and communities of color. This became painfully clear during the Trump presidency, which laid bare both the strengths and limitations of American democracy while offering painful lessons in what happens when multiracial, participatory, and representative democracy falls victim to such forces. The assault on democracy today, fueled largely by lingering vestiges of Trumpism, takes the forms of voter suppression and intimidation, widespread gerrymandering and election subversion, the whitewashing and erasing of history, and efforts to silence voices of dissent, protest, and truth. The very best qualities of the American democratic character and spirit are being eroded under an avalanche of lies, half-truths, propaganda, disinformation, conspiracy theories, distorted reality, and a growing culture of political violence; the tragic repercussions are becoming increasingly evident in democracies throughout the world. Black Christians have always been the most important voices of conscience in this society[19] and prime movers in ensuring a healthy leveling of civil and political liberties. If this is to remain the case, we must take the lead in reclaiming the kind of values-infused culture that affirms, cherishes, and elevates truth, civility, honor, rationality, and other ingredients that are essential to the workings of true multiracial, participatory, and representative democracy.

The proclamation of the Word and Christian education in Black church traditions have always been about truth telling and truth sharing. Jesus's powerful and captivating words in the Gospel of John (8:32, KJV)—"And ye shall know the truth, and the truth shall make you free"—are often heard in Black Christian circles. These words are especially meaningful today in a culture that is becoming increasingly enslaved by untruth. Falsehoods have become mainstream and normal in our culture, even at the highest levels of the nation's political and religious life; all too many seem comfortable with the blurred lines between truth and lies. Much of this is part of the lingering effects of Trumpism, which consistently reminds us that the old rules and standards regarding truth and truth telling are no longer applicable, and which bombards us with terms like "alternative truths," "alternative facts," and "alternative reality."[20] But there are, indeed, absolute and objective truths, or those truths that are universally accepted and affirmed; when a society cannot agree on fundamental truths and facts, it no longer has a shared sense of what is right and wrong, real and unreal, or rational and irrational. This is the clear and present danger haunting America and, indeed, the world.

Black church traditions teach us that the lifelong quest for truth is liberating and empowering, that this is essential for the integration and health of the personality, and that enslavement to untruth can only lead to death and destruction. Those traditions, more than any other in the nation's history, are also known for producing prophets who are unafraid to speak truth to power. The society is in dire need of such ethical and transformational figures today.[21] The only question is whether the contemporary Black church can take the lead in radiating the kind of moral and spiritual power required to save us from the most devastating effects of what social and cultural critics are calling "the post truth age."[22] Clearly, this is one of the greatest challenges confronting American religious institutions, and particularly Black Christian communities, in the twenty-first century.

The answer to the Black Christian identity question hinges in large measure on the degree to which this and other aforementioned challenges are met today and tomorrow. But in order to meet and respond to such challenges forthrightly and effectively, Black Christians must be clear about our history and heritage, about who we are as people of faith today, and about what we are called and equipped to do in terms of ministry and mission in a rapidly changing society and world. This is immensely important since there is so much debate surrounding the current identity and state of the Black church and about where it stands in relation to its rich history and traditions. Eddie S. Glaude Jr., the James S. McDonell Distinguished University Professor of Religion and African American Studies at Princeton University, made the sweeping claim, in a blog in 2012, that "the Black Church, as we've known it or imagined it, is dead." Glaude focuses especially on what he views as the decentering of Black churches and "the myth" that they are "necessarily prophetic." In other words, the claim is that "this venerable institution" called the Black church has ceased to be "central to Black life" and can no longer be legitimately seen as "a repository for the social and moral conscience of the nation."[23] Thus, Glaude seriously questions an image of the Black church that extends throughout American history and that was consistently upheld and affirmed by scholars like W. E. B. Du Bois and Carter Woodson[24] and that permeates the writings, sermons, speeches, and conversations of Martin Luther King Jr. and countless other freedom fighters.

Glaude's pronouncement of the obituary of the Black church was greeted with a storm of criticism from some academics and churchpersons and a call for more serious thought and reflection by others, for his claims, at the very least, struck at the heart of the Black Christian identity question. "The Black Church may be dead in its incarnation as an agent of change," wrote Anthea D. Butler, who teaches religion at the University of Pennsylvania, "but as the imagined home of all things Black and Christian, it is alive and well." Butler went on to assert that "I will go out on a limb and say that the Black Church will never be truly 'dead' as long as we have a nation invested in racial symbolism."[25] Jonathan L. Walton, who taught in religious studies at the University of California, Riverside, at the time, acknowledged that it is "a stretch to suggest that the Black church is dead," but quickly noted that "unless Afro-Protestants become less consumed with building institutions characterized by tribal racial insularity, autocratic cult of personalities and/or idolatrous inward-oriented, henotheistic theologies, it might as well be." Walton also conceded, and rightly so, that Glaude's claims about the death of the Black church "can be read as both a descriptive proclamation as well as a prophetic challenge."[26] "Glaude is correct, something has died," declared Ronald

B. Neal, then a professor in religion and philosophy at Claflin University, "though it's not the Black Church." "What no longer lives and cannot be resurrected is *The Myth of the Black Church*," Neal added. "May it rest in peace."[27] William D. Hart, who taught religious studies and African American studies at the University of North Carolina, Greensboro, perceptively concluded that "if the Black Church is dead, then it is dead because the 'universal church' is dead, because God is dead in the sense that Nietzsche meant when he put those words in the mouth of 'a madman.'"[28] In yet another response to Glaude, Josef Sorett, who was teaching in African and African American studies at Harvard University at that point, promptly asked: "What work does one accomplish by claiming that 'the Black church is dead,' and who is the intended audience for such a claim?"[29] In a fitting climax to the opinions offered, Edward J. Blum, a professor of history at San Diego State University, concluded that Glaude's "essay, as I read the ending, is just as much a proclamation of the Black church's death as it is a call for its resurrection, but in a more progressive form.... This echoes Du Bois, Frazier, and Wilmore,"[30] Blum added.

Eddie Glaude's claims about the demise of the Black church are clearly premature, and they shimmer before a mountain of evidence that suggests otherwise. It is a bit of an overstatement to conclude that the Black church is dead because it no longer has a prophetic posture and zeal, for this assumes that the life of that institution, throughout its history, has been defined, necessarily and exclusively, by its function in the realm of the prophetic. The prophetic quality has never been the one and only characteristic of the Black church. The sum total of the Black church is far more than that. Moreover, it is one thing to claim that the Black church is not sufficiently prophetic, and yet another to conclude that it is dead. The validity of one claim does not necessarily lead to the validity of the other. We hold that the Black church is still very much alive in many ways—physically, spiritually, liturgically, socially, and in terms of its importance as a source of identity, a refuge, and a support system for a people who still confront the harsh realities of white supremacist attitudes and structures daily.[31] That institution also still affords opportunities for self-help and self-expression, and it remains the place in which African Americans can receive due recognition and exercise leadership and authority.[32] We also feel that the very existence of the Black church is in some measure not only a prophetic critique of the evils of white supremacy and white nationalism but also a testimony to the continuing desires of Black people to speak for and govern themselves.

To assert that the Black church is still alive is not to suggest that all is well with it. While that institution is not dead, it is being redefined and is, thus, in the midst of what might be called a definitional crisis. Much of this crisis is attributable to a problem already discussed, namely, the loss of much of its prophetic voice and spirit. Martin Luther King Jr.'s critique of the church in *Letter from the Birmingham City Jail* (1963) has become increasingly applicable to the contemporary Black church. All too many Black clergy and laity have become silent and noncommittal in the face of the lingering "big lie" about the outcome of the 2020 presidential election, government mendacity, and abuses of power at the highest levels of political and governmental life, and some have become what King called "arch-defenders of the status quo."[33]

This became painfully evident during the Trump years as some of the nation's leading Black clergy cozied up to and became bold voices for the former president despite his assault on truth, his appeasement of and support for white supremacists and nationalists, and his apparent lack of respect for the rule of law, the Constitution, and American democratic norms and traditions.[34] Bishop William Barber was the most courageous and persistent among those very few Black clergy who were willing to stand up and speak truth to power.[35] We witnessed firsthand what can happen when Black religious leaders become enablers instead of prophetic critics of bigotry, intolerance, and injustice. This loss of the prophetic and sacrificial spirit, which was so prominent during the freedom crusade of the 1950s and '60s, is at the root of the contemporary Black church's definitional and/or identity crisis.

This crisis has been triggered, to a significant extent, by the gradual decline of Black neighborhood churches. Driven by safety concerns, and determined to escape the epidemic of drugs, guns, rising crime, and gang violence, Black congregations in many parts of the country have moved out of the inner cities or Black urban areas to more suburban and less populated settings. This trend, which is likely to increase with time, is most unfortunate since neighborhood churches have long served as the epicenter of Black community life. They have traditionally functioned as social service centers, or what Gayraud S. Wilmore calls "social welfare agencies," fulfilling a broad spectrum of needs for the rapidly growing Black urban populations. They have provided counseling, food, shelter, childcare, recreation, and so much more.[36] The increasing departure of neighborhood churches means that many of them are not likely to actualize their full potential as social change agents. Also, this may constitute the removal of the last best hope for inner city dwellers, who are already struggling under the weight of economic deprivation, grinding poverty, and a chronic lack of resources and support systems.

The rise of the megachurch phenomenon is yet another explanation for the Black church's current definitional and/or identity crisis. The growth of megachurches, which claim an average weekly attendance ranging from 10,000 to 20,000 congregants, and which mirror the corporate structure in terms of their organization, management, and mission outreach, are redefining the Black church, and they are increasingly setting the standard for how we do church. They are indeed the new face of the Black church. Moreover, Black megachurch leaders—such as Bishop T. D. Jakes of the Potter's House in Dallas; Creflo Dollar of World Changers International Church in College Park, Georgia; Joseph W. Walker III of Mt. Zion Baptist Church in Nashville; and Michael Moore of Faith Chapel in Birmingham, Alabama—operate as CEOs with dozens of clerical staff, and they have emerged as national celebrities while assuming center stage in the culture.[37] These vast bodies listed must be understood and evaluated in terms of how they conform to and deviate from what we call the Black church tradition and also from the standpoint of how they impact the quality of life in Black neighborhoods.

Black megachurch pastors are likely to claim without hesitation that they are standing in the very best tradition of the Black church. Bishop Jakes and the late Bishop Eddie L. Long have been included among the inheritors of Martin Luther King Jr.'s mantle, and Creflo Dollar is among the new and rising generation of televangelists who are "extending King's ministry by emphasizing issues such as economic empowerment." "Dr. King stood for the freedom of all people," Dollar declares, "I believe that deliverance from debt is an integral part of that freedom." "When a man is out of debt," Dollar adds, "he is better able to accomplish God's divine purpose for his life by being a blessing to others."[38] Paul S. Morton, formerly the presiding bishop of the massive Full Gospel Baptist Church Fellowship International, agrees. He maintains that "teaching Black people better money management is the 'next dimension' of King's ministry."[39] Clearly, the emphasis of megachurch gurus is always on the next phase of the freedom movement or that phase beyond the civil rights crusade of the '50s and '60s. "I'm not against marching," Bishop Jakes maintains, "but in the '60s, the challenge of the Black church was to march." Jakes continues: "And there are times now perhaps that we may need to march. But there is more facing us than social justice. There's personal responsibility, motivating and equipping people to live the best lives that they can."[40]

There is indeed some substance to such claims, and no one can deny that the megachurches are true to the Black church tradition in some ways. Their message of personal responsibility and economic self-help and empowerment is grounded in that tradition. To a considerable degree, Black megachurches, blessed with enormous financial resources, have assumed some of the functions of government through nonprofit agencies and faith-based initiatives. They spearhead charitable ministries and create new opportunities for ministry and mission in such areas as social welfare,

114

childcare, affordable housing, services for the elderly, health care, and education. Much like the large, urban Black congregations from the first half of the twentieth century—Reverdy C. Ransom's Institutional AME Church in Chicago; H. H. Proctor's First Congregational Church in Atlanta; L. K. Williams's Olivet Baptist Church in Chicago; and Adam Clayton Powell Sr.'s Abyssinian Baptist Church in New York—Black megachurches serve as "social welfare agencies."[41]

After Hurricane Katrina in 2005, these institutions mobilized to help thousands of Gulf coast residents who needed food, shelter, health screenings, and other basic necessities. By providing homeless shelters, health care screenings, food banks, soup kitchens, counseling services, educational initiatives, and other social service and charitable good works with varying degrees of vigor and success, the megachurches are honoring a tradition that stretches back to the earliest Black churches and Free African Societies.[42] The lingering effects of the current global pandemic COVID-19, is likely to impact their social services ministries in even greater and more positive ways with the passing of time. But the megachurches' efforts are not as beneficial to the poor and needy as they could be because too many of their leaders and lay constituents refuse to actively protest against the structures of economic injustice while assuming that charity or philanthropy alone is enough to solve certain kinds of socioeconomic problems. King's words, uttered during a critical stage in the struggle for civil rights, are relevant here: "Philanthropy is commendable, but it must not cause the philanthropist to overlook the circumstances of economic injustice which makes philanthropy necessary."[43] Evidently, King was making a distinction here between those who become satisfied with treating the symptoms of poverty, neglect, and injustice and those concerned about curing "injustice at the causal source."[44]

The megachurches have also increased the connections between the sectors of the Black church and the larger human family across the globe, and this is important in view of the nature of the times. That connection has always been there, to some extent, primarily through foreign missions, but the megachurches—with their satellite facilities and networks, television airtime, and computer websites—are able to speak to the world on a constant basis. Black megachurch pastors have an international platform, and their messages, though seriously lacking in prophetic content and tone, reach people in virtually every corner of the globe each week. Hopefully, this will ultimately contribute to a climate in which African Americans are more mindful of the need to develop an international perspective and to view themselves as global citizens. This should be regarded as a critical part of what it means to be Black and Christian in the twenty-first century, especially since the most rapid growth of Christianity today is in Africa, and that continent, as Gayraud S. Wilmore often said, "holds the future of Christianity in its hand." "I am astonished at how ignorant African American Christians seem to be of what is happening in Africa today," Wilmore declared a few years ago.[45] Martin Luther King Jr. also constantly stressed this need for Black Americans to "develop a world perspective" because he saw his people's struggle in America as part of a "worldwide revolution in progress."[46] The armed conflict in the Darfur region of western Sudan, the Boko Haram-related violence in Nigeria, the recent Russian invasion of Ukraine, and the suffering and death experienced by the people in these and other parts of the world merely reinforce this need for African Americans, who have a deep sense of what it means to be persecuted, slaughtered, and displaced, to claim their world citizenship while supporting the freedom struggles of people everywhere.

There are also levels on which the Black megachurches deviate from the Black church tradition. The emphasis on bigness on the part of their leaders has always been considered by many among the faithful to be contrary to the Gospel of Jesus Christ, and the massive numbers of these bodies mean that the degree of impersonality within their ranks is not only immense but also not necessarily good for people who grew up in congregations in which the members knew and related to each other on a first-name basis. Megachurch pastors, after years of leadership and service, only get to know a select few of their members by name. Furthermore, megachurches too often equate success with numbers, thus forgetting that the quality of ministry and mission is always about service and should never be judged by the numbers of their memberships.[47] King's words, though spoken more than a half century ago, are instructive at this point. "We worship that which is big—big buildings, big cars, big houses, big corporations," he complained, as he thought primarily of Black pastors who routinely bragged about the sizes of their congregations and their bank accounts. "We find our great security in bigness." King went on to denounce the very premise on which some megachurch leaders today claim legitimacy, power, and success:

> This numerical growth should never be overemphasized. We must not be tempted to confuse spiritual power and large numbers. Jumboism, as someone has called it, is an utterly fallacious standard for measuring positive power. An increase in quantity does not automatically bring an increase in quality. A large membership does not necessarily represent a correspondingly increased commitment to Christ. Almost always the creative, dedicated minority has made the world better.[48]

King's words are equally relevant and useful for critiquing the megachurches' tendency to overemphasize the gospel of individualism and materialism. Black church traditions have never been completely united on this issue. Such a gospel was affirmed and widely preached by Black spiritual churches in the late nineteenth and early twentieth centuries and by prosperity pastors such as Roosevelt Franklin, Frederick J. Eikerenkoetter (Rev. Ike), and Johnnie Colman in the mid- to late twentieth century. It still echoes through the proclamations of megachurch leaders. But too much stress on the gospel of individualism and materialism is encouraging the type of selfish ambition, competitive situations, and elitism that breed what one of the authors of this essay has long called structures of privilege within the Black community—structures of privilege that divide African Americans along class lines, that undermine service toward positive ends, and that are actually antithetical to the traditional communal values of the Black church.[49] But there is also a tradition in the Black church that declares that an excessive stress on individualism, materialism, selfish ambition, elitism, and classism is inconsistent with the Gospel and biblical revelation. Those who take this stand have long insisted that the primary emphasis should be placed on communal and spiritual values instead—the kinds of values that foster group cohesion, cooperative economic ventures, and racial uplift and empowerment, though not to the total neglect of the individual and the material.

King was a representative of this latter tradition. This tradition seriously questions Creflo Dollar's view that "people would make a decision to live their lives by the principles of the Word of God, all of the social ills in our society would cease to exist."[50] This declaration simply reflects the classic, one-sided view that has long kept Christian conservatives from properly emphasizing a social and prophetic gospel: namely, that if the church simply converts and transforms individuals, this will automatically translate into the transformation of society for the better. The best of our faith tradition reminds us that efforts must be made to transform not only the individual but the communal and social aspects as well. The Black megachurches' gospel of individual conversion, prosperity positivism, entrepreneurial spirituality, and materialism has some merit, but in order to meet the needs of people who are still victimized by the structures of white supremacy, it must reclaim a greater stress on the type of spirituality that takes more serious account of the communal, interpersonal, social, public or political, and prophetic dimensions. In other words, being Black and Christian today demands that we choose not the entrepreneurial spirituality of the megachurches but the more balanced spirituality and the prophetic model represented by churchpersons from Richard Allen and Sojourner Truth down to Martin Luther King Jr., Jeremiah Wright, and Bishop William Barber, in more recent times.[51]

The leadership model and lifestyles embraced by these figures made it possible for them to speak truth to power while identifying with and serving the needs of the poor, exploited, and marginalized. This cannot be said today of the media and megachurch pastors who, despite finding ways to connect with and sway large numbers of people on a spiritual and emotional level, tend to accept the status quo while being routinely absent from those Jericho roads of life on which people are suffering and dying daily. The megachurch pastors are captivated more by the seductive lure of materialism than by the call to prophetic witness and activism, and they have become filthy rich. They draw enormous salaries, live in multimillion-dollar homes, wear high-priced clothes, and drive expensive cars.

Relishing in extravagant lifestyles and in an "abundance of life" biblicism and theology, some megachurch leaders are consummate exhibitionists who advocate a puritanical moral code; revel in showering their congregants with pristine, otherworldly images; brag about their vast power and networks of personal influence; promote a consumerism devoid of radical, public piety and discipleship; and scoff at any concept of the church as prophetic community, suffering servant, or sacrificial lamb.[52] The fact that some of these megachurch pastors serve churches that have begun to exhibit the authoritarian features of a cult—or movements associated in earlier times with the likes of Father Divine, Daddy Grace, and Prophet Jones—is all the more cause for concern, especially for those of us who see the need to reclaim an ecclesial vision consistent with the highest and best values in the Black church tradition.[53]

Being Black and Christian in the twenty-first century has little to do with skin color and being a devoted affiliate of a particular church or denomination. It is not reducible to simply dissent on matters of race, equal rights, and social justice in the United States. As suggested at points throughout this essay, it is about affirming and honoring one's place in a long and rich faith tradition that takes seriously not only the personal and interpersonal dimensions

119

of spirituality but also the public and prophetic aspects. It has to do with a progressive outlook on humanity and the world in which we live and radical faith praxis in a twenty-first century society and world that are becoming wiser and more hostile, divided, and violent each day. It is about challenging and protesting against today's evil systems, structures, and institutions and doing constructive ministry and mission at points where human need is most pronounced. In short, being Black and Christian means thinking through and understanding what our raison d'etre as the body of Christ is at this particular time in human history.

Chapter 7

Transatlantic Bridges:
A Tribute to Forrest Harris's Global Involvements

R. Drew Smith

A 1999 essay by Black religion scholar Gayraud S. Wilmore outlines "unmet needs" pertaining to "the future of African American religious thought and praxis," particularly related to the global scope of that work. Among the needs Wilmore identified was "a renewed contact and bonding with African, Caribbean, and Black Latin American churches, mosques, intellectuals and religious leaders" and the "religiously oriented African Diaspora" in England, the European continent, and elsewhere. Wilmore's 1999 observations left off with a challenge to African American religion scholars: "The time is ripe for our church people and theologians to forge new, mutually beneficial relationships with brothers and sisters abroad."

The Transatlantic Roundtable on Religion and Race (TRRR; https://religionandrace.org), founded in 2010 with leadership footing in South Africa, the US, and the UK, represents one recent effort at living into Professor Wilmore's challenge. Hundreds of persons from almost thirty countries and more than one hundred academic and community institutions have now participated in TRRR. Each individual and institution with which TRRR has worked has helped shape its direction.

One active participant has been Forrest E. Harris, who has brought to his TRRR involvements wisdom and expertise deriving from his decades of scholarly, pastoral, and academic administrative leadership, as well as a systematic and demonstrated commitment to the "beloved community" and "world house" toward which

Martin Luther King Jr. pointed—and which serve as guiding principles for TRRR.

On behalf of my fellow Transatlantic Roundtable on Religion and Race co-conveners, I am pleased to highlight some of Dr. Harris's multiple involvements in TRRR's work, both because his active participation has proven very valuable to TRRR undertakings and because of what his involvement suggests about his commitments, in general, to global intersections of religion, race, and justice. This essay will highlight aspects of the global arenas and dynamics with which Dr. Harris has been involved, examining specifically TRRR's focus on Black Atlantic intersections of the religious, social, academic, and community-based endeavors of our people. The essay explores these matters against an historical backdrop of challenges and breakthroughs that for fifty years have signaled possibilities for socially impactful intersections of religion and public life across the Black Atlantic.

Bridging Worlds, Grounding Worldviews

Martin Luther King Jr.'s final book, *Where Do We Go from Here: Chaos or Community?*, concludes with a chapter titled "The World House" that outlines key aspects of his global vision. In this world house we have inherited, says King, we are "a family unduly separated in ideas, culture and interest, who, because we can never again live apart, must learn somehow to live with each other in peace."[1] Decades later, diversity and difference have become far more apparent, and so too have the possibilities for conflict—and for a broadening and deepening of community.

TRRR's work embraces these diversities and community-building challenges with emphasizing how ways religion engages social difference related primarily to race, class, and ethnicity. TRRR mobilizes leaders and practitioners to advance research, dialogue, and action in response to social challenges stemming from social differences. Although centering on religion, TRRR's scholarly activities are interdisciplinary while seeking to ground its scholarly dimensions in everyday Black struggles through attention to contextualized cultural immersions and issue engagement. These are issues that have been central to the thought and activism of Dr. Harris.

Immersions in Context

TRRR's conference themes and settings have been attentive to context, reflecting time and place through themes such as post-racialism for the 2011 conference in South Africa, multiculturalism for the 2012 conference in the UK, race legacies and repair for the 2016 conference in Trinidad, and conflict and peacemaking for the 2019 conference in Kenya (with a special emphasis on TRRR-funded research undertaken in South Sudan).

The parallel hyper-racialized histories of the US and South Africa and the racialized colonial legacy of the UK helped framed TRRR's direction from the outset. Key Black theology proponents and Black religion scholars were featured in TRRR's initial conferences, including James E. Cone at TRRR's 2010 conference in the US; Allan Boesak (South Africa), Walter Fluker (US), and R. David Muir (UK) at its 2011 conference in South Africa; and Anthony Reddie (UK) and Carol Duncan (Canada) at its 2012 conference in the United Kingdom. TRRR also engaged in strategic collaborations from its earliest days with the Samuel DeWitt Proctor Conference's (SDPC) impactful racial justice network, including annual participation at TRRR conferences by Proctor conference delegations headed by SDPC cofounders Iva Carruthers and Jeremiah Wright. These delegations frequently were inclusive of SDPC board member Forrest Harris.

These initial conferences were shaped by an awareness of sporadic progress across the Black Atlantic in mitigating racial and ethnic conflict some sixty or more years beyond the US Civil Rights Movement and the formal decolonization of most Global South nations. TRRR work was also heavily influenced by the legacies of apartheid affecting South Africa's democratic transition from white minority rule and the ongoing indignities faced by African descendent and global Black majority communities living in Europe under the guise of multiculturalism. TRRR deliberations were initiated out of these twenty-first-century, sociocultural complexities and contradictions, with the 2011 dialogue taking place at the University of South Africa (one of the higher-educational institutions allied with apartheid policies during the freedom struggle) and the 2012 conference beginning with a session hosted at the British House of Lords by one of its members. At this session, Coretta Phillips, Marla Frederick, Iva Carruthers, and Forrest Harris were among those who led a comparative discussion of Black and ethnic minority criminalization.

TRRR's 2013 Ghana conference further engaged racialized transatlantic historical and contemporary contexts with its focus on tragedies and atrocities associated with Black enslavement. The conference dialogue and engagement were situated in deep traditions of religious and theological critiques of enslavement, colonialism, patriarchy, and other forms of social captivity and drew on presentations from leading scholars focused on these issues, such as Mercy Oduyoye, Kofi Opoku, Akosua Ampofo, and Kwabena Asamoah-Gyadu. As part of the program, conferees traveled to the Cape Coast castle sites where enslaved Africans were imprisoned while awaiting passage to the Americas and to the nearby Assin Manso Slave River Site, where the enslaved were provided their last bath before being sent to the castles. These were places of painful remembrance for TRRR conferees, and one of the memorial tributes rendered was a prayer of lament and consecration at the river site. TRRR conferees requested that Dr. Harris provide that prayer—which he did in a way that powerfully invoked the pathos of the context and the enduring spirit of the ancestors.

Following conferences in South Africa in 2014 and the UK in 2015, TRRR held its 2016 conference in Trinidad, a country whose rich legacy of Pan-African organizing and theorizing produced four of the leading advocates of Black empowerment to emerge during the latter nineteenth century and across the twentieth century. Henry Sylvester-Williams, born in Trinidad in 1869, was a lawyer living in London when he founded the African Association (1897), an organization committed to Pan-African unity throughout the British colonies. George Padmore, born in Trinidad at the dawn of the twentieth century, became head of the Negro Bureau of the Communist Trade Union International and, after leaving the Communist Party, spearheaded the mobilization of thousands of anticolonial activists across the Caribbean and Africa. A contemporary of Padmore was the radical social theorist and historian C. L. R. James, who was born in Trinidad in 1901. He left Trinidad in the early 1930s for England, where he became active in socialist Pan-Africanist organizing efforts, subsequently in the US, and finally back in Trinidad. The most contemporary of these Trinidadian-born activists, Stokely Carmichael, was born in Port of Spain in 1941, where he lived until relocating to New York City, later becoming head of the Student Nonviolent Coordinating Committee and a spokesperson for Black Power during the 1960s before moving to Guinea and founding the All-African People's Revolutionary Party.

The work and spirit of these Trinidadian leaders were an inspirational backdrop to TRRR's conference deliberations on race and community repair. The 2016 conference was hosted by Rose-Marie Belle Antoine of the University of West Indies Faculty of Law and by Trinidad pastor Ronald Nathan, both of whom provided important insights on contemporary affairs in the region. This was also true of other key conference speakers with deep connections to the region, such as Sylvan Lashley (interim president of Trinidad's University of the Southern Caribbean) and two of that university's distinguished alumni, David Williams (Harvard) and Gosnell Yorke (Copperbelt University). The Caribbean region's vibrant reparations advocacy reverberated throughout TRRR's Trinidad conference discussions, and this has been an issue to which Dr. Harris has paid close attention as well.

TRRR's 2019 Kenya conference focusing on Black Atlantic social divisions took place at a time of significant conflict in South

Sudan, Somalia, and the Democratic Republic of Congo and on the heels of post-election violence in Kenya following its 2017 presidential election. The Kenyan location of TRRR's conference (including its setting at the Hekima College Institute for Peace Studies and International Relations) heightened alertness by conferees to peace and conflict issues within the region (and beyond), as did informed accounts and analysis from African religious leaders and scholars who presented at the conference. Cameroonian national ecclesial leader Babila Fochang spoke on emerging civil conflict in Cameroon, Kenyan social scientist Connie Martinon provided an assessment of Somalian political instability, and South Sudanese journalist Lucy Poni and Kenyan Peace Studies scholar Elias Opongo shared findings from TRRR-funded research on religious peacemaking in South Sudan. TRRR's South Sudan research occurred at a time of important developments in the South Sudan crisis—one year after the signing of a major peace agreement between South Sudan's warring parties and a few months prior to a September 2019 dialogue on peace consolidation convened in Nairobi by the African Council of Religious Leaders— Religions for Peace.

An important component of TRRR conferences has been direct engagement with local community groups through immersion activities and dialogues. For example, during the 2015 UK conference, TRRR conferees participated in structured dialogues and fact-finding visits in Tottenham, a working-class suburb of London whose history includes race riots in 1985 and 2011 in response to a controversial death of a Black person at the hands of police. TRRR conferees met with local religious and civic leaders who represented Black and ethnic minority groups on the frontlines of social struggle, comparing social change strategies from our respective national contexts. During the 2014 South Africa conference and the 2019 Kenya conference, TRRR conferees met with local leaders working to bring about change in two of Africa's poorest urban settlements.

South African scholars Itumeleng Mothoagae and Mokhele Madise facilitated the visit to Diepsloot, an "informal settlement" of 140,000 mainly shack dwellers near Johannesburg, while the Kenyan visit focused on Kibera, the largest slum in Nairobi and largest urban slum in Africa. Similarly, during TRRR's 2017 US conference, participants engaged with local community leaders in Baltimore's Sandtown neighborhood (where Freddie Gray was killed by police in 2015). Discussions were held about the severe social challenges being faced in this neighborhood and the ways residents were attempting to respond. The depth of poverty in these three places and the determination of the local populations to bring about change set a high bar for our conference deliberations, as they always do, coming at the very beginning of our conference gatherings. Where present, Dr. Harris has spoken into these occasions a needed empathy and moral indignation toward the severity of human struggles and with proposals emanating from a pastor's heart and college president's hopefulness regarding potential reforms and improvements.

With more than two decades at the helm of an historically Black college with deep historical ties to the Civil Rights Movement, Dr. Harris has brought to his TRRR involvements a well-formed appreciation of the relationship between context and learning and an affinity toward TRRR's commitment to that intersectionality. As president of American Baptist College in Nashville, Dr. Harris developed student contextual learning strategies, such as the Social Justice, Equity, Advocacy and Leadership initiative, a curriculum that "links undergraduate coursework with secondary school enrichments and civic education for youth from low-income neighborhoods." In addition, he has provided continuing education opportunities for local clergy that connect them to curricular resources to aid in planning and implementing community social change activities. Commenting on the college's commitment to learning experiences that integrate theory and practice and that connect with broader worlds and publics, Dr. Harris states, "An aspect of the academic endeavor is to critically engage history and traditions in order to discover how we should progress toward the future." Cognizant that the college's history and traditions incorporate alums at the forefront of civil rights activism, such as C. T. Vivian, John Lewis, Diane Nash, and James Bevel, the college actively celebrates their legacies as a means for "reigniting a powerful flame on the relevance of these iconic figures to the current times and forecasting what could happen in the future of social activism."[2]

That same spirit of *sankofa* (retracing steps while looking toward the present and future) has guided TRRR activities—with TRRR engagement of targeted Black struggle contexts seeking to place those situations encountered on the ground into broader historical and geographical context. These have been undertakings of solidarity and of mutual learning across social, cultural, and physical boundaries, and TRRR has benefitted from a tremendous network of educators like Dr. Harris in this educational work.

Analytical Content

The broad reaches of TRRR's issue-engagement and public-awareness initiatives have been signaled in its campaigning and advocacy initiatives. The latter has included petitions endorsed and circulated transnationally on matters such as democracy and peace in the Sahel region (2012); twenty-first-century captivities, including modern-day slavery (2013); and solidarities in the struggle against Ebola in West Africa (2014). Dr. Harris was a lead endorser of these campaigns, and his generative support alongside other institutional presidents and executives immeasurably strengthened these campaigns.

Dr. Harris's engagement with the global struggles of Black people has been shaped and influenced by social justice-oriented scholarship. Drawing especially from Christian ethics, he has brought a scholarly commitment to what he refers to as a "liberative praxis" that urges close and careful readings of Black social and spiritual life as source materials for social theorizing and theologizing. He draws from justice-oriented Black intellectual traditions, including those of progressive Black social scientists, such as W. E. B. Du Bois, and of Black liberationist theologians. In doing so, what distinguishes Dr. Harris's analysis from many others within these progressive schools is his sustained commitment to the religious and social experience of everyday Black folks as an authentic gauge of the resonance of religious and social theorizing.

Dr. Harris's body of scholarship and work in the theological academy point also to a twenty-first-century moral positioning and praxis signaled by Black theology's existential wrestlings. Black theology of liberation, as it has been descriptively labeled, achieved formalization and traction beginning in the late1960s via the writings of James Cone and additional African American theologians. Dialogue ensued at about the same time between US Black theology scholars and African theologians on overlapping concerns. While these conversations (and those with theologians focused on other Global South contexts) were limited throughout the 1970s, they were expanded in subsequent decades.[3] As it relates to these efforts at expansion, TRRR builds most directly on initiatives and organizations whose dialogues span the Black Atlantic and aim to connect scholarly activity to social urgencies and community needs, including work emanating from theological consultations facilitated during the late1960s and early1970s by the US National Committee of Black Churchmen and the All Africa Conference of Churches (AACC); conferences and general assembly gatherings of the Ecumenical Association of Third World Theologians (EATWOT) convened yearly from 1976 to 1979 and every 4 to 6 years since; and meetings and mobilizations by the Circle of Concerned African Women Theologians, which began in 1980 as AACC, EATWOT, or World Council of Churches gatherings before formally launching as CIRCLE in 1989.[4]

TRRR shares with these endeavors a commitment to bridging divides in the disciplinary, sectoral, and regional geographies of this theologically minded social engagement work. TRRR is also concerned with a more systematic groundedness of this work in the lived realities of communities facing pronounced social difficulties. This theological engagement work aligns with a growing emphasis within scholarly realms on demarcating connections between scholarship and the social worlds out of which it comes and to which it speaks. Theologies in these instances have effectively and systematically examined social subjectivities, particularities, and ramifications of theological worldviews although they have not always been quite as exacting in applying their theoretical propositions to practices addressing social urgencies on the ground. Black theology has proceeded along a continuum toward more explicit social applications, both with respect to embracing more gender-explicit frameworks and more explicit economic doctrines.

With respect to the latter, for example, Cornel West outlines five stages through which the Black theology of liberation has evolved on its way toward a comprehensive global economic critique, with the first three critiquing aspects of race and culture, the fourth critiquing US capitalism, and the fifth critiquing capitalist civilization. Dr. West resists limited cultural critiques along this continuum for their "lack of a social vision, political program and concrete praxis which defines and facilitates socioeconomic and political liberation."[5] Other African American theological scholars have conveyed convictions in their own terms about the need for a more rigorous socioeconomic analytics within Black theology, including James Cone, Katie Cannon, Keri Day, and Obery Hendricks—as have African theological scholars such as Jesse Mugambi, Itumeleng Mosala, Sunday Bobai Agang, and Vuyani Vellem.[6] Dr. Cone states, for example: "There is little in our theological expressions and church practices that rejects American capitalism or recognizes its oppressive character in third world countries. The time has come for us to move beyond institutional survival in a capitalistic and racist society and begin to take more seriously our dreams about a new heaven and a new earth."[7] Likewise, Dr. Agang calls for a repositioning of African theologies, centering social problems in ways "going beyond the surface issues to the underlying causes rooted in social structures and prevailing worldviews."[8]

The Transatlantic Roundtable on Religion and Race has emphasized greater socioeconomic (and political) grounding within theological and church ministry realms and has facilitated intersectional spaces that bring scholars into conversation with community stakeholders and with each other in ways that cross cultural divides, including those between Black theologies and African theologies. Part of the affinity between Dr. Harris and TRRR's work has been its trans-African vantage points on social and theological matters and its opportunities for expanding understanding of the diverse ways Blackness is conceived across the Black Atlantic. Affinities have stemmed also from TRRR's efforts at cross-regional integrations of analysis and applied dimensions, especially were concerned with economic structural issues.

Dr. Harris's presentation at TRRR's 2015 University of London conference reflected his emphasis on socioeconomic context and greater theological responsiveness. Addressing TRRR's assembly of leaders from such contexts as Angola, Nigeria, South Africa, Finland, the US, and the UK, his presentation championed "the movement of justice in the world for the poor" while examining ways "black liberation and womanist theologies and the black churches in North America and Africa map the road to justice." Citing the need for greater commitment to "liberation and spirituality to free the minds, bodies and spirits of oppressed people for public agency in service of love and justice" and for diligence by leaders in truth-telling that facilitates "public policy and structural changes," he placed a specific challenge to the theological sector:

> The continent most deeply entrenched in poverty is Africa, where more than half of the people live in extreme poverty. Black Liberation and Womanist theologies have sought to map a path for liberation and spirituality to reconstitute black people's global situation of poverty and injustice to hopeful possibilities for justice. These theologies have been hard pressed to make visible the cultural diversity of racial and sexual identities

amidst the globalization of capitalism and Western privilege that seek to render black bodies invisible.... There is a liberationist faith to make visible a spirituality that values people, their differences, cultures, and human rights to live and flourish.[9]

Dr. Harris's remarks captured the spirit of that occasion and of the work undertaken by many others with whom TRRR has been privileged to collaborate over the years.

Race-based economic disparities have been a consistent focus within TRRR deliberations. Building upon content from TRRR's 2015 conference on repairing community, TRRR's 2016 Trinidad conference emphasized the persistence of social divisions and disparities. One of the opening 2016 plenary sessions featured National African American Reparations Commission (NAARC) convener Ron Daniels (Institute of the Black World 21st Century) and commission member Iva Carruthers (Proctor Conference), along with TRRR co-conveners Rothney Tshaka (University of South Africa) and William Ackah (Birkbeck, University of London). The panel discussed NAARC reparations objectives, including reparations funding toward development of Black housing, land-based economic development, communications infrastructure, wealth generation, and health.[10] Panelists outlined the relevance of these objectives for Black communities in the US, Caribbean, UK, and South Africa as well as steps required for achieving these objectives. Several additional conference presenters also addressed reparations, including multiple presentations focusing on: (1) land dispossession in Zimbabwe and South Africa; (2) wealth expropriation in various African contexts; (3) theological support for reparations; and (4) reparatory preconditions to racial reconciliation. Socioeconomic repair was placed in a fuller theoretical perspective via a presentation by biblical scholar Obery Hendricks on Martin Luther King Jr's socialist inclinations, with a plenary session led by sociologist Jualynne Dodson and Michigan State University's Africa Atlantic Research Team detailing contemporary community development strategies within socialist Cuba.

A concern, therefore, with systemic and structural change has been the theoretical plumbline extending across TRRR's work. Whether advocating for institutional transformation, public policy reform, or economic restructuring, TRRR participants have given voice and visibility to local and regional Black Atlantic socioeconomic challenges and pursuits—as viewed and engaged from religious vantage points. The intersectional advocacy TRRR has fostered builds upon historic mobilizations rising from centers of ideational and spiritual ferment and crucibles of Black struggle. Many TRRR participants have given intellectual expression and embodiment to this, from South African theologian Allan Boesak's 2011 TRRR calling forth a theological "restlessness" that resists global "enslavement of people" and a "maintenance and justification of imperial and colonial designs" to Hendricks's 2016 Trinidad reflections on the "revolution of values" King believed necessary to "restructure the architecture of American society" and make "Beloved Community" possible; to Jesse Mugambi's chronicling of African liberative traditions as conveyed through 2019 TRRR presentations on several of his notable publications, such as *Prophetic Christianity and Church-State Relations* (2004) and *The Church and the Reconstruction of Africa* (1997).

Indeed, a distinctive quality common to TRRR participants has been a bridging of theory and practice—exemplified in their individual walk and their collective work. In this respect, TRRR participants place before each other and before communities they engage in a challenge rooted in their own story and in its broader implications. TRRR participants speak out of a deep embrace of location and of its strivings—as has Dr. Harris.

Rooted in historic Black institutions (educational and ecclesial) and closely tied to the burdens these institutions have shouldered in the cause of Black liberation, Dr. Harris concluded a chapter he contributed to a TRRR volume with a "Social Justice Credo" that calls for greater strides toward: (1) a theological literacy that reveals and sustains liberation; (2) education that develops Black civic capacity; (3) health and health care that facilitates a higher quality of Black life; (4) a social policy agenda that invests resources in ways that can help all people to achieve their potential; (5) legal redress of injustices toward women and on matters bearing upon gender and mass incarceration; and (6) commitments to egalitarian democracy and civil and human rights.[11] To some this may seem a sweeping agenda, but to Dr. Harris, and to many within the TRRR network, it reflects the kind of comprehensiveness demanded of our time and the kind of audacity required of those who would seek to lead.

More Rivers to Cross

These are times that demand global thinking in every respect—measured not only in geographies but also in the scope of intellectual and moral vision. We bring pieces through our personhood and groupness to this larger global mosaic, and we should be intentional about ensuring content that contributes to the broadest possible good. TRRR strives for that kind of intentionality and has been fortunate to journey in solidarity with persons such as Dr. Harris in these pursuits.

A 1970 Ike and Tina Turner song conveyed a truth about prospects for change pertinent to that time and to our present time: "Working together we can make a change. Working together we can help better things." When we learn to work across our boundaries and become truly global actors and leaders, change becomes more possible. We must each do our part, and we owe gratitude to Dr. Harris and all others who have endeavored to be faithful to that calling.

Chapter 8

Cultivating Leaders, Proclaiming Justice, and Healing Communities

Peter J. Paris

The American Baptist Theological Seminary (now the American Baptist College) was founded in 1924 as the successor to the Roger Williams College for African Americans that, incidentally, had a relatively short life. By contrast, this school's founding emerged from the dream and tireless work of Sutton E. Griggs, a prominent civil rights activist, writer, and preacher who was the corresponding secretary for the National Baptist Convention, USA, Inc. In 1913, he was the first African American to address the Southern Baptist Convention, which met in St. Louis. In his speech, he asked the convention for financial help to actualize a dream he had about a theological seminary for Black individuals. The money was provided, and the college opened with Griggs as its first president (1925 to 1926). The oldest building on this campus, recently renovated, was named to honor his memory. After the school converted from a seminary to a liberal arts college in the 1970s, it gained HBCU (Historically Black Colleges and Universities) status in 2013.

During the early 1960s, the civil rights protest activity of its students brought national publicity to the school. Four of its students were iconic leaders in the Nashville sit-in movement: the late Congressman John R. Lewis, James Bevel, Julius Scruggs, and Bernard LaFayette. They were all mentored by the leading luminaries: the Reverend Kelly Miller Smith Sr., who was also their homiletics professor; the Reverend C. T. Vivian; and the Reverend James Lawson. Lawson was an authority on Mohandas Gandhi's philosophy of nonviolence and a student at Vanderbilt Divinity

School from which he was later expelled because of his leadership in the Nashville sit-in movement.

Though the Southern Baptist Convention did not admit Black students to its own seminaries, it supported this segregated Black school financially until 1996, when it turned its assets over to its board of trustees. Prior to the mid-1950s, however, the American Baptist Theological Seminary was the only theological seminary in the South that admitted Black students.

Since 1999, this institution has been privileged to have Dr. Forrest E. Harris as its president. I was honored to serve as the speaker at his installation and am honored once again to deliver the Garnet-Nabrit Lecture on the subject "Cultivating Leaders, Proclaiming Justice, and Healing Communities." It is a fitting topic because it reflects both this school's mission and its president's vocational life.

As a pastor, scholar, administrator, teacher, and preacher, Dr. Harris's moral and spiritual formation occurred in the racially segregated South where he was born and has spent his life. His experience in both segregated and desegregated institutions prepared him well for his life's work. After gaining degrees from Knoxville College and this school, Dr. Kelly Miller Smith Sr. and I were privileged to work with him at Vanderbilt Divinity School as he pursued the Master of Divinity and Doctor of Ministry degrees. We easily discerned his potential as an excellent theological leader. Many view the Doctor of Ministry degree as a way to legitimize their use of the title *Reverend Doctor*. Its true purpose is to give clergy additional tools with which to enhance their respective ministries, and that is exactly what Dr. Harris sought in his pursuit of the degree. Consequently, his life and work have benefited not only this school but also Vanderbilt University and the city of Nashville as a whole.

In addition to his local, national, and international denominational work and his membership on several boards of trustees, Dr. Harris has been an active member of five significant academic associations: the American Academy of Religion, the Society of

Christian Ethics, the Society for the Study of Black Religion, the Samuel DeWitt Procter Conference, and the Transatlantic Roundtable on Religion and Race. In each of those societies, he has delivered papers and found relevant conversation partners relative to his professional interests and concerns. What a pleasure it has been to see him and his wife at those gatherings, including at the Society for the Study of Black Religion's "Walking the Spirit Tour in Paris" this past summer while they were en route to the Baptist World Alliance meetings in Zurich, Switzerland.

Some people accuse scholars of living in ivory towers far removed from ordinary life, studying and writing about esoteric topics in which ordinary people have no interest. While that may be true for some, it is far from the truth for many, including Forrest Harris, who believes that any topic can become a subject for academic inquiry. Whenever that subject includes practitioners, the latter's experiences should be a necessary component in the research. Such has been the case with the Black churches since Black scholars first began studying them in the early part of the twentieth century.

Dr. Harris's vocational interest in building bridges between theological seminaries and the churches that they serve has been an integral part of his work throughout his leadership roles in this institution and Vanderbilt University Divinity School, as exercised respectively in the following ways:

> (a) through his relational work as president of this college, dean and professor of the Practice of Ministry, and director of the Kelly Miller Smith Institute on Black Churches Studies at Vanderbilt University;

> (b) by bringing nationally acclaimed religious leaders and scholars to Nashville for dialogical conferences on a wide range of relevant subjects with the city's white and black communities;

> (c) as the author of three significant books, numerous lectures, and many published essays, sermons, and even eulogies in

137

church publications, university journals, and occasional op-ed articles in local newspapers;

(d) most important, Harris's voice has been heard in the midst of this city's social crises, including the tragic act of violence that claimed the lives of four persons in 2018 at the Waffle House in Antioch, Tennessee.

Inspired by the late Kelly Miller Smith's 1983 Lyman Beecher lectures at Yale University that were published in 1984 by Mercer University Press under the title *Social Crisis Preaching*, Harris's book *Ministry for Social Crisis* moves the subject from its focus on homiletics to that of ministry as a whole. In accord with Smith's thesis that social crisis preaching is necessarily prophetic, Harris argues that prophetic ministry invariably expresses the essence of the theology and praxis of the Black church tradition. Forrest Harris's major contribution to the academic study of Black religion is confirmed by the following: the distinguished biblical scholar Brian K. Blount, my former colleague at Princeton Theological Seminary and now the president of Union Theological Seminary in Richmond, Virginia, anchors his acclaimed study of the Gospel of Mark, entitled *Go Preach! Mark's Kingdom Message and the Black Church Today*, on Harris's understanding of the Black church. Accordingly, he writes:

> Forrest Harris points to a duality in the life of the African American church. Two interrelated but also competing traditions exist within the same body. The survival tradition leans toward self-affirmation, internal spiritual freedom, and social accommodation. The liberation tradition proclaims self-help and self-reliance, and demands interior and exterior freedom, moral resistance, and the social conflict necessary to acquire them. The church is its healthiest when there is an ongoing dialogue between these when the two poles serve to complement, extend and complete one another.[1]

I fully agree with Blount's claim that unless Christian ministry emerges out of a deep awareness of the context in which the church is located, it will lose its proper focus by favoring an alternative stance of passivity and irrelevance. Like Harris, Blount calls for the necessity of grounding one's theology in contextual thought whereby the person is viewed as integrally related to the community that, in turn, challenges all Black churches to embrace a worldview in which they constantly seek and promote social justice in all their thinking and acting. This means that the Black churches will not wait on God to act, but trusting in their understanding of God as one who never ceases acting in love and justice, they will act on God's behalf to liberate God's people from all forms of injustice.

Now, if a church's mission is informed by, and expressive of, God's love and justice, everything the church does will be shaped by that orientation. Such a prophetic consciousness will guide its Sunday school teaching, youth work, men's and women's societies, worship, prayer meetings, Bible studies, preaching, singing, community work, and every other activity it undertakes. In short, when the prophetic ethic of the kingdom of God becomes the church's overriding ethic, everything the church does will reflect that ethos. Consequently, no one type of activity will be viewed as prophetic with other practices viewed as either pastoral or spiritual, but everything the church does will be expressive of the pastoral and prophetic vocations fully united. In other words, in the Black church there will be no division between the pastoral duties of nurturing, educating, counseling, healing, feeding and clothing the poor, on the one hand, and the prophetic actions of social criticism, community organizing, public advocacy, and nonviolent protests on the other hand. Rather, the two will function together as diverse functions in the service of love and justice for all. The most active Black churches in America's mid-twentieth-century Civil Rights Movement manifested such unity in both their internal and external practices.

Yet, then and now, there were and remain tensions and conflicts from young people who have felt and continue to feel that the desired changes fail to occur fast enough. In the early 1960s, that conflict resulted in the youth forming their own organization, the Student Nonviolent Coordinating Committee (SNCC). It is important to note that the group's embrace of the term *nonviolence* in its name marked an ongoing familial relationship, one that Stokely Carmichael and Dr. Martin Luther King Jr. never ceased demonstrating despite their strategic disagreements.

Tensions also occurred between older civil rights organizations like the NAACP and the Urban League, who had put their trust respectively either in the legal system as the agent for racial justice or economic development and its concurrent expansion of job opportunities. Yet their mutual shunning of public protests did not prevent the possibility of limited cooperative actions between these conflicting approaches through diplomatic negotiations. Clearly, many churches, both white and Black, remained firmly opposed to the use of nonviolent direct resistance in confronting the system of racial segregation and discrimination.

Let us not forget, however, that in the middle of the 1950s, two iconic Baptist ministers became national exemplars of radically different forms of public ministry. While the Black Baptist preacher Martin Luther King Jr. was leading the 1955 Montgomery bus boycott against the system of racial segregation, the white Southern Baptist evangelist Billy Graham was conducting one of his longest extended crusades in Madison Square Garden in New York City. It lasted for sixteen weeks. Clearly, those who followed either of those leaders had radically different views of church leadership. Most seminaries at the time were more likely to support Graham's approach rather than King's.

Further, during that same period, Vanderbilt Divinity School was quietly integrating its basic ministry degree program by admitting Joseph A. Johnson, who later became a bishop in the Christian Methodist Episcopal Church (then called the Colored Methodist Episcopal Church). Vanderbilt's secretive action went almost unnoticed since its admission process for that degree was an internal matter rather than a university-wide process. Nonetheless, for the next several years, whenever Johnson went to Rand Hall for meals, a faculty person was designated to accompany him lest something untoward should happen which, fortunately, never did. But when Johnson later entered the PhD program, the divinity school once again used tactics that helped desegregate its own internal life without publicly challenging the university's wider policy of denying admission to African Americans.[2]

Clearly, a basic condition for leadership is the ability to understand one's situation fully in order to have a complete grasp of the basic problems that either need repair or replacement. Those who view social problems as wholly spiritual in nature invariably seek leaders who only advocate spiritual solutions rather than those who strive to influence public policies aimed at social change. The former often view prayer and moral character as the primary remedies for social change while passively hoping for divine intervention. The latter view the combination of prayer, moral character, and public advocacy as the most efficacious means for social change. In the 1950s and thereafter, the Billy Graham evangelistic crusades represented the former approach while Martin Luther King Jr.'s nonviolent resistance movement represented the latter. It is important to note, however, that at that time, many African Americans were attracted to Graham's style and opposed to King's style. In those years, the Reverend Dr. Joseph H. Johnson, president of the National Baptist Convention, USA, Inc., was among Dr. King's most prominent Black opponents.

Though many Black Americans celebrated the gains of the Civil Rights Movement that culminated in the Civil Rights Act of 1964, the Voting Rights Act of 1965, the Fair Housing Act of 1968, and the various domestic programs of the Johnson administration, few knew at the time that a major social decline was taking place among African Americans. Thus, in his book *Ministry for Social Crisis: Theology and Praxis in the Black Christian Tradition*, Dr. Harris reminded his readers of the findings of William Julius

Wilson, the esteemed urban sociologist at the University of Chicago and later at Harvard University. Wilson, in his book *The Truly Disadvantaged*, revealed that for twenty years following the Civil Rights Movement, the social conditions of urban Black residents deteriorated at an alarming rate. During that period, poverty among African Americans failed to drop while steady increases occurred in the incarceration of Black men, unemployment, teenage pregnancies, school dropouts, and single-parent households. In addition to that social decline, the administrations of Richard Nixon, Ronald Reagan, and George H. Bush deliberately acted to dismantle affirmative action and human services programs.[3] Perhaps the most insidious act of all was President George H. Bush's successful nomination of Clarence Thomas to the Supreme Court to replace the iconic Thurgood Marshall, the architect of the 1954 *Brown v. Board of Education* decision that had overturned the 1896 *Plessy v. Ferguson* separate-but-equal doctrine. The deliberate neglect of the gains of the Civil Rights Movement by neoconservative politics supported by fundamentalist white Christian churches greatly diminished the progress of the Civil Rights Movement. That realignment of federal power would soon gain expression in Donald Trump's ascendancy to the presidency in the 2016 national election.

Let us not lose sight of the fact that it took a long while for African Americans to discern that the gains of the mid-twentieth-century Civil Rights Movement had benefited only the Black middle class, who alone were enabled to flee from the center cities while leaving poor African Americans to fend for themselves in the midst of a pervasive blight that affected housing, health, education, jobs, criminal justice, and the mass incarceration of Black men—all of which soon characterized the ethos of the nation's inner cities.

Since leaders must always embody the basic values of the people they lead, those who train leaders must understand the social context in which they are training the next generation of leaders. Though good leaders share many of the same characteristics, those with identical training can also serve opposing goals when engaged on opposite sides of a conflict. As in sports, the military, business, politics, and numerous other professions, similar strategies, tactics, and skills can be used to pursue opposing goals.

For example, during this country's bitter Civil War, most of the officers of both the Union and Confederate militias received their basic training at the United States Military Academy at West Point. All were trained by the same instructors to support the West Point motto, *Duty, Honor, and Country*, as well as the seven army values of duty, respect, selfless service, honor, integrity, loyalty, and personal courage along with additional military values of physical fitness, teamwork, and the will to win.

Now, every student of the Civil War knows that Commanders Ulysses S. Grant and Robert E. Lee were classmates and among West Point's most distinguished graduates. Yet their moral characters were formed in quite different social contexts that ensured different worldviews. In short, their worldviews and moral characters were formed long before they arrived at the academy. Since it has never been the mission of the academy to change either the worldviews or moral commitments of its cadets, teaching them how to think and act strategically has been and remains the school's sole purpose.

Theological education is similar in that students come to the seminary morally formed. Though their training in seminary may change their thinking about many things, their basic moral formation is not likely to change in such a short period of time. Thus, the art of cultivating Christian leaders is not unlike that of cultivating leaders in any other sphere of life, whether it be sports, the arts, science, politics, business, etc. Effective leaders demonstrate a love for the field, have some talent for grasping its basic principles, show an aptitude for its practices, and embody a cooperative spirit with the ability to inspire others by their commitment and integrity. Most of those attributes are likely to be discernible at an early age and are capable of being perfected through their love for disciplined practice until they become second nature. All practitioners readily recognize this truth. This is why recruitment officers who seek various types of talent spend enormous amounts of time searching for appropriate candidates whom they can persuade to join their enterprise. Clearly, the best recruiters are alumni/ae who, knowing both the school and the candidate, can rightly judge whether the two are a good fit.

Those who seek prophetic leaders must search for them in the right places, namely in those churches where evidence of prophetic leadership is readily visible. Though prophetic leaders may come from other contexts, one should not expect that to be the case. The biblical prophets, from Moses to Jesus, were spokespersons for God's justice; whenever justice is substituted for injustice, communities are healed. I join with you in praising Forrest Harris for his work of cultivating students to proclaim and to do justice as the only effective means for healing communities. Certainly, there can be no greater vocation than this.

Chapter 9

Theological Education for the 'Hood

William Myers

Introduction

I write this essay in honor of Forrest Harris as a witness to a brother whose life has been dedicated to the church and the academy, to the people in the 'hood, a people, in the words of Howard Thurman, "whose backs are against the wall." Harris was not only called and trained to do this work but he was also born, nurtured, and reared in it.

The very crucible of his formation is eloquently and passionately captured in his own words:

> I am a child of the Black Church and a product of Black Christian faith through the agency of my parents' faith, piety and public witness. They loved the Black Church. The last prayer I heard my father pray before his death in 2010 was for the faith of the next generation. After a long life of practicing a liberating faith, raising a family of nine children, confronting racism, facing oppressive confrontations, and resisting social humiliation, my father closed his eyes to immortality with the dream of Jesus and the Black Church still vibrantly alive in his soul. His faith lived on in the future of Black Christianity. With my mother and siblings who remain, I live with this faith daily to testify that the God of Black faith is a liberating and saving reality for the life of future generations. I seek to do the reclaiming of liberation and prophetic justice to make real what people need physically, socially, spiritually, and academically for wholeness of life.[1]

Harris and I have crossed paths across three decades in a variety of venues—the American Academy of Religion, the Society for the Study of Black Religion, and the Samuel DeWitt Proctor Institute. As important as all of these spaces are, there is a unique intersection in the life of the church and the life of the academy where we plant not one foot, but both feet in each on behalf of our people in the 'hood—the least of these, the left out, the let down, the last to get a seat at the table. We do not just seek to give them a voice in all the spaces we are privileged to enter. We seek also to help prepare present and future generations to traverse and fill the spaces of the Black church and academy in order to join the battle and the struggle for liberation of our people that is inclusive in terms of race, gender, class, and sexual orientation.

Here is a life dedicated to the cause of preparing leaders to serve the underserved, to lead those who seek liberation, and to pick up their cross daily. Harris has spent all of his life dedicated to fulfilling that charge in both predominantly white and Black spaces in the life of the Black church, at historically Black colleges and universities (HBCUs) as well as predominantly white academic institutions. HBCUs, and most especially the religious and theological schools, have historically been underfunded and understaffed. Leaders of these institutions—presidents, vice presidents, deans, and faculty—have chosen to truly be laborers of love in these spaces. Undoubtedly, they have never been compensated as they deserved or as they might have been elsewhere.

Yet we must also admit that predominantly white institutions, including theological spaces, have not always been welcoming to Black bodies. Not only has this been the case in their hiring practices, but it has included their curriculum and pedagogy as well. These institutions of the academy, inclusive of schools and societies, have been anything but inclusive of Black bodies' experiences, history, traditions, culture, ethos, or presence. When Black people discovered that they were not welcome in the white church, in protest they charted their own path. So, it would be in theological education as well. The most comprehensive historical analysis to date

146

of Black Church Studies is the work of Lewis Baldwin, retired historian at Vanderbilt Divinity School.[2] Although Black Church Studies would have its inception in the twentieth century, proto-Black Church Studies existed in Black academic institutions like Shaw, Howard, Payne, and others[3] in the nineteenth century. The Black Church Studies inception cannot be untethered from the Civil Rights Movement and Dr. Martin Luther King Jr.'s assassination, that is, the fight for liberation of Black people. The early progenitors and activists in the struggle were scholars and theologians such as Henry H. Mitchell and Gayraud S. Wilmore, both of whom died in recent times, Mitchell at the age of 102 (January 18, 2022) and Wilmore at the age of ninety-eight (April 18, 2020). It is part of my cherished memories to have known both of these men as dear friends and colleagues across many decades.

A great irony and paradox is that while resisting the very essence of the cultural differences of Black Church Studies, these programs started in predominantly white institutions. Yet what Wilmore observed more than a half century ago remains palpable in many of our predominantly white institutions today. "White faculty had to be convinced that what we were doing was significant."[4] A dear colleague of mine called me frequently until his death telling me how much time he spent in his office putting Black students back together again after white faculty kept telling them that a Black Church Studies curriculum was not a serious undertaking. Henry Mitchell was the first Black professor to hold a faculty position as professor of Black Church Studies as well as first director of the oldest Black Church Studies Director at the oldest Black Church Studies program in the nation at Colgate Rochester Divinity School. Mitchell not only felt that the curricular differences were inadequate for the training of Black students to do ministry in the Black community, but he also felt that the cultural differences were a major factor in the need for a Black Church Studies program and curriculum. Toward that end, he was instrumental in designing and shaping the first Black Church Studies program in the nation.[5]

The Historical Background for the Founding of the McCreary Center for African American Religious Studies and the Black Church Studies Program

I grew up as a child of the church. My early childhood years were spent at St. James AME Church, from the age of five to ten, in Meridian, Mississippi. When I left for Cleveland when I was ten, I wound up at New Mount Zion Baptist Church, where I have been the pastor for the last twenty-five years. Ever since I was five years old in Sunday school at St. James, I have been fascinated with reading and studying the Bible. So much so that by the age of eight, I was writing to the American Bible Society, accumulating materials to increase my knowledge.

When I arrived in Cleveland, along with my younger brother to join my mother, we wound up at a storefront church that had just started two years earlier. We met the Reverend Carey McCreary, the founding pastor, who became my surrogate father, father in the ministry, and uncle. McCreary was a genius at getting children engaged in ministry. He did not see them as second-class citizens in the life of the church who had nothing to offer. He was a highly gifted man with extraordinary prophetic gifts that not only allowed him to see the future but also to see the potential in children. He saw my gifts and interest in studying the Bible and finance, so he opened opportunities for me to grow in those endeavors. By the age of twelve, I was engaged in helping with the finances of the church. By fifteen, I was teaching a Sunday school class for young adults; at sixteen, I was teaching the adult class; by seventeen, teaching the ministers class, and by nineteen, managing all of the church's finances.

After growing up poor in Mississippi and receiving public assistance in Cleveland with my younger brother and mother, I made up my mind to never be poor again. I knew the route to accomplish this was through education. I finished at the top of my class in a business high school program. Next, I obtained bachelor's and master's degrees in business with a concentration in finance while working at a major bank starting at nineteen years old. After the completion of my master's degree, and with many years of banking experience, I started teaching finance part time at a local community college while working full time at the bank. Yet I never lost my love for the study of the Bible. So, as soon as I finished my MBA, I started working on my MA in Biblical Studies at Ashland Theological Seminary, which had opened a campus in Cleveland. After completing my master's, teaching finance at college, and having risen to the pinnacle of the field of finance as vice president of the investment department, I was living my dream. The two fields of study that I loved the most were wide open to me.

Then the tension began. The bank could not understand why I was doing all this study at seminary. The exact quote was always, "What does this have to do with finance? Are you planning on becoming a preacher? Are you leaving the bank?" While I always laughed it off, it really was not a laughing matter. The sting of poverty was real for me, which motivated my pursuit of the financial field of study, or, as I would often say, "my millions." But so too was my deep abiding love for the study of the Bible. This tension within was also a vivid reminder of the prophecies over me by the old ladies in the neighborhood back in Mississippi: "Now, you take Big Bubba there, Lord knows that boy gonna be a doctor or teacher one day." Many might want to interpret this in a variety of ways, but it was clear in my spirit exactly what they were talking about. From the age of five on, I have always known that I was destined to teach at the university level. I thought it would be Bible, but as I grew older and the desire to never be poor grew stronger, I became open to the possibility that maybe I would teach finance. What I knew for sure was that the internal tensions were not going away: my days at the bank were probably numbered. Therefore, I took a leap of faith, left the bank, and headed off to seminary full time to complete the Master of Divinity and Doctor of Ministry programs. Even at this point, however, I had no intention of giving up my pursuit of my millions. My plan was to get those degrees and teach Bible as an avocation while making my millions on Wall Street to fund my avocation. Such were my plans. God had something different in mind. Those baby steps were key, however, in order for God to get me to see and become open to his plan.

Well into my doctoral program, a key question and observation became crystal clear to me. The question: what will be the nature of my project? The observation: whereas the student body was 33 percent Black (nearly 50 percent at present), there were no Black professors, readings, or assignments. Another observation was: most of the excellent pastors and ministers in Black churches did not have seminary degrees. In addition, I knew many lay people like me who had calls upon their lives and wanted further education but just did not see seminary as it was as the place to get what they needed. Eureka! My project: the creation of a Black Church Studies institute contextually designed to help train Black ministers and pastors to meet the needs of the Black community through the Black church. Upon the completion of my doctoral degree, God dropped other shoes.

The first shoe to drop was Ashland Theological Seminary offered me a job as a professor. What now? As a classmate buddy of mine asked, "Why would you take that, considering what you could make in the financial field? Don't you know seminaries pay poverty wages?" How do you settle this conflict? How about a good old biblical Gideon fleece, doctored up a bit with an MBA class financial analysis, which in summary amounted to this: God, if this is your will, here is the minimum I need to live and take care of my family with no frills or thrills. If their offer comes back with this amount, which I had surmised would not, I will consider that this is your direction for me now. It came back $1,000 more! The second shoe to drop. You know you need another doctoral degree—the Ph.D. for the discipline you want to teach in—Bible—it is necessary. So, it was off to the University of Pittsburgh the day after graduation at Ashland Theological Seminary to complete that degree while also starting to teach at Ashland Theological Seminary. The third shoe to drop. (Yes, I have three feet.) On my ride to Ashland for my graduation, a conversation arose with McCreary, who was going with me to celebrate my graduation. I had not told him anything about the nature of my doctoral studies, but he told me about two visions he had had, one on the way down and the other on the way back. The first one was, "Doc, I had a vision last night, and the Lord said to me, that boy is going to start a school for me, and I want you to build him a building to hold it. And, Doc, he showed me right where to put it."

On the way back, McCreary told me the answer to a vision he had been trying to understand his entire life. He received the answer at my graduation. He said when he had been called to preach, he had had a vision in which he was in a church and the Holy Spirit told everybody to leave. When he got up to leave, the Holy Spirit said, "Not Carey McCreary." The Spirit came up to him and gave him a Bible and said, "Go preach my word to the doctors and lawyers." McCreary then told me, "All my life that was the one vision I couldn't understand because I said who am I to preach to doctors and lawyers, I don't have any education." He then said, "But when I was sitting out there in the audience, when you walked across that stage and that man handed you your doctor's degree, the Holy Spirit said to me, 'See, didn't I tell you that you would preach to the doctors and lawyers? You didn't know when I sent him to you as a boy that he was going to be a doctor.'"

The Foundational and Developmental Years: 1982 to 1989

And so, McCreary's vision was the impetus for constructing a building for the McCreary Center for African American Religious Studies. I named it in honor of my mentor, who died in 1997 after forty years of service as the founding pastor of New Mount Zion Baptist Church and was one of the McCreary Center's greatest advocates.

The focus of my Doctor of Ministry project was to develop a model for contextual theological education for particular African Americans whom seminaries had overlooked, namely ministers and laity without bachelor's degrees. Not only was the curricular design in focus, but so too was the location. It needed to be located in the 'hood, that is, an inner-city Black neighborhood. As important as the curriculum was, the ethos, culture, disparities, issues, needs, dreams, and desires of the community would be self-evident as students came in and out of the community. Every day, as they came and left the community to which they had been called to serve, they could not help but be reminded of why they were there, unlike when they went to school in the plush opulence of the surrounding suburbs. One was a reminder of people who had more than they needed while the other was a reminder of people who had far less than they needed.

I examined every seminary curriculum as well as primary institutes that I could find in an attempt to understand what had been done toward that end. I contacted people such as Henry Mitchell and Gayraud Wilmore[6] and had long conversations with them about their experiences. The examination of what seminaries and institutes offered or did not offer helped me with the curriculum design. The conversations with Mitchell and Wilmore helped me with the matter of contextual concerns. I published an article about this matter of theological education, unity, and context in 1984, much of which I would disavow now. I was young, naive, inexperienced, and misinformed at that time. Mitchell and Wilmore were right. I was wrong and had to modify my course of action radically and quickly. I finished my course of study, the project, the degree, and graduated in the spring 1984. I founded the McCreary Center for African American Religious Studies that summer as well and entered the joint PhD program in Religious Studies at the University of Pittsburgh/Pittsburgh Theological Seminary. I also joined the faculty of Ashland Theological Seminary in 1984. I was not only the first African American hired as a full-time faculty member, but I was also the first-full time faculty member hired for our urban center in Cleveland. My uncle and pastor of our church be-gan the construction of the building that would house the McCreary Center in July and completed it in September 1984.

In the fall of 1984, I started teaching a few theological courses myself at the McCreary Center, which were offered to both clergy and laity who did not have the requisite requirements to enter sem-inary. Eventually, I brought in other African American scholars and trained practitioners to give lectures. Initially, it was all free. Our first move into charging was $35. An event occurred in the summers of 1985 to 1988 that was so impactful for me that it would not only forever change my theological pedagogy but also it radically advanced my activism and advocacy for what would hap-pen at McCreary Center and what would take place at Ashland Theological Seminary. The gathering on the St. John's University campus in Collegeville, Minnesota, launched the Afrocentric Hermeneutics movement that would forever change biblical stud-ies in the academy forever. It was not just the first critical engage-ment of biblical studies by African American scholars that we pro-duced, nor was it the first section in Society of Biblical Literature and American Academy of Religion (SBL/AAR) we started, or the movement itself. More importantly, it was the Black colleagues I met for the first time in this discipline, the stories of our journey we shared, and the lifetime friendships we created. It changed my pedagogy, zeal, perseverance, and urgency forever.

After that first summer, I returned to the campus of Ashland Theological Seminary with a fire within that some things had to change. Here was an institution where one third of the student body was Black. In our extensions in Cleveland and Detroit, classes were often 100 percent Black and few were less than 80 percent Black. Yet there was not only no degree with a Black focus, there were no courses, books, or assignments that focused on anything Black. I had been a graduate of this institution three times, and now I was a faculty member as well. In other words, I was a partic-ipant in this madness in more ways than one.[7] Something had to change, and it had to change quickly. Therefore, I presented to my

153

department a new course that I wanted to teach: African American Biblical Interpretation. For the first time, in 1987, I created and taught a course at the seminary that focused on Black people and their engagement of the Bible. However, after the second and third year, when we started the writing of *Stony the Road We Trod*, one course was no longer enough. So, I approached President Fred Finks and told him that what we were doing was unacceptable for our Black students. We needed an entire curriculum; we needed a degree. I said that we were doing these things at the McCreary Center, so I knew how to do it. I will never forget how supportive Finks was in this endeavor, not just at the beginning, but throughout his entire tenure as president at the seminary and university. He told me that if I designed the curriculum, he would make sure the faculty passed it. I did and the faculty was unanimous in their support. It passed in 1989.

The Partnership and Accreditation Years: 1990 to 2016

The Black Church Studies program at Ashland Theological Seminary was launched in 1990 and held at the McCreary Center, in the middle of the 'hood, located in the poorest ward in Cuyahoga County. The design of the program had two foci: it was integrated in all the courses in every department and every discipline, and it had three levels of independent and interdependent components: a diploma of theology, a master's in ministry, and a Doctor of Ministry, all in Black Church Studies. All three of these courses of study, while independent, also built upon each other, allowing students to continue from one to the other. At least half of the curriculum consisted of Black Church Studies courses except for the Doctor of Ministry degree, which was 100 percent Black Church Studies courses. The diploma of theology in Black Church Studies, the first of its kind at Ashland Theological Seminary, and perhaps in America, was designated for students who did not possess a bachelor's degree. This was a stand-alone diploma that was also granted by Ashland Theological Seminary, and the students graduated at commencement along with the master's and doctoral students. I had observed that other institutions had what was called a certificate that could be attached to a master's degree by taking a few additional courses in Black Church Studies. My design was different. It was intended to be more thorough and rigorous, more integrated and capable of preparing those students for theological study at graduate level in seminary. Further, I determined that the term *certificate* was insufficient both for the community it was trying to reach and for the import of its curriculum. The design has remained intact and endured the test of time for more than three decades. I have remained the director of the program from its inception to the present day.

I drew upon my colleagues from all across the nation. The majority of those colleagues from the "Stony the Road" book project have taught at the McCreary Center in the program many times, as well as many, many others I met over the years. Several local colleagues also taught. Many of these colleagues continue to teach to this very day. It is the collaboration that is important in this effort. I want the students to see that and emulate that in their ministries. This is a unique aspect of this program. No student would be able to go to all the institutions where the Black scholars taught, so I decided to bring Black scholars to the students. You name them, they have been to the McCreary Center. Many of them have left us and joined our ancestors while many are still with us to this day, but the memory of all of them grace the center's hallways and classrooms. Thousands of students who have taken classes in Black Church Studies at the McCreary Center remember it with transcendent joy as a life-changing experience. I remember with equal joy those diploma students who may not have ever had the opportunity to go to seminary and matriculated successfully. More than three hundred of them completed that course of study. Some went on to obtain master's degrees, while others continued on to obtain the Doctor of Ministry degree in Black Church Studies as well. During this period of time, I was pleased to work with Dean Dale

Stoffer, a historian in our Theology and History Department. Stoffer's thorough and tireless work, with the full support of President Finks, led us to have the McCreary Center accredited as a campus site where all the Black Church Studies courses could be taught. This was one of the highest moments in the McCreary Center's history and one of the most shining moments in Ashland Theological Seminary history. Yet darkness always lurks in the background, awaiting its moment to pounce and dispel the light.

The Painful Years:
2017 to 2018

We were rolling along quite nicely, at least in Black Church Studies, although some dark clouds had been stirring in the distant skies moving ever menacingly closer year after year. Our numbers started to plummet across the board at Ashland Theological Seminary, deficits began to rise, budgets became strained, and personnel were let go, including the president of the seminary. History was made at the seminary. The first Black president was hired as well as the first Black dean. In some ways, we all celebrated those historical events. Although they did not know how much I had to do with certain aspects of their prior careers, I celebrated the moves as well. I went overboard in trying to welcome both of them and made every effort to help them be successful. I do not know to this day if that is how they would characterize my efforts, but that is the truth. I was in for a rude awakening. First thing out of the gate upon each one's arrival was the destruction of the Black Church Studies program. I must say, however, that in the case of the dean, who came shortly after the president, I believe she was merely carrying out the dictates of the boss who had hired her. This is a painful story, so I shall not linger long on it or wallow in the sordid details. However, it is a crucial part of the program's history, so it can't be ignored as if it did not happen. It was not painful merely because something sorely needed was being taken away from those who needed it most or because it had been hard-fought for and difficult to retain; the most painful part was that the program was being dismantled by one of their own kind. In the end, though, the Black religious community of Northeast Ohio—pastors, students, and alumni—rallied to the defense of the Black Church Studies program at Ashland Theological Seminary. They said, "We are not having it. We will bring the full weight of our community against the entire university." In the end, the seminary relented, but the damage had been done. They had, without faculty knowledge or anyone else's knowledge, as far as we knew, the McCreary Center delisted from accreditation and stopped holding classes there. Then, one by one, the new dean and the new president were released. Whether it is because of what was done to the Black Church Studies program, we will never know. It was never acknowledged. Both of them were gone, but so, too, were aspects of the Black Church Studies program and partnership between Ashland Theological Seminary and the McCreary Center—gone forever, never to return as it once was.

The New Birth: 2019 to 2022

We were all left to pick up the pieces that were shattered in so many inexplicable ways that they are too numerous and difficult to categorize. However, as it relates to the McCreary Center, some are obvious. These things are gone: accreditation, Black Church Studies-degree classes, financial support, and a shared partnership. Could it be put back together again? Another search began for a new president for the seminary. Another history-making moment was the hiring of the first Latino president. Further, he had participated in training at an institute and had great appreciation for them. This seemed great. We were joyous again. Within a matter of months, however, he was struck with an illness that, despite months of recovery, required him to withdraw. We were all so very hopeful, most especially the Black and Latinx communities. We looked forward to the most historic changes since the creation of the seminary. Dr. Juan Martinez was a shining light, a breath of fresh air, a great person who came with a great vision, but a vision that never got an opportunity to develop. How do we begin again? With one of our own, that's how. He served in the Biblical Studies Department with me. I was on the search committee that recommended him to our faculty. He was selected to lead us. When the presidential search began, it was made clear that there was no intention of restoring the partnership as it once was, with accreditation or degree courses being held at the McCreary Center. We needed to find a different way of working together.

Now the McCreary Center would go its own way: we would continue to train and prepare students for seminary, but now our students could apply for admission to Ashland Theological Seminary in the Bachelor Exempt Program. The McCreary Center was now free to carve out a new trail in its own way. During this time, after more than three decades at the helm of the center, I decided to step aside and allow some younger people to take over. One of my former students, whom I had mentored from the diploma program through the Doctor of Ministry program, took the mantle, along with a number of my students who were placed on the board. I wrote the new MOU (memorandum of understanding) that formalized the relationship between the McCreary Center and Ashland Theological Seminary. With two people at the helm of both institutions who both received their initial training in a theological institute and who have a great appreciation for them, I see nothing but light ahead. However, the McCreary Center, with its new president and CEO, Dr. Crystal Walker, has a new birth and can go wherever the Lord leads her. I see nothing but light ahead. Ashland Theological Seminary has a new leader at the helm, Dr. John Byron, who will appreciate all of these Black students following the same path he took to seminary. I see nothing but light ahead.

I remain on the faculty at Ashland Theological Seminary as well as the director of the Black Church Studies program, closing in fast on my fortieth year. The end of my journey, I'm sure, is also closing in fast, but I remain in the struggle until the Lord gives me release. I remain in the fight and struggle in and for the 'hood, until I can fight no more. For the sake of posterity and the cherished memory of those who served as lecturers, preachers, and teachers at the McCreary Center, many who have gone home to glory, I memorialize their names here (deceased=d):

Richard Allison (d)
Randall Bailey
Katie Cannon (d)
Rick Carson
Mack King Carter(d)
Gloria Cheney
James Cone (d)
Timothy Crow
Miguel De La Torre
Kelly Brown Douglas
Cheryl Kirk Dugan
Riggins Earl
Andrew Edwards
Cain Hope Felder (d)
Walter Fluker
Cheryl Townsend Gilkes
Jacquelyn Grant
Robin Hedgeman
Obery Hendricks
Dwight Hopkins
Carrie Hudson
Paul Kaufman
Luke Keefer (d)
Arthur Kemp (d)
C. Eric Lincoln (d)
Lawrence Mamiya (d)
Clarice Martin
Marvin Mickle
A.G. Miller
Henry Mitchell (d)
Russel Morton

Otis Moss, Jr.
Felix Muniz
William H. Myers
Evelyn Parker
Anthony Pinn
Roderick Pounds, Sr.
C. Shelby Rooks (d)
Mitzi Smith
R. Drew Smith
Emilie Townes
H. Dean Trulear
Crystal Walker
Renita Weems
Dennis Wiley
Regginia Williams
Zachery Williams
Gayraud Wilmore
Vincent Wimbush
Ben Witherington, III
Jeremiah Wright

Chapter 10

Clearing the Barriers

Karen F. Brown Dunlap

My mother spent much of her last years, her final months, worrying about the seminary. She'd rest her head between her forefinger and fist and say, "I hope the seminary can make it."

Mary S. Fitzgerald devoted her career to teaching English, French, Black Literature, and sometimes music at the American Baptist Theological Seminary (ABTS). The school hired my father, Rev. Charles H. Fitzgerald, as an instructor fresh out of graduate school. He rose to dean and pastored a nearby church before moving to an executive role with state Baptists.

The seminary's identity, to my mom, was that of a small school doing noble work but barely surviving financially. It was beholden to two Baptist denominations: one Black, one white. She worried that funding would dry up and the little school would cease to exist. Mom didn't live to see ABTS take on a new identity.

Wise leadership under President Forrest Harris and changes in the times led the seminary to become American Baptist College (ABC), a school with an expanded mission and new sources of funding. Staff secured the school's designation as an historically Black college as increased federal allocations assisted these schools. It celebrated its place in the Civil Rights Movement when the nation and the home city of Nashville recognized its alumni C. T. Vivian and John Lewis.

The school has much to celebrate, but challenges persist. ABC navigates changing relations with constituencies, gentrification in its community, and the tempests of problems that other schools and organizations face. These include general economic uncertainty, political and social fissures, and a new generation of students with changed expectations. Church-affiliated schools face additional hurdles as some denominations fracture and church membership declines.

This essay explores lessons on leadership, some from ABC and its neighborhood in Nashville. It presents short profiles of leaders who made a difference, acting from various positions and stages of life. It addresses specific challenges today, including how to preserve the best of the African American identity while, faced forward, pursuing new directions and ventures. It suggests steps to bring others along, to help determine strategies, and to build community.

The Question of Identity

Innovative, entrepreneurial leadership runs deep in the DNA of ABC and the neighboring Haynes community, going back at least as far as a man whose name lives on.

Rev. William Haynes (1850 to 1933) was born on a plantation east of Nashville. Haynes's father was the plantation owner, his mother, a slave. His father educated him and deeded him land in the Whites Creek Road area of Davidson County. Rev. Haynes later purchased additional land.[1]

William Haynes was a minister, banker, realtor, lawyer, author, and community leader. At least four ongoing churches in Nashville list him as founder or former pastor[2] He was deeply involved in the Baptist Sunday School Publishing Board, one of Nashville's two national Black Baptist publishing houses. Haynes was the primary force in moving Roger Williams University (originally known as Walden College) from the Peabody-Vanderbilt University area to the present site of the American Baptist College and Baptist World Center, property he originally owned.

Haynes acted to improve education among Black people to "obliterate illiteracy"[3] and particularly help children. This led to the founding of Haynes Elementary School in 1931, half a mile from

ABC. The school was located on land that he sold to the Davidson County Board of Education for $500. In later years, the remainder of the tract was donated to the school board for a high school and football field. The school housed grades 1 to 12 from 1938 until the last graduation in 1967. With desegregation, officials converted it to a junior high school.

As a pastor, Reverend Haynes encouraged members to save and offered banking services. That led to him joining R. H. Boyd and about nine others as founders of the One Cent Savings Bank and Trust Company, which continues as Citizens Bank and Trust. Records of many Nashville Black businesses in the late 1800s and early 1900s often show Haynes as a board member or a founder.[4] His son wrote of the respect white citizens showed his father as he transacted business in town.[5]

Haynes's belief that "everybody needs a home of his own" led him to buy, sell, and develop housing areas in northeast Nashville, where he lived. In addition to a school and a street, at least five neighborhoods carry his name, most built after his death: Haynes Heights, Haynes Meade, Haynes Manor, Haynes Garden, and Haynes Park. Attorney Richard Jackson, vice president of ABC, speculated that only Andrew Jackson exceeds Rev. Haynes in having his name attached to local entities.

Rev. Haynes and his first wife had a son and daughter. The daughter died while young; the son, J. C., became principal of what is now Ford Greene School and followed his father as a pastor. He and his second wife raised eleven children: their eight, two adopted daughters, and his son.

Leadership Lessons from Rev. William Haynes

William Haynes knew who he was. Haynes was biracial but did not seem confused about who he was or his mission. His purpose was uplifting African Americans. Few leaders today seem to struggle with racial identity, but many quietly question who they are. They question their calling, ability, role with various constituencies, even their values. Leadership requires solid footing in personal identity and mission.

Haynes wisely used resources to meet the needs. Because his father gave him extensive land, Haynes was far ahead of most Black individuals at that time. He had much, and he used much to help many. The challenge for many leaders today is how to do much with little. God provides the answer in Exodus 4:2 while giving Moses leadership training: "What is that in your hand," God asked (NIV). The point was to focus on available resources, not on the lack of resources. Be confident and resourceful in using whatever is at hand to meet the needs.

Haynes's efforts helped immediate and long-term needs. Guiding a congregation to budget and save money addressed immediate needs while taking a step toward building generational wealth. Starting an elementary school not only addressed an immediate need for literacy but also provided jobs, inspiration, and education for generations.

Finally, Haynes didn't just have vision. He got things done.

The Present Situation
We've Come a Long Way...

Black people have made great progress over the years, maybe more than most ancestors could have imagined. The Pew Center reported that in 1965 there were no Black US senators or governors and only five members of the House of Representatives. In addition to a Black US president and vice president, state and local elected officials include many Black mayors and police chiefs. Pew called the political progress of the Black community an "upward yet uneven trajectory."[6]

The same can be said of other areas. For example, Black academics have become presidents at predominantly white universities, but the percentage of Black university presidents overall hovers at around 10 percent.[7] More importantly, the appointment of a few folks to top positions has not lifted masses of Black people from poverty.

We Still Have a Long Way to Go

The wealth gap is one of the most telling and painful measures of Black standing. White families had a net worth of about $180,000 in 2018 while Black families had about $20,000, according to the National Urban League's annual report on "The State of Black America."[8]

Then there are the vestiges, the remnants, of past discrimination that contribute to the income gap, such as unfair housing and education practices. Combined with ongoing and new biased acts—for instance, in lending, hiring, and injustice—we still have a long way to go to achieve equality in society.

A Fractured Society

In the 1960s, the Haynes community included Black professionals who owned or directed Nashville's Black bank, publishing houses, and other businesses as well as university faculty and administrators. Contractors patterned their own houses and expansive yards after the rich, white community. Within two miles of the Black elite, residents lived in frame structures with outhouses. By the 1970s, as segregation ended, top Black students left for white colleges that now welcomed them, and many moved away for jobs. Higher-income residents moved to integrated communities. By the 1990s, neighborhoods that looked progressive in the '60s were beginning to look worn. Some residents maintained their homes beautifully, but as a whole, the community began to sag. Grocery stores closed, the school was converted from grades 1 to 12 to a middle school with students from outside the area, pillars of the community died, and the community gained a reputation for looking unkept and fostering crime. This is the story of so many Black communities.

An Endangered Community

By 2010, city developers realized this marginal community was ten minutes from downtown and on the Cumberland River. Gentrification followed, sucking up stretches of homes and demolishing wooded areas. Landlords sold properties and their tenants found themselves looking for homes in a new, costly market. Homeowners who choose to stay watched huge projects spring up next door. New residents arrived with different habits and expectations. Sweeping changes blew in almost daily, and those changes affected the culture and maybe the community's name. Politics also threatened as legal moves promised to make voting more difficult and divided long-standing Black districts.

A Need for Spiritual Renewal

The USA's women's 4 x 400 relay team blew out their competitors at the 2021 Olympics. Four individual medal winners came together and not only dazzled in their run but also brought Black beauty in a range of physical builds, skin tones, and ages. Allyson Felix was thirty-five; Athing Mu was nineteen.[9] Their talents would not have mattered if they had not accomplished one requirement: they passed the baton, one to the other, without fumbling.

A malaise has settled in the spirit of African Americans. The causes are many, but some of it is embedded in failing to pass along "the dream." The dream speaks of goals and purpose. Each generation must interpret its position, but progress calls for a firm grasp and a smooth handoff to the next generation. Something has faded in the soul of Black people. There is a need for renewal of the spirit.

Black America shares the anxiety others feel about an out-of-whack climate, never-ending international conflicts, a political divide, false information that increases the divide, uncivil discourse, deteriorating trust in most institutions (especially the church), a widening income gap[10], uncertainty about life-sustaining careers for some, and uncertainty about surviving day to day for others. The reasons for the African American malaise run deeper.

A lost sense of self causes many to drift. Needed emotional support wanes when communities disperse and history fades. Busyness saps time to pass on family and race history. Schools do not fill the gap, and children grow up not knowing from whence they have come. Many children do not know what and how their ancestors overcame, nor do they develop the pride, strength, and purpose to contribute to society.

A loss of spiritual faith is seen in declining church membership and the growth of the "nones," those who respond in surveys by saying their chosen faith is "None."[11] Church sanctuaries are often a picture of female senior citizens and empty pews. New megachurches draw younger crowds with energetic services. Still, so many have lost faith in biblical teaching or never had it. *New York Times* columnist David Brooks explored the falling away of young people from the largely white evangelical churches. He quoted Russell Moore, who resigned from a leadership position in the Southern Baptist Convention: "We now see young evangelicals walking away from evangelicalism not because they do not believe what the church teaches but because they believe that the church itself does not believe what the church teaches."[12] Could the same be true of African American churches?

Finally, the African American community needs to heal. Better diet and health practices would go a long way, but the healing needed is much deeper. In the book *What Happened to You? Conversations on Trauma, Resilience, and Healing*, Oprah Winfrey talks with Dr. Bruce D. Perry, child psychiatrist and neuroscientist. She says this:

> When I think about the African American community, I see how trauma can trace back for generations—all the way back to slavery. Hundreds of years of internalizing the trauma of racism, segregation, brutality, fear and the dismantling of the nuclear family—all of it reacted and repeated over and over at the

microlevel of the individual and eventually seen and felt at the macro level of society.[13]

Rage, alienation, diminished hope, and an urge to quit run deep in our communities. We need to heal.

A Resilient Community

Despite all, Black people show resilience. They turned out and stood for hours to vote in recent presidential elections. They march to say Black lives matter. They feed the hungry, care for children, and maintain difficult jobs, often with low pay. They run on.

Three Examples of Change-making Leadership

Courage. Diane Nash lived a life of change even before she arrived at Fisk University in Nashville. She had youthful thoughts of becoming a nun, later won a Chicago beauty contest, and took classes at Howard University. At Fisk, she planned to become an English teacher, but things changed as life in Nashville exposed her to segregation. Nash was stunned by the practice and dismayed by talk of challenging racism through nonviolent protests. I think she thought change came through nonviolence was not the American way. Eventually, she supported the method when she did not see another path for overcoming discrimination.

Nash joined Fisk, ABC, and Tennessee State University (TSU) students in evening training sessions on her campus. Fellow students admired her organizational skills and made her chairperson of the new Student Nonviolent Coordinating Committee. Soon, the federal government noticed her. In 1961, US Attorney General Robert Kennedy called his assistant, John Seigenthaler, and bellowed, "Who the hell is Diane Nash?" He told Seigenthaler to convince Nash to call off planned Freedom Rides by college students deep into the segregated South. Seigenthaler recalled that he grew irritated while telling Nash to change the plans. He finally said, "Young lady, do you understand you will all be killed?" She calmly replied, "Sir, we have already signed our wills." Seigenthaler, who became a nationally respected journalist and a voice for justice, commended the students' courage and impact.

In the 1960s, Diane Nash was pregnant when jailed for leading nonviolent protest training. She and her husband, ABC student James Bevel, led voter registration drives in Mississippi and were among those planning major marches with Dr King. Later, she was active in antiwar protests and pushed for fair housing back in Chicago. Nash still lectures, receives awards, and inspires a new generation, including leaders of the Black Lives Matter movement. In 2017, she called nonviolent protest the most important invention of the twentieth century.[14]

In an interview, Nash said she was amused when people called her courageous because she and others were so often afraid. Two elements pushed them past fear: "Segregation was so horrible," she said. "We were committed to do whatever was necessary to end it." The other element was individual, internal transformation. "We changed ourselves into people who could not be segregated," she said. "Once you change yourself the world has to fit up against the new you."[15]

Leaders around the world face physical threats if they stand up for what's right, but that's not the usual problem today. The more common challenge today might be risking something else: status. Leaders who stand for justice might lose a promotion or a pastorate, an election, a choice place at the high-prestige table, or comfortable relations with neighbors and colleagues, an academic title, or a hard-fought-for grant. Whatever the challenge, leadership requires courage.

Character. Dr. Jamye Coleman Williams loved the African Methodist Episcopal Church. Her father was an AME minister; her mother, a religious writer. She attended Wilberforce University, founded by the AME Church, and later taught there, then served on the board of trustees.

At the 2000 AME General Conference, Williams led in offering a resolution calling on the church to finally elect a woman as one of the twenty-one active bishops. She declared that the meeting should not end without that step.

The Washington Post reported: "For the last 20 years or so, women in the AME Church have been fighting that lock on power. 'We're just asking for our slice of the pie,' said Jayme Coleman Williams, the first woman elected as one of the church's 13 general officers, who serve in administrative positions."[16]

The New York Times wrote: "Jamye Coleman Williams, one of the sponsors of the resolution and a retired church officer, said: 'In our church, the majority of members and the majority of seminary enrollees are women. So, it is not fair to deny them full inclusion. It's sort of like the civil rights battle, where nobody wants to give up power.'"[17]

Williams was often the smallest person in the room, but you wouldn't notice. She wasn't loud, but she was powerful. Before the conference ended, Vashti Murphy McKenzie was elected bishop. In the conferences that followed, four additional women were elected bishops with Williams coaching, persuading, and encouraging. She carried out the battle with her trademark tools: preparation, a savvy strategy, and fierce determination while dipping into a reservoir of respect grounded in her character.

Speakers at the funeral of Dr. Williams in January 2022 included the four women bishops. The fifth had died. Bishop E. Anne Henning-Byfield described Williams as "a moral compass, a bold, courageous leader."[18]

Jamye Williams demonstrated leadership for change, but her greater life contribution might have been as an educator. After attending Wilberforce, she earned a master's degree at Fisk University and a doctorate at the University of Ohio. She and her husband, Dr. McDonald Williams, taught at Wilberforce, then joined the TSU faculty and produced a book on famous Black speakers.[19]

Williams taught rhetoric, the art of persuasive speech and writing, including Aristotle's belief that ethos, or character, is key to persuasion. She quoted Ralph Waldo Emerson: "Your actions speak so loudly, I cannot hear what you are saying." Her actions as a teacher went far beyond classroom lectures. Bishop Byfield said, "She saw us; she knew us. She was willing to invest in us, and she was determined to bring out the best in us."[20]

An East Nashville high school student came to TSU on scholarship and was offered a local TV network job before she finished her college senior project. Williams, her department head, wished her well. That student was Oprah Winfrey. On Williams's 100th birthday, Winfrey sent a video message from South Africa to say thank you.

During their years as educators, Mac and Jamye Williams stood for justice. They marched with students, served in and recruited for the NAACP, and engaged with and gained awards from Nashville interracial civic groups. In retirement, they moved to be near family in Atlanta: a daughter and grandson, his wife, and their two daughters. They remained active, Jamye as a much-sought-after speaker. She gave an address at Fisk when she was nearly 100. McDonald Williams died in 2019 at age 102; Jamye followed him in 2022 at age 103.

Willing to Bearing Witness. Darnella Frazier set out on May 25, 2020, on what she called "just a normal day for me walking my 9-year-old cousin to the corner store." It was about 7 P.M., and her cousin had been waiting to go to the store. Near Cup Foods, at the corner of 38th and Chicago, in Minneapolis, they walked into a crowd calling out while police held a man face down by the patrol car. One officer pressed his knee on the back of the man's neck as the man kept saying, "I can't breathe."

Frazier, seventeen, reacted as many young people would: she pulled out her cellphone and started videotaping the police and the man, George Floyd. Then she did what many would not do: she held the camera with a clear angle and a steady frame for more than eight minutes, capturing the scene.

Frazier went home and posted on Facebook, "They really killed somebody at Cups.... I'll post it tomorrow.... The police really killed him, bro, right in front of everybody."[21] The next day she posted the video. The world was shocked and reacted.

Frazier's role was simply bearing witness. She didn't turn away from someone in distress. She remained and then presented the story to the world. Her English teacher said Frazier had "presence of mind and steadiness of hand."[22] Merriam-Webster dictionary defines bearing witness as "to show that something exists or is true." Sometimes the key is just being there.

Journalist Soledad O'Brien learned about the concept long before she became a CNN reporter and ABC morning host. Once, when a teenager, she went to get her mother from the high school where Estela Marquetti O'Brien taught. As Soledad and Estela, an Afro-Cuban, walked down a nearly empty school hall, they converged with a student running down the hall and the principal. The Black student looked guilty and scared; the white principal appeared ready to give the maximum penalty. Estela came to a stop and observed. The principal smiled, assured her that everything was all right, and waved her along. Estela stayed, waiting until the student was calmly addressed and dismissed. Soledad wanted to move on much earlier. She was us.

Years later, Soledad O'Brien covered the aftermath of Hurricane Katrina in New Orleans. Day after day, she told the stories of people who had lost everything, who didn't get the help they expected, who didn't know their next steps. She let them tell their stories. When she and the TV crew prepared to fly out of Louis Armstrong Airport, people who were gathered there broke into spontaneous applause. She had been there to bear witness for them.

Darnella Frazier was traumatized as she watched a policeman murder a man. She was still traumatized when she testified at the officer's trial a year later, but she testified. In June 2021, the Pulitzer Prize board awarded her a special citation "for courageously recording...a video that spurred protests against police brutality around the world."

A Vision of Leadership

We need leaders today who master the following challenges.

Teach Us to Walk with the Wind. John Lewis told a story from his childhood that helped guide his leadership. He said his aunt provided care for his cousins, sister, and him in a shabby Alabama house. One day, an unusually strong storm came and shook the little house, threatening to take it off its base. The children were frightened, but his aunt had them hold hands, stretch out across the room in a line, and walk together back and forth. Lewis said that as they walked with the wind, their little bodies, working in unison, provided safety by holding the house down.

Maybe the biggest challenge for leaders is to shepherd folks to sacrifice a certain independence in the interest of building kindred spirits by, at least metaphorically, holding hands. Even more difficult is to guide folks in walking together in the same direction. That calls for wisdom, patience, and prayer, but it happened in the 1960s. It can happen again.

Become Part of the Community. My strongest personal memory of the Civil Rights Movement as a child was seeing our Wednesday, midweek Bible school teachers come to teach us with their heads and arms bandaged. They were seminary students who attended class; went downtown to join lunch-counter protests, where they were beaten; and then came to Roger Heights Baptist Church to teach community children.

Over the years I began to question my memory. Then a lifelong friend, Linda, told me she wanted to visit John Lewis in his Atlanta office to say hello to her midweek Bible school teacher. She remembered the excitement of community children each week as they arrived, the classroom where her group met, and how Lewis told Bible stories. Those who are willing to invest in communities change lives. Most never become widely known, but many are long remembered by the people they touch.

Institutions can get comfortable in a community without being a part of the community. They exist in a different world with, maybe, occasional planned ventures into the neighborhood, like benevolent tourists who come to visit without really knowing the natives' language or culture. Being a part of the community means knowing the names, problems, and points of pride; being comfortable in its shops and homes and offering a place for fellowship; solving problems and growing together. The Oprah Winfrey book on trauma and healing says most healing happens in community.[23] People build resilience and steady themselves in the company of fellow humans who share their history, take time with them, and care.

Strategize for a Multifaceted Attack on Problems. People with "a long way to go" can benefit from multiple ways to get there. A voting convoy focuses on grooming potential candidates, inspecting ballot issues, presenting slates of candidates, registering voters, and making sure they vote. The institutional fleet builds contacts, networks, and relationships within corporations, schools, nonprofits, the judicial system, and other branches of government. The civic/social caravan utilizes membership in groups to promote needed change.

Success means casting a large net and developing leaders, engaging people at all levels of society to play a role. Effective leaders aren't necessarily figures who stand out as "The One." They are those who cultivate leadership skills in others. Delegating spreads the load and gives others a chance to step up and offer fresh ideas. Delegating risks mistakes so it requires mentoring and a tolerance for not getting things right every time. The key to the strategy is to have a large number of people willing to speak up and show up for a planned outcome.

Keep Telling the History. In addition to everything else, the leader must be something of a griot, the one who keeps telling the tribe's history. Leaders must keep telling stories of the trials, the successes, and the outstanding figures.

My father was born to a fifteen-year-old, single mother. Relatives kept him in church; he worked hard, and Third Baptist Church in Toledo helped send him to Morehouse College. He was impressed by the college's president, Dr. Benjamin E. Mays and saved administrative papers and commendations he received from Dr. Mays. He and my mother, who attended Atlanta University, talked about the elegance and dignity of Dr. and Mrs. Mays. That made history real to me and others, and I pass it on.

The Haynes Manor community was not the only area named for an important figure, the streets in the area bear names of outstanding Black people. Few residents know that. Young people walk down (Hiram) Revels, (Carl)Rowan, (James) Baldwin, and (Faith) Ringgold[24] and drive down streets with no clue of the lives being honored. It happens in most communities. Schools, bridges, and parks bear the names of those who made great contributions. Black history is all around us. We need to teach it to the young. Lift their spirits by letting them know the greatness in their past and present.

Focus on the Present and Boldly on the Future. Leadership requires attention to present needs while imagining and planning for what's ahead. Stay abreast of changes. Know of technological advancements. Learn from the young and be excited about the next big thing. This gives others the confidence to lean into the future.

Be Strong and of Good Character. It is interesting that the Lord's leadership lessons for Joshua (Joshua 1:8; NIV) repeatedly stressed strength and courage but not character. But then, Joshua had shown his integrity earlier in the biblical story. Character was not a problem then, but it is a huge problem now. Ministers, politicians, corporate and educational leaders crash in personal failures. Meanwhile public confidence deteriorates, standards crumble, and the Christian faith seems like stories from a dusty, old book. Leaders must practice what they teach and preach to draw others to their messages. Character matters.

Conclusion

When I grew up at American Baptist Theological Seminary, the campus ended in a half-circle gravel drive with two rows of small student family apartments on one side, and thick, foreboding woods on the other.

Individual students in "the movement" would slip through the trees and brush, sit down by the river on the other side, and meditate. Maybe Bernard Lafayette, James Bevel, or John Lewis would process teachings on nonviolence, ponder the future, and pray.

Decades later, President Forrest Harris had the woods cut down, revealing a view of the Cumberland River that is simply beautiful. It was always there, but only a few could see it.

Leaders guide by clearing the barriers of past trauma and current threats. Their courage and strong character, presence of mind, and steady hand draw others along in community to healing, victories, and maybe better days than we've ever imagined.

Chapter 11

Black Pastoral Leadership:
Tradition, Experience, and Vision

Wallace Charles Smith

I am honored to participate in this work, honoring the ministry and the tireless work of Dr. Forrest Harris.

I met Dr. Harris in the 1980s. He was a highly effective pastor in the Knoxville area and president of the local NAACP. His ministry exemplified much that I share in this essay. Black pastors have always functioned as priests, proclaimers of the Word, and community leaders. The friendship that Dr. and Mrs. Harris shared with my wife and me is a blessing we continue to celebrate. In this essay, I want to share what I discovered through academic research and what I observed in my own ministry.

Unlike those in the medical profession, the most influential pastors are not specialists but generalists. Dr. Harris exemplifies the best of this tradition. To God be the glory!

For several centuries, the Black church has been the spiritual, economic, and political bulwark for Black people. Although it has faced enormous challenges, the church remains a venerable anchor within Black culture. Unlike in many European cultures, the Black pastor is not just a servant to the congregation. Harkening back to slavery, they are the chiefs of the tribe, emotional healers, and prophets. Servant leadership is but one aspect of the equation. Servanthood never outweighs other leadership components. Black church pastors live this multifaceted expectation of Black congregations. It is no wonder that Dr. H. Beecher Hicks accurately describes the preacher/pastor as the man nobody knows. In my experience of more than fifty years of pastoring Black Baptist churches, this is an apt description of the challenges of pastoring in an African American context.

My mentor at the Calvary Baptist Church in Chester, Pennsylvania, was Dr. J. Pius Barbour. He was erudite and witty and served as the unofficial dean of Black students at Crozer Theological Seminary. Among his mentees was Martin Luther King Jr. Dr. Barbour's ministry tilted to the academic. However, when I worked with him as his student assistant, I became aware that his primary connection with the congregation was through his careful attention to his members' needs. As much as he read and quoted Shakespeare or Plutarch's writings, he never neglected his priestly office of providing support and comfort to those in need. I succeeded Dr. Barbour at Calvary and learned a valuable lesson. In my first few months as pastor, there was a great hue and cry in the city about a public safety issue that emerged when the city, for budget reasons, closed the fire station that served the predominantly Black community. Citizens demanded a public meeting at which Black residents expressed outrage toward the city government. I could not attend because of a commitment to be out of town. The next day my phone blew up with members calling to reprimand me for not being present at the meeting. In Black churches, many parishioners want to have a close personal relationship with their pastors and expect them to be there during their unique life crises, funerals, weddings, and other events, but community leadership is also an important part of a pastor's job description.

Community leadership was significant to the members of my second church, First Baptist Capitol Hill in Nashville, Tennessee. Dr. Kelly Miller Smith Sr., a principal leader in the Civil Rights Movement and legendary figure in the Tennessee Southern Christian Leadership Conference, was nationally recognized as a civil rights icon. After Dr. Smith's death, I became pastor of First Baptist and learned another aspect of his leadership. To the members of First Baptist, this nationally recognized civil rights leader was known for his deep commitment to pastoral ministry. He visited the sick, attended to families in crisis, and was constantly available for counseling and support.

Members of First Baptist Capitol Hill knew him fondly as a pastor who would come to their bedsides in hospitals, at homes, or in any crisis, no matter what hour of the day or night. His civil rights leadership garnered national recognition, but what made him a beloved pastor was his commitment to visiting the sick, attending to families in crisis, and being available for the ministry of caring.

Shiloh Baptist Church of Washington, DC, where I serve as senior minister, has a long history of pastors leading their parishioners in justice issues. Fourteen formerly enslaved people established Shiloh in 1856 under the leadership of Rev. John Walker. Dr. J. Milton Waldron, Shiloh's third pastor, was a founder of the Niagara Movement but was never officially honored by the movement because he supported Woodrow Wilson. The latter had promised Black voters better treatment during his presidency. Unfortunately, that did not prove to be accurate as he would never sign an anti-lynching bill and previewed D. W. Griffith's racist movie *Birth of a Nation* right in the White House. Some people blamed Dr. Waldron for misleading Black people politically.

In 1983, Dr. Henry C. Gregory III, my predecessor at Shiloh, evidenced another aspect of pastoral leadership: vision. When he led the congregation to build the first Black family life center in the nation, he worked with architects and contractors as well as the occasional member who did not capture the vision or see the need to build such an innovative structure. Pastor Gregory lived between his God-given vision and the frequently complex realities of congregational polity and financial realities. The multifaceted world Black pastors inhabit can make accomplishing God's will challenging to a pastor's leadership skills and abilities.

When I reflect on the church's work, I recall Michael Green's words in his book *Evangelism in the Early Church*: "Christians were always in trouble, always broke but deliriously happy." At the Hampton Minister's Conference in 1985, one of the presenters stated that the soul of successful pastoral leadership is to be with people when they laugh and be with them when they mourn. I have never come up with a more concise or appropriate definition.

In addition to being an organizer, counselor, political leader, and builder, the moment's needs often determine a pastor's reactions. One must handle the challenges and issues that arise in an instant.

Slavery and Multifaceted Pastoral Leadership

Community leadership during slavery required pastors to assist in helping fugitive slaves to freedom, mainly through the Underground Railroad. During Reconstruction, pastoral leadership encompassed keeping members safe from the terrorism of night riders and the Ku Klux Klan. Pastors participated in and directed civil rights efforts during the civil rights era. Now pastoral leaders are working on economic development and the skillful use of political power. In the long history of the Black struggle, rarely have pastors been able to concentrate on specific components of ministry. They must be generalists since circumstances may determine the shape and focus of pastoral ministry. Martin Luther King Jr. accepted the pastorate at Dexter Avenue Baptist Church in Montgomery, Alabama, intending to become the first African American preeminent theologian to gain his reputation within the walls of academia alongside such European scholars as Paul Tillich and Reinhold Niebuhr. The Montgomery bus boycott demanded of him something other than a distinguished career in the halls of academia.

Let me discuss some generalist concepts that, regardless of calling or circumstances, represent those skill sets that make a pastor effective in many different arenas. Those areas would be the prophetic, the priestly, and the kingly.

Hebrew Scripture establishes religious leadership as many-sided, starting with the Sinai event. As we have stated, a pastor must be a practical theologian, a warrior for justice, and someone who cares for members and attends to them as often as necessary.

Pastors are in a unique relationship with parishioners. They encounter members at their most joyful times, such as weddings, baby dedications, and graduations. Pastors also interact with members at some of their lowest moments, such as the death of their parents, spouses, and children. With the high rates of incarceration and death due primarily to street violence, grandparents often reach a point in life where their golden years give way to being parents again. Pastors often stand with people at significant breaking points with no answers to life's tragedies. Why was a teenager with such promise gunned down on a street corner? Why did some particularly insidious form of cancer end a beloved spouse's life? Why is the underground economy of drugs one of the few ways young people can climb the economic ladder, with all the concomitant risks of incarceration and violence constantly looming?

Pastors stand with members at the breaking points in life more than any other profession. We often have no answers that come close to addressing the crying needs of those living on the margins. At that point, pastors' consolation allows us to become another member of the family. Often, we hear the anger of Martha and Mary, "Jesus if you had been here, our brother Lazarus would not have died" (John 11). Black pastors have been the ones who stand in the gap and provide comfort, hope, and healing at the most challenging times in a Black family's life.

African Tradition and the Black Pastor

Several years ago, I visited the site in Ghana where many captured Black people viewed their homeland for the last time before embarking on the fearful pilgrimage to the Americas. Most had no idea how their lives would change if they survived the Middle Passage. Those not thrown overboard as shark bait would survive to enter a new world where unspeakable cruelty and indescribable horror awaited them. They were separated from family and tortured for the slightest infraction.

One writer stated that slavers' biggest mistake was introducing these enslaved people to Jesus. Enslavers did this to encourage the enslaved person's cooperation. But these captured people experienced Jesus differently than their masters expected: rather than obedience, they found liberation. Such biblical entreaties as "slaves, obey your masters" were listened to politely without the slightest disagreement. After the slave catchers went to bed for the night, these African American people would sneak to the hush harbors to their underground churches, usually located at the river shores where slave quarters were built. Here, they worshipped in their style and customs. Harold A. Carter, in his book *The Prayer Tradition of Black People*, pointed out that the enslaved people often carried washtubs to meetings so if a shout came upon them, they could cover their heads with them so as not to give away this underground praise.

The Black pastor filled a natural role that went back to Africa. The role of the chief was multifaceted. When someone came to him with their back covered with keloid scars from severe whippings, in his role as a father, he comforted them and encouraged them never to relinquish their hope. Because the Bible taught them, as James Cone entitled his theological treatise, that God was on the side of the oppressed. The theology of the enslaved people was that the same God who sent Moses to liberate the Hebrews from Egypt would eventually lead Black folk to freedom.

The Black preacher was a healer in the lineage of Elisha and an encourager in the style of Barnabas. He was also a freedom general like Moses who believed that, when the time came, God would part the Red Sea of incarceration. As freedom general, the Black pastor involved himself in efforts to aid his members to escape. The songs selected for the underground meetings were laced with coded messages to instruct people where and when escapes could happen. Worshipers sang "Deep River" to alert the enslaved people that an escape by the river would come that evening. "Ride in the Christ" informed folk that a wagon was coming for an overland escape. The Black preacher led in facilitating escape.

Also, the Black preacher often welcomed assignments as carriage drivers. After the carriage driver deposited the master's family at the church, the driver would sit by a window and overhear the preaching of the Word. He did not internalize Paul's messages as the master hoped. The carriage drivers and others heard something entirely different. They overheard the powerful words of liberation as written in the Book of Daniel. Daniel refused to give up his traditional prayers, although he fully realized this would lead to certain death. Daniel's faith taught him that God would provide an appetite suppressant to eliminate the lion's hunger. In that same Book of Daniel, they could quietly rejoice when Shadrach, Meshach, and Abednego responded to the king's order to bow down before his golden image by saying, "O king live forever. Still, we will never bow to your image because our God can deliver us. But even if God chooses not to, we still will not turn to your vision" (Daniel 3). The shouting part of this liberation sermon was that even though the furnace was heated seven times hotter than before when the king came to the furnace the following day, he saw that the furnace had not harmed the Hebrew children. Inexplicably, there was a fourth one with them in the furnace, and the fourth was likened unto the Son of God. The slaves overlooked the texts of terror, but the stories of victory over bullying domination became the corpus of the Black canon of freedom.

Following the Civil War came the era of Reconstruction. During this time, the Democrats made a political deal with the Republicans that removed Union forces from the South, leaving Black people to the mercy of those who had once "owned" them. Southern politicians and law enforcement ensured their dominance through terror campaigns enforced by the White Citizens' Council, the Ku Klux Klan, and other white terrorist groups. At this time, Black churches and pastors provided vital support for those living in Reconstruction, which was just slavery by another name.

During this era, schools and hospitals were built. Again, the church and pastors led the way through the partnership with Northern Baptists to build hospitals and colleges. Teaching the formerly enslaved people to read and write was a significant priority. Unfortunately, when the Union troops exited the South, many efforts to rebuild the slaves' lives came to a grinding halt.

While Black citizens did garner political power and gain majorities in state and federal elections, Jim Crow laws, which were passed as early as 1865, caused these gains to erode quickly. Dr. Peter Paris cited the speech of Dr. E. C. Morris at the National Baptist Convention in 1900. Dr. Morris addressed the violence toward Black people during Reconstruction:

> We all regret that racial conflicts have taken place in any part of this glorious land, and the spirit to disregard the country's loss has grown in the last decade to marvelous proportions. But this disregard for the law does not represent the best element of our citizens or the true spirit of Americanism. Crime should and must be punished, but there is no doubt that the utter disregard for law and order has produced a feeling of unrest all over the country, presented a serious problem for both the white and black races in the United States.[1]

With the brutal expressions of terrorism facing them, the Black church and pastors toiled tirelessly to help Black people through these rough times.

In the 1950s and '60s, leaders of the Civil Rights Movement drew on Black churches as the touchstone in the quest for freedom. Dr. Martin Luther King Jr. assumed the Montgomery bus boycott's headship and utilized the Black church's historical role in pursuing freedom. During the civil rights era, historic Black church resistance to oppression merged with an activistic social agenda. These twin forces merged as movement leaders creatively altered the words of the traditional Black hymns to address the contemporary liberation struggle. One example is "Ain't Going to Let Nobody Turn Me 'Round," which originally contained the lyric "Ain't going to let nobody turn me around walking up to Beulah Land." In the civil rights era, it became, "Ain't going to let nobody turns me around, walking up the freedom way."

In the post-civil rights era, the centrality of church leadership began to erode. First, there was the Black Power movement. Then, along came the hip-hop generation, the first in Black history not to get its music from the church but from the streets. This shifting reality, by necessity, required new pastoral leadership. For all of the good the Civil Rights Movement did, an unfortunate result was that the liberation theology that deeply informed the Baptist Convention preaching gave way to conservative teaching in many independent seminaries and Bible schools. These seminaries taught spirituality and politics do not mix. They taught that the goal of deliverance should be individual salvation, not societal or corporate. It was then a short walk to prosperity gospel, with such slogans as "Name it and claim it." The declining political influence of the Black church gave way to televangelism, with the mark of success being how high one's ratings were on the Christian Broadcast Network.

The Black Pastor and Contemporary Issues

Just as pastoral leadership has changed over the centuries, congregations have also changed. From the ringing shouts of slavery and the mournful moans of worshipers, Black churches have become corporate entities with budgets, financial statements, and audits. Throughout Reconstruction, church administrators were the deacons. Most churches did not have full-time pastors during this era, as one pastor often served several congregations. As the church moved from the rural South to the urban North, deacons and pastors often experienced leadership tension. These disagreements resulted from pastors and deacons struggling with who should function as primary decision-makers. As the twentieth century unfolded, the need for sound business practices led to the development of finance committees composed of trustees, an office often required by local laws. The emergence of trustee boards produced another challenge for the Black church. Deacons and trustees were often at odds with each other and the pastor. The idea of constitutions and bylaws, ignored by the more rural churches, became a requirement in the churches of the urban North. More and more churches began settling their polity issues through litigation. In an increasingly litigious society, constitutions and bylaws became essential, and secular courts often determined their rulings based on how warring factions did or did not adhere to constitutions. Since we live in a much more litigious society than in the past, the selection of officers today is not determined as much by spiritual gifts, such as teaching, as it is by the candidate's understanding of boards, property management, legal knowledge, and fiscal abilities.

Now, Black churches are facing the new challenge of gentrification. Post-World War II America went from an agrarian society to a suburban one. White flight became a descriptor as Black men and women in increasing numbers moved from the rural South to the urban North. Chicago, Detroit, New York, Philadelphia, and Washington, DC, became enclaves for Black migrants. Racism had convinced the white population that living with members of the Black community was socially and economically dangerous. The height of white flight after the riots following the assassination of Dr. King was primarily built on this false narrative. Concurrent to this were the redlining procedures that shut Black individuals out of the housing market in all but specific, predetermined neighborhoods. Unscrupulous realtors exacerbated white fears by a process known as blockbusting. As Black people moved into the cities, unscrupulous realtors led white people to believe that if Black families moved into their neighborhoods, violence would increase and property values would drop precipitously. The result of all this was Black political power rose immensely.

Powerful politicians like Adam Clayton Powell in New York, Harold Washington in Chicago, and Coleman Young in Detroit began to exert extreme control within the Democratic Party, the party of choice for most Black Americans. Not accidentally, white politicians schemed to develop ways to destroy Black political power. In Washington, Mayor Marion Barry, the African American mayor citizens nicknamed "Mayor for life," was brought down by scandals conjured up and implemented by political operatives working on behalf of the right-wing power structure. Black Washingtonians were not shocked when the incarceration of Mayor Barry led to the emergence of Black mayors who were all too willing to do the bidding of these shadowy white businessmen and politicians. Evidence of the success of this insidious plan is that the new power elite who ran the city was all too willing to capitulate to the white power structure. The rise of gentrification became the method attracting white people to the district.

Washington, DC, once known as "Chocolate City," is now mocha city and only affordable for the wealthiest; it is now an area where most Black and brown people cannot afford to live. Only the richest can live in the city in which they grew up. The cruel irony is white flight drew the red lines around inner cities. As white people extricated themselves from so-called urban problems and fled to the suburbs, Black people followed that pattern. In Prince George's County, Maryland, one of the wealthiest predominantly Black areas in the nation, Black homeowners paid exorbitant prices for their houses. They now often live in neighborhoods where their properties are underwater because the value of their homes in the suburbs nosedived. In contrast, the properties of the white newcomers in the city skyrocketed.

An issue that the Black church has faced over the years is female leadership. Going back to slavery, men and women stood on equal footing. The master was no less cruel to women than men. Women were in the fields picking cotton and tobacco, similar to men. A Black woman would give birth and be expected to continue working as soon as possible. Black women had children sold away, never to be seen again. Through all the slights and indignities, these women stood alongside their men when it came to the issues of justice and freedom. Black women were never allowed on a pedestal, as elite white women had been. The male-dominated society believed white women were too delicate for manual labor.

They were placed on pedestals and treated as frail and fragile creatures to attend to by their mates and servants.

During Reconstruction, as Black men wandered the roads in search of work, Black women assumed educational leadership, worked hand in hand with the Northern missionary societies, and built orphanages, churches, and schools. In addition, Black women took in laundry, sewed, and cooked for white people to keep their families afloat. Yet during Reconstruction, Black women were increasingly relegated to a subordinate status and denied leadership roles. Madam. C. J. Walker became a millionaire and one of the wealthiest Black women in society but still endured the slights of Booker T. Washington, who insisted her revolutionary hair care for Black women was not original.

The newly forming conventions were utterly male dominated. Often, women like Nannie Helen Burroughs pushed men to be more assertive in claiming their God-given rights of full citizenship. Although women in the conventions played a dominant role in organizing and fundraising, the men who led the conventions never gave them space on the program to speak. The Women's Auxiliary was the only place where women served as leaders. Even the largest and most affluent congregations followed this procedure. Again, the mission societies, auxiliaries, and choirs were where women achieved leadership roles.

Today, male baby boomers continue the trend of keeping women in subordinate positions. In the roles of pastors, deacons, and trustees, women remain underrepresented. Although Black churches are well over 65 to 75 percent female, women are rarely considered suitable leaders. It is incumbent upon male pastors to take a strong position and utilize our pulpits and our educational opportunities to begin helping our congregations see that this is not God's will. Too often, we have isolated texts from Paul to insist that God did not give leadership roles to women. Male leaders must teach the congregation that Paul's rigid patriarchal style was because he was a man of his era. In Jerusalem, as well as all of the ancient Near East, male domination was the norm. But having said that, the text of Galatians 4 indicates that Paul was indeed ahead of his time. If we take the lordship of Jesus seriously, although there were no women among the Twelve, women like Mary Magdalene were part of Jesus' key leaders. When we share with our congregations the need to develop women in ministry and leadership, we must never fail to preach and teach that the first witness at the resurrection was a woman, Mary. Nor should we overlook the fact that when the Lord instructed her to tell the disciples that he rose, he made her the first Christian preacher.

Another challenge facing the Black church is sexual orientation. I am convinced that President Bill Clinton's approach to homosexuality, "Don't ask, Don't tell," came from the practice of Black churches. Black churches have always had dominant gay leaders who have functioned as principal figures in the music ministry. Almost since the beginning of the free Black church, these persons were vital worship leaders. Even in Western Africa, the griot, the keeper of the tribe's history, was often a hermaphrodite, preventing confusion of leadership roles with the chief. From Reconstruction down to the present day, many churches have handled these matters by looking the other way.

With the recent gay pride initiatives around the country, remaining closeted is no longer acceptable to those in the gay community. Contemporary Black churches must develop a new hermeneutic that addresses the more homophobic biblical texts that deny all equal status. In previous times, racists used the Bible to support slavery. Will we not permit gay men and women to be a part of the church? Will we commit the same mistake as nineteenth-century slavers? Indeed, the Black church, since the Second World War, has been content to ignore the challenge. As baby boomers' leadership passes off the scene, the new emerging leadership, the Gen Xers, do not treat gay people as pariahs. Instead, they embrace them as totally eligible for all leadership positions. Our traditional churches that dominated the Black religious landscape are witnessing a reduction in the numbers of youth and young adults because of a lack of tolerance.

Kelly Brown Douglas, a professor at Howard University, offers that homosexuality is not a sin; the sin is homophobia.

> A Black sexual discourse of resistance is also constrained to make clear that homophobia and concomitant heterosexist structures and systems (those structures and systems that privilege heterosexuals while discriminating against nonheterosexuals) are sin. In other words, it is not homosexuality but homophobia that is sinful. Just as White cultural exploitation of Black sexuality has impaired Black people's ability to affirm their humanity and what it means to be created in the image of God, so has Black homophobia done the same to numerous gay and lesbian Black persons. Since Black gays and lesbians have internalized the venomous rhetoric of homophobia, they have become alienated from God.[2]

Historically, the Black church experienced many challenges, such as political and economic injustice. The goal for pastors must be to ensure that the image of God is not denied to any of God's children. As the Black church led for equality and justice, it must now advocate for the rights of all, whether straight or a member of the LGBTQ+ community, to share equally in God's sacred image.

Chapter 12

Forrest Harris Sr. as the Watchman on the Wall: The Promise of Our Ideals and the Realities of Our Time in the Black Church's 11th Hour

Stacey Floyd-Thomas

Son of man, I've made you a watchman for the family of Israel. Whenever you hear me say something, warn them for me. If I say to the wicked, 'You are going to die,' and you don't sound the alarm warning them that it's a matter of life or death, they will die, and it will be your fault. (Ezekiel 3:17-19 MSG)

I've posted watchmen on your walls, Jerusalem. Day and night they keep at it, praying, calling out, reminding God to remember. (Isaiah 62:6 MSG)

What is it about the prophetic witness and liberation theology of the Black Church tradition that strikes at the heart of American curiosity, social outrage, and the audacity of hope? To be sure, media coverage concerning the Black Church in recent years has paid more attention to stereotypical sound bites, the commercialization of its singing talent, and the steamy sex scandals of few of its leaders without lending attention to the ongoing legacy of empowerment and enlightenment for which the Black church was once esteemed. Even Black scholars, practitioners and activists like Ivy League professor, Christian practitioner, and political pundit, Eddie S. Glaude Jr., have maintained, on the one hand "The Black Church, as we've known it or imagined it, is dead."[1] On the other hand, "Those of us who are not in the battleground states, those of us who are in blue states or red states, we should just leave the ballot blank" during critical times when we, as Black Christians, currently are facing the erosion of rights and the erasure of history won by faith, blood, and ballot. Without question, we collectively are in for the fight for our lives.

In times like these, it is not enough to teach, preach, or pontificate. As a womanist scholar, one who exists in a world where 'all the women are white and all the Blacks are men,"[2] I have had very little access or reliability to allies whose words do not wound and whose words were bonds in which I could cash in. Within the realm of the Black church, collegium, and community, my male interlocutors were very few who were willing to shine forth rather than shapeshift. So many had fallen prey to the wiles of fame, the fears of the retaliatory white male gatekeepers flexing or the solipsistic navel gazing that pulpits and publishing houses can do in drawing them in as to not only turn on others but turn in on themselves. Let's face it: to matter in our worlds as Black folk is to wax poetic in a fashion that often does not impact reality.

Yet for many of its faith practitioners, the Black Church tradition still is a necessary institution for Black social uplift and spiritual empowerment that evokes a sense of needed affirmation, peoplehood, and the prospects of social transformation. But institutions are only as enduring as the individuals that inhabit them, and in particular of the leaders that give definition to the work, worth and witness that those people matter and that the institutions in which they place their faith and fortitude live up to it as the God they serve keeps the promise to link divine justice to social justice. Such is the case of a 21st century watchman is Rev. Dr. Forrest E. Harris, Sr.

It was the 11th hour of a dark, stormy night in October 1992 when I, along with a group of enthusiastic seminarians, embarked on a challenging pilgrimage literally driving up the rough side of the mountain to make our way from Atlanta, Georgia to Nashville, Tennessee. More than thirty years ago, we were steering northbound on US 75, a highway that is beautifully scenic by day, yet we failed to keep in mind was that this open road could become more treacherous and fearsome because of some curvy roads and steep hills with falling rocks to possibly block our trek. As if that was not enough to keep one's heart racing along the way, it will slow you down when driving in the dark night as rain sheets fall. With slippery highways and heavy cargo causing us to lean to one side, as gravity took its hold, it was little wonder that just prior to our entry our van was leaning to one side as we sped up as we were going slow motion found us crashing in "the buckle of the Bible belt," as my colleague A. J. Levine rightly named it. As a young Black female seminarian, I was inspired by former U.S. President Jimmy Carter during my brief tutelage with him to pursue a path as an ethicist rather than a lawyer. Additionally, under the guidance of my mentor, Dr. Robert M. Franklin—at the time he was an ethicist as well as Director of Candler's Black Church Studies program—me and my fellow Black seminarians were driven to witness and engage with individuals whom we had previously only known through written words.

As fate would have it, at Vanderbilt University Divinity School, a gathering of African American religious leaders convened to explore the profound question, "What does it mean to be Black and Christian?"[3] As acknowledged by the subtitle of the conference proceedings, the meeting was intended to bring the pulpit, the pew, and the academy together into national dialogue. Harris writes that this, "is an identity question that lies at the center of the Black community's struggle for liberation." The battle to interpret this question is being waged by clergy and with Black Christian lay people who fill the seats on any given Sunday. Meanwhile, Black religious scholars and theological educators are engaging in this enterprise to help them relate their scholarly research with the spiritual lives of everyday people.

Living circa the late first and early second century AD, the Roman poet and satirist Juvenal wrote scathing attacks on the vices and failures of the imperial Roman society of his era. Even if you do not know this ancient writer by name, he is probably most famous for posing the following famous for this question: *Quis custodiet ipsos custodes?* (Who watches the watchmen?) In many ways, built into Juvenal's deceptively simple query suggests a threefold concern rooted in the reality and responsibility of the so-called "watchman." On the one hand, there is a requirement of accuracy for the one who watches because this person has a reasonable mastery of their sensory input. Put another way, the watcher can be trusted to give a clear determination of what has been observed. Next, the watchman is worthy of the title because this person is accredited. With time and experience dedicated to the required task at hand, the interpretation of the genuine watchmen is part and parcel of his very existence. Last but not least, the seeds of doubt firmly embedded within the human predicament demand that we require accountability to ensure the oversight of that which they have been entrusted to protect and preserve. This means the watchman's viewpoint and valor are not taken for granted but have been validated because they have been repeatedly put to the test and have been validated.

When I think of how the Rev. Dr. Forrest E. Harris, Sr., once a pullman porter who tirelessly with elegance and esteem lugged baggage, served passengers, and attended to the tedious traffic of strangers without being derailed by the stench of racism or internalized oppression during the summer months between his school years, it is little wonder that while many would have complained, with the mission of completing college on his mind, he found not only prized wages, but met and married the woman who would be his lifelong wife. So, too, he has lived up to and into his vocational calling as a leader in the field of Black Church Studies. He has been such a pullman turned watchman dedicated to safeguard this sacred institution even amid its 11th hour crises.

While this disparity amplifies the real issue that underlies the rancorous crisis of race, culture and religion illustrated by the 11 o'clock hour on Sunday as the "most segregated hour of the week," it also highlights urgent responses to the unaddressed mandates of a nation divided and a people at the crossroads of peril and promise. As the Black Church wrestles with its "eleventh hour" both in terms of the media frenzy of this current political climate and also an internal assessment of it, to quote Rev. Dr. Martin Luther

King, Jr., "where do we go from here," this conference hopes to offer interventions into this critical moment in our nation's history as one of its greatest institutions of moral conscience and freedom fighting lies in the wake of public ruin and private pain.

Social justice praxis and ministry formation has been the rubric under which the Kelly Miller Smith Institute on Black Churches which has offered conferences, theological seminars, and intensive programs for over four decades to address the moral and social complexities of the communities that Black churches serve. To better understand Forrest Harris as both a fervent devotee and fierce defender of the Black Church tradition as sacred community, one needs to know that he was part of a large and loving family as well as being endowed with a strong sense of the viability of African American civic institutions of church, education, and communal uplift. He was born to his beloved parents, W.T. and Sallie Mae Harris, and reared in Memphis with his eight brothers and sisters (including his twin brother Frank), his grandchildren and relatives. He is married to Jacqueline (Jackie) Harris, who had her own lauded career as a registered nurse for decades. They have four grown children and four grandchildren. Harris received the Bachelor of Arts (B.A.) degree from Knoxville College and a Bachelor of Theology (B.Th.) degree from American Baptist College (ABC). He earned both the Master of Divinity (M.Div.) and Doctor of Ministry (D.Min.) degrees from Vanderbilt University Divinity School. In 1985, the Vanderbilt University Divinity School faculty established the Kelly Miller Smith Scholarship for Ministry in the African American Church. Roughly a year later the Kelly Miller Smith Institute on Black Church Studies (KMSI) was created in posthumous tribute to the late Rev. Dr. Kelly Miller Smith, Sr., who was a paragon of the Nashville civil rights movement and served as an assistant dean of Vanderbilt Divinity School from 1968 until his death in 1984. with Forrest Harris serving as its founding director since that time.

In 1999, Harris was inaugurated the tenth president of his alma mater, American Baptist College (ABC). Assuming the leadership mantle of a private, Christian liberal arts educational institution (while manning the post of Black Church Studies at Vanderbilt Divinity School), ABC has consistently benefited under his 25 years of leadership and the exceptional breadth of expertise he brings to the position. Harris cultivates a philosophy of educational "vitality," investing in strategies and approaches deeply connected to teaching and learning innovations for diverse students. Harris holds the distinction of ranking among one of the longest-tenured leaders of the nation's Historically Black Colleges and Universities (HBCUs). During the last quarter century, his leadership is distinguished for making a significant contribution to the academy and the church by merging academic liberation theology with social justice activism and ecclesial praxis. During his tenure as ABC's president, he has led the development of countless new programs and initiatives at the College. He remains deeply committed to sustaining and enhancing ABC's academic distinction by building upon its unique strengths as a Historically Black College with a focus on social justice advocacy, combined with the College's strong legacy in civil rights leadership throughout the institution's history. Harris has succeeded in advancing innovative teaching and in amplifying ABC's partnerships in the United States, the Caribbean, and on the African continent. Through the auspices of both KMSI and ABC, Harris has continually devoted time, resources, and attention to launching initiatives shaping the future prophetic Christianity within the Black Church tradition for the 21st century and beyond.

From the colonial era several centuries ago to the current age of cell phones, cloud computing, and cryptocurrencies, Black churches in America have played a pivotal role in American society and culture. As a central part of Harris's lifelong mission and mandate has been offering resources and reflections on how Black churches have not only been important to African Americans but have also impacted the nation and the world as well. Although often overlooked and trivialized, the institutional, inspirational, intellectual, and improvisational power of the Black Christian tradition has made immense contributions to the nation and the world. While severely battered and bruised by white supremacy and colonized Christianity from the outside and misogynoir, elitism, colorism, ageism, homophobia, and transphobia within, Black Christianity nevertheless has been the backbone of Black communities for several centuries. Historically speaking, a sad but true reality of the Black Church tradition has been the fact that the struggle against dehumanization in and of itself has been the secret of some of its greatest successes.

Arguably over the past 400 years, through its efforts to overcome slavery, segregation, and even now sociopolitical division, Black churches have often stepped up to meet the challenges of changing times and have done so in ways that combine the pastoral and the prophetic. Many of the most capable and community-oriented churches continue to provide social services such as meals for homeless people, housing for the elderly, clothing share closets for the needy, childcare / afterschool programs, prison ministries, health care ministries, and programs supporting survivors of domestic abuse and intimate partner violence among other efforts to make the wounded whole.

Yet Black churches in America are changing. They are losing members—as are white mainline churches—even though roughly 80 percent of Blacks maintain that religious identity and spiritual practice remain very important to them. Nevertheless, nearly half say Black churches have less influence than they had 50 years ago, but they believe Black churches should have a greater role in society, according to Pew Research polling data. The necessary paradox of our initiative is that we are striving to provide theological and ministerial resources that will both address the present need of our moment in time as well as stand the test of the ages. To speak to such a dramatic set of concerns, the challenge is how to have a Word that is relevant to Black Christians in the 21st century. In other words, how do we profess a religious tradition that endured through slavery and segregation to a generation addicted to cyberspace and cell phones?

When I was given the great honor and opportunity to address this watchman in our midst as a living legacy while providing a historical sources and trajectories of Black preaching amid social crisis, I naturally began wrestling with the very premise of the idea. At first glance, I often thought the presupposition of the phrase "social crisis preaching" represented an oxymoron. To clarify my own thinking and concern about this matter, I had to go back and refer to the best source I know regarding this matter. In 1983, Rev. Dr. Kelly Miller Smith Sr. delivered the prestigious Lyman Beecher Lectures at Yale University. Roughly a year later, these lectures served as the basis for his final publication, *Social Crisis Preaching*. In that text, he offers the following statement:

> The social crisis sermon is never properly a museum piece of social oratory. Nor is it appropriately an animated discussion of current social issues. Rather, it is a call to action. It is preaching on the highest order. It is quality preaching…Quality preaching is the efficacious proclamation of the genuine Word of God. It is adherence to the mandate found in 2 Timothy 4:2: "preach the word, be urgent in season and out of season, convince, rebuke, and exhort, be unfailing in patience and in teaching."

Thus, as I understand the point raised here by Harris's mentor, preaching that is both good and sound ought to always speak to the perils and predicaments we face as people, to which Harris would add Black Christianity's mandate to "Social Crisis Ministry, Theology, and Praxis". To my mind, is there any need for preaching that does not speak to either the problems that surround us or the evil that plagues us from the cradle to the grave? Is there any moment of our mortal existences that are completely impervious to the misery and suffering that befalls all of us as human beings humbly yet exquisitely made of flesh and blood by our Creator? Most importantly, Black theologian and mystic Howard Thurman's classic statement gets us to ponder, "What does the religion of Jesus have to say to those with their backs against the wall?"[4] In other words, is there ever a time that preaching the Gospel of Jesus Christ is not supposed to speak life to a dying world? Faced with this dizzying array of questions, I ultimately came to embrace the notion that every time the Word of God is uttered to the churched and unchurched alike, it is in the context of crises, both great and small. However, the larger question is whether that preached message allows women, men, and children to receive a timely and credible word that allows them to see Christ amid the crisis of life.

For Harris, the Church becomes impotent and irrelevant when it serves as the quiet, uncritical sponsor of the status quo. Today, however, we find that Black churches have fallen into a strange sort of trap by supporting a social order that supports privilege, power, and prosperity, arguably violating our own senses of democracy, moral agency, and love. On the one hand, in its spiritually oriented emotionalism and its yielding to classism, on the other hand, Black churches have fallen short of their full potential as prophetic agents of social justice and peace both locally and globally. This shortcoming is perhaps especially conspicuous in the Black church's scarce response to the overwhelming chaos and violence of social dislocation that afflicts our families and curses our communities. The lack of a concerted and effective response from Black pulpits is likewise perplexing regarding societal ills that affect our households. What must we ask ourselves is whether the American myth of a level playing field in a post-Obama era has clouded our vision or has even a mitigated sense of power and a transient notion of privilege simply undermined our interest in true liberation? King asks a critical question: "Is organized religion too inextricably bound to the status quo to save our nation and the world?"[5]

When I think about the consequences, I see the great and growing pain of a generation under extreme pressure. Recently while my husband, daughter, and I were visiting with our good friend and her sons at their church during Sunday worship, I was struck by a moment that saddened me greatly. The church's choir and music ministry were performing a wonderful rendition of "No

Weapon," a contemporary gospel song based on Isaiah 54:17 and popularized by Fred Hammond when I saw the troubling sight of our godson weeping uncontrollably. As a student in one of Nashville's premier magnet schools, this young Black man with a brilliant mind, a bright future, and a loving, nurturing support system, yet found the stresses of life were too crippling for him to bear. If this is the case for him, what would happen to the countless young women, men, and others who do not have similar life chances and advantages working for them? In the words of philosopher Cornel West, the prospects for this latest generation are largely defined by a sense of nihilism: they are "rootless, dangling beings." As such, these young Black women and men have existences in which they do not respect the lives of others yet do not fully appreciate their own reason for living. Watchmen like Forrest Harris have been vital to safeguarding many of our Black youth so they do not plummet headfirst into despair.

In the face of such doom and gloom, there are also signs of hope looming on the horizon of our imaginations. The mobilization of thousands of people of good faith and conscience drawn from all walks of life who are called to commit themselves to public service, community activism, and volunteerism in their heroic attempts to combat the twin evils of apathy and cynicism. One of the greatest fears of chronicling the roots of social crisis within African American Christianity is bearing witness to how many times we fail to learn the lessons of a rich and storied past that is both our history and heritage. An oppressed people who abandon the knowledge of their own history of deep, intimate faith or who fail to grasp the myriad of lessons embedded in such experiences will only yield to the perpetual domination of others. Vincent Harding argues, "The story of the African American struggle for freedom, democracy, and transformation is a great, continuing human classic whose liberating lessons are available to all of us, especially those who are committed to work and sacrifice for the creation of a better country [and] a more hopeful world."[6] Therefore, writing this history of African American religious faith and belief in general and the Black Church tradition in particular assists in the process of invoking the past to inform the present in the hopes of inspiring a better future.

Within the purview of Harris's work building institutional bulwarks of the Black Church tradition in academic terms, Black Christianity ought to respond to suffering, division, or conflict with self-directed claims of divine favor in terms of God's grace and mercy. Moreover, there is a critical breakdown between the pastoral concerns and the prophetic consciousness of this sacred enterprise. This breakdown occurs when the pastoral word is not merged with the prophetic imperative in ways that allow the faithful believer to see themselves and the conditions of possibilities in their lives as part of an ongoing relationship between God and humanity in its entirety. Specifically, instead of viewing all the unrest and tragedy around us as opportunities for Christians to respond to God's call for loving and serving our neighbors to the fullest, too often the preached Word that is coming forth from Black preachers is taking its marching orders from "prosperity gospel," "neighbor theology," and "bible-olatry" among other gimmicks that oversimplify the calamities of our world to one common denominator: all catastrophic events are divine punishment for human immorality and all material gains are God's symbol of human merit.

Thus, the beauty of the debate surrounding Rev. Dr. Jeremiah A. Wright Jr.'s "Confusing God and Government"[7] sermon fifteen year ago lies in the ways in which has served as an act of *disruptive theology*. By this, I am referring to social crisis preaching as a prophetic mode of God-talk brought about when urgent utterances invoke a point of collision between *chronos* (human conception of time) and *kairos* (divine conception of time) to create a rupture in the status quo wherein we, as a people and a nation, can have a moment of truth and clarity. Whether one stands in agreement and solidarity with disruptive theology, prophets are necessary to shake this nation as well as the Church out of the zombie-like trance it has been under for so long. Rather than running from Wright's

201

statements, African American religious leaders and their congregations needed to see this moment as an opening, an opportunity in order to revive a much-needed conversation about the role and responsibility of the Black Church tradition to confront the powers that be on all matters that affect the chances for human flourishing, especially this nation's ability to wage war and make peace in this world. Even though many church leaders might use the expression "speak truth to power," it is now time to make that statement more than a convenient catchphrase.

Ultimately, God's story for Forrest Harris is not simply for the formation of the Christian church in human history. It certainly calls for the formation of the Church, but ultimately, God's story is God's caring encounter with humanity and loving embrace of the world. Social crisis preaching and social crisis praxis proclaim the character and content of God's story so that the Church may reflect the divine grace it has received thus far and, in turn, participate in the divine encounter. Thus, taken to its logical conclusion, social crisis preaching as liberation praxis is fueled by God's care for the world, involving the pursuit of human liberation through justice and through relief from suffering. In closing, history is replete with the need for the Black Church to live up to the standard of linking divine justice to social justice by what we often regard as "afflicting the comfortable and comforting the afflicted." Proclaiming the unmitigated Gospel of Jesus Christ ultimately requires finding the synergy within Black Church tradition between the pastoral and prophetic to overcome the Church's seeming surrender to the false idols of privilege, power, and prosperity. The challenge for us here and now is how to transform this understanding into ways in which those of us who care about prophetic activism, preaching, teaching, and living in accordance with the Gospel could preach, teach, and live through these trying times....watchmen that work the work while it is day and watch out at night so that the institutions we make sacred—and the individuals that inhabit them—will not be made ashamed.

Chapter 13

Doing Theology on the Run:
An Essay in Honor of Forrest Harris

Walter Earl Fluker

There are few friends and colleagues in my life whom I have been more fortunate to meet and grow alongside than Forrest Harris. Forrest is both tall in physical stature and a towering figure in pastoral leadership, public intellectual life, and professional academic career. I often marvel how the long-distanced run of his career, from our early days at Vanderbilt Divinity School to his professional stature as a pastor, public intellectual, and college president, is an apt metaphor for his prophetic witness and creative performance as a *bricoleur*. One of the rewarding tasks of my professional life has been the opportunity to witness the velocity, versatility, and vitality of the transition from his early corporate background to theological education, which he refashioned and reconfigured while he was on the run.

Our friendship, which includes a thriving collegial and professional relationship, has continued over the years in his professorial and public leadership roles at Vanderbilt, throughout the country, and in international settings. I served as his professor in at least two seminars, "The Religious Thought of Howard Thurman" and "Models of a Metaphor Community," while I was at Vanderbilt Divinity School. In these settings, I was most impressed by his agile mind, creative sense of the moment, and his ability to grasp the relevance of what is seen and heard in the moment and to translate acoustic repetitions into actionable agenda. His first major conference at Vanderbilt, sponsored by the Kelly Miller Smith Institute, came about as part of a lecture and class discussion on the tension, if not tragedy, of "On Being Black and Christian." Anyone who knows anything about Forrest Harris's work as an administrator, practical theologian, and public leader remembers the impact that this conference had on the academy and church. Academic and pastoral leaders benefitted immensely from the presentations, discussions, and reflections that were a part of this most impressive series. The Kelly Miller Smith Institute found its distinctive signature and Forrest's inimitable voice in the crux and implementation of this work. Among preachers on the national scene, he is second to none. Among *practicing* practical theologians, he has few peers. His three books, *What Does It Mean to Be Black and Christian: Pulpit, Pew and the Academy in Dialogue* (Townsend Press); *Ministry for Social Crisis: Theology and Praxis in the Black Church Tradition* (Mercer University Press); and *What Does It Mean to Be Black and Christian: The Meaning of the African American Church* (Sunday School Publishing Board), attest to the scholarship and wisdom he developed over the long years while he was on the run!

In this brief essay, I suggest that Forrest Harris's ministry of teaching, preaching, and pastoral and institutional leadership serves as a critical resource for a new generation of scholars, pastors, activists, and freedom fighters who are engaging the long and complex history of race in the US while negotiating deep systemic issues of state violence, gender and sexual inequities, health, education, economics, demographic locations, and more. Religious scholars, theologians, and church leaders must take a good look at the ways in which this new moment calls us to join Forrest Harris on the run.

Doing Theology on the Run

In this tribute to my dear friend and colleague, I return to an earlier project[1] and argue that religious scholars and Black church leaders need to begin with the basic consideration that our theological constructions have always been, and will continue to be, contextual and constructive; that is, we must *do* our theology on the run. Like the herald who is running in Habakkuk 2:2–4 (KJV)[2], we are called to run errands of resistance that are a part of our existence as *run-*

aways and to search for new visions and read them within what Howard Thurman called "the divine context."[3] Yet more is expected of the runner. She must *prophesy* and *publish* the disenchanting yet good news that our freedom is going to take much longer than we thought, and that it will come not by a magical hand of fate. Rather, it will come because we continue to struggle, resist, reconstruct, and reimagine our futures as we run toward our destinies in hope of our resurrection and revelation as the sons and daughters of God.

Our greatest theological leaders of the past century did their theology on the run. During the Civil Rights Movement, Otis Redding's 1961 song "Shout Bamalama" best described the context in which Black religious leaders did their theologizing. A verse from the song goes like this:

> The preacher and the deacon were prayin' one day
> Along come a bear comin' down that way
> The preacher told the deacon to say a prayer
> He said, "Lord, a prayer won't kill this bear"
>
> I gotta make it, baby
> Shout "Bamalama"
> I gotta run for it
> Well, well, well
> Nobody's gonna set him down
> He's down in Alabama
> I'm shoutin', "Bamalama"
> We shall be free!

These religious scholars' and church leaders' contextual and constructive tasks grew out of their immediate present much like the story of the African savanna. Every morning, the gazelle wakes up running because if it does not run, it will become the breakfast of some pride of lions. And every morning, the lion wakes up running because she knows that if she does not catch the gazelle, her family will go hungry. Everybody in the savanna wakes up running, and so must we!

Our biblical stories are replete with prophets and others who woke up running and encountered God at *crossing(s)*—those liminal spaces fraught with peril and possibility.

- Moses woke up running away from Pharaoh's house and hid out in the Midian desert until he bumped into a fiery bush at a *crossing* and returned to Egypt and *crossed* the Red Sea to liberate his people.

- Elijah woke up running from Ahab and Jezebel after he called fire from heaven on Mount Carmel and hid in the wilderness until Yahweh summoned him to *cross* the desert near Damascus and appoint a new order of government and religion.

- Jacob woke up running from Esau and *crossed* the Brook of Jabbok, where he bumped into a night demon who established his future as Israel, the prince of the nations.

- Rahab, the Canaanite, hid two spies on the run at the *crossing* of Jericho, and her extended family escaped doom by waiting inside a house marked with a red thread.

- Hagar was on the run *crossing* the desert of Paran with her infant child, escaping from Abraham and Sarah, and was met by an angel by a spring of water who told her to return home and promised her that she would become the mother of a great people.

- David woke up running from the terror of Saul and *crossed* over into the precincts of Adullam and hid in a cave and returned as King of Israel and Judah.

- Yes, even those frightened disciples of Jesus woke up running after the crucifixion and *crossed* into their destinies on the Day of Pentecost, where wind and fire scattered them to the corners of the earth, witnessing and testifying to what they had seen and heard.

In our own times, we have witnessed prophets who woke up running. Martin Luther King Jr. *woke up running*. He was haunted by the "fierce urgency of now." King's short life was a biography of running. He completed college at nineteen, graduated seminary at twenty-two, and received a PhD at twenty-six, by which time he was already the established leader of the Montgomery Improvement Association. From 1957 until his assassination, he traveled more than six million miles to deliver more than 2,500 speeches. In the short span of thirteen years—from 1955 to 1968—while he was running, he changed the leadership equation: public leadership no longer belonged to the strict province of position, power, and privilege, but to the marginalized moral minority—those whom King labeled "transformed nonconformists."[4] In this short time, King, and those brave known and unknown souls who struggled with him, expanded the moral grammar of American history and culture from parochially applied democratic principles to concrete proposals for inclusiveness and action. He was running a social justice errand in the divine context, and while running from his fate, he *woke up* to his destiny. King woke up running and so must we!

Running, Runagate, Resistance, and Reconstruction

Vincent L. Wimbush's 2011 essay "Interpreters—Enslaving/ Enslaved/Runagate"[5] provides a window through which we might engage in word play; that is, playing and privileging the notion of *running* as in *runagate*, a term made popular by the Black poet Robert A. Hayden. Hayden's 1962 poem "Runagate Runagate" uses Harriet Tubman and the symbol of the *runaway* to reveal the dangers, determination, terrors, crossings, moods, and strategies of enslaved Africans who escaped the master's house in pursuit of freedom. They were running for both freedom of the body and the liberation of consciousness for the birth of subjectivity—running away *from* and running *to* something *strange*, not yet realized, but imagined as a new future, a new situation, a new being, a new way

207

of interpreting the world—a world where one is saved from the horrors of enslavement of the body and mind.[6]

Wimbush centers the narrative on Frederick Douglass, the runaway from the Great House Farm, where enslaved Africans were trapped in an ideological circle of biopolitical incarceration in which their bodily, psychic, epistemic, social, and political worlds were fixed—bound by law, social norms, and customs that prevented them from seeing beyond their bondage. He became a preacher in the African Methodist Episcopal Zion Church (AMEZ), where he created a "Sabbath School" and secretly taught his fellows to read and write—seeing literacy as a pathway to freedom. More was at stake, however, for the young Douglass. He was able to imagine himself as *free*—so he ran away—but as he ran, he strategized about how he could return to liberate his fellow bondspersons from the Great House Farm. Wimbush writes,

> As Douglass looks back to the Great House Farm, he does not romanticize the situation of the slaves. He indicates that he has come to understand that the chief dilemma that slaves faced was not the physical domination, as demeaning as it was, but the not being seen, not being heard, not being understood, not being communicated with in broad terms befitting the dignity of humanity, not being able to communicate the complexity of sentiments and feelings, and being cut off from everything— except, ironically, the Great House Farm. Enslavement meant being able to sing, perhaps, but only within the Manichaean- prescribed circle in which Black was overdetermined as, among other things, "unmeaning jargon." This was for Douglass intolerable. He would escape it.

And indeed, he did! With Wimbush, I suggest that as Douglass ran away from his fated ideological and physical bondage, the bounded consciousness of the Great House Farm, he ran toward his freedom, the "negation of negation,"[7] and discovered his destiny to publish, to reveal and imagine that his story of bondage and freedom would also be the future-story of his fellow enslaved Africans. Thus, taking a cue from Wimbush's excellent essay, I am arguing that doing theology at the beginning of this century demands that we, like Douglass, make a run for it and invite others to run with us to an imagined future! Douglass is an archetype of the African Americans and colonized peoples of the world who have had to escape the Great House Farm, "the house that race built,"[8] where certain groups of people understood their place in the architecture of Western civilization. Here, my concern is with the *demos* that are not accounted for in the configuration of power, those relegated to animal life with sound (*phônê*), "unmeaning jargon," but who cannot speak. Nonetheless, these bodies dare to speak, break, shift, run, and redefine the spaces they have been assigned. Because they dare to speak as an act of resistance (*logos*), they reveal the process of equality because only a free human can speak.[9] But how do we speak, prophesy, within this psycho-cultural, theo-ethical, and existential-aesthetic as *runagates* when so many of our churches and leaders are still engaged in "unmeaningful jargon" and wandering about in the Great House Farm?

We begin first with *context*. Oppressed and colonized people begin the theological task by responding to the primary theological and ethical question of context; i.e., "What's going on?" Marvin Gaye was not the first to ask that question. Black theology is a contextual and constructive practice in God-talk, in reconceptualizing, reinterpreting, and reimagining narratives, language, signs, and symbols about divine activity *in situ*. Our progenitors of Black theological discourse and practice—Frederick Douglass, Harriet Tubman, Sojourner Truth, Ida B. Wells, Pauli Murray, Adam Clayton Powell Jr., Ella Baker, Fannie Lou Hamer, Malcolm X, Albert Cleage, Martin Luther King Jr., and James Cone—constructed their theologies on the run.[10] So, what might contextualization of theological truths look like on the run? How might we, as Cone suggests, appropriate the great biblical stories and lessons of antiquity and refashion them to our social existence and historical needs? Shall we continue to "debate religion on an abstract theological level" or live our "religion concretely in history"? I think we can and must do both—debate abstract conversations and live religiously in the concrete circumstances of history. A rereading of the ancient text of Habakkuk is an example of what is possible in doing both, which is captured in the metaphor of "doing theology on the run."

Lessons from Habakkuk: A Meditation on *Running*

The inquirer in Habakkuk 1:2–4 is suffering in the circle of the Great House Farm of Babylonian captivity.[11] The prophet is exhausted from and exasperated by the ongoing oppression of his people and cries out to the God of Judah, "How long?" We are familiar with the anxiety and trauma expressed in this text. The prophet's question has a ring of despair, exhaustion, and aggravation. He is interrogating the contradictions of logic—the God of Judah is the God who rescues and delivers, but for some reason it appears that God is not acting in the way that logic would demand—Is God on our side? Why doesn't God, the all-powerful and all-loving, act on our behalf? Is God a white racist? Hear the lament of W. E. B. Du Bois as he raises his cry in the aftermath of the Atlanta Riot of 1906.[12]

> Bewildered we are, and passion-tost, mad with the madness of a mobbed and mocked and murdered people; straining at the armposts of Thy Throne, we raise our shackled hands and charge Thee, God, by the bones of our stolen fathers, by the tears of our dead mothers, by the very blood of Thy crucified Christ: *What meaneth this?* Tell us the Plan; give us the Sign!

> *Keep not Thou silence, O God!*

> Sit no longer blind, Lord God, deaf to our prayer and dumb to our dumb suffering. Surely, Thou too art not white, O Lord, a pale, bloodless, heartless thing?

> *Ah! Christ of all the Pities!*

In the throes of social misery and strained theological contradictions, the inquirer in Habakkuk takes a defiant stand and lifts himself up on the walls of the high tower:

I will stand at my watch
  and station myself on the ramparts;
I will look to see what he will say to me,
  and what answer I am to give to this complaint.
Then the Lord replied:
"Write down the revelation
  and make it plain on tablets
  so that a herald may run with it.
For the revelation awaits an appointed time;
  it speaks of the end
  and will not prove false.
Though it linger, wait for it;
  it will certainly come and will not delay.
"See, the enemy is puffed up;
  his desires are not upright—
but the righteous person will live by his faithfulness."
  (2:1–4, NIV)

A critical point of departure in the reading of this text is to understand that the watcher, the one standing on the tower, is a representation, an alter-consciousness of the herald, the one who is running. This symbol of the visionary is multivalent, both depictions of consciousness are simultaneous—*the one who sees is also the one who runs.* There is a *watching self* and a *running self.* The *watching self* sees a theocentric vision of the existential context through the lens of the divine context. The herald, *the running self*, is looking at and reading the revelation while she is running—but both the seer and the runner are aspects of the same inner and outer moorings of the Spirit that is speaking to the situation.

Second, the watcher and the runner can be imagined as one and the same. I am placing emphasis not on the watcher who sees the vision, which is important, but rather upon the one who is *watching* and *running.* We are called to write, read, and prophesy on the run! The compartmentalization of writing, reading, and running is non sequitur in lived experience. Like Douglass, we are constructing theology on the run! Who are these *watchers/runners*

211

for us? What is the internal dialogue between the watcher and runner who is called to prophesy? What might the watcher be saying to the runner? And what might the runner be saying to the watcher? How do we construct our theological worlds without falling into a dichotomous conundrum that renders us (the church) immobile, fixated, and powerless in this terrible moment that threatens Black life and existence—a moment when we must be on the run? What might an attempt at an embodied, unified consciousness like look like for us—who must read, write, run, and prophesy as we imagine a new moment of embodied theological discourse and practice for our time in order to escape the privileged, abstract Manichaean theological level and live our religion concretely in history?

Howard Thurman's exposition of the *Book of Habakkuk* is helpful.[13] He suggests "a principle of alternation"[14] in consciousness activates in consciousness the practice of *involvement* and *detachment* in a fluid movement of the spirit. Involvement (for our purposes, *engagement*) and detachment (*waiting and resting*) are not discrete, separable moments of consciousness, but one fluid intersubjective reality that is wrought through discipline and practice—which Thurman, in other places, calls "the tools of the Spirit."[15] How might we, in our time-space relationships, both personally and collectively, become watchers and runners without falling into the traps of dilemma, wandering in exodus, and burning in the perpetual hellfires of negation? We must reimagine the future as we remember, retell, and relive our stories. The *watcher/runner* must reimagine theological discourse for this new time and rhythm as *runagates* who escape the bondage of ideology and culture and the political, economic scenarios that doom us to a perpetual lake of fire where we burn day and night, where our children are killed by the State, where a global pandemic has ushered in and given permission to the principalities and powers of this Great House Farm to unleash their hounds of hell on the poor, the left out and left behind.

Congregating, Conjuring, and Conspiring
in Common(s) at the Crossings

Might I offer, in conclusion, some reflections on what might be possible with respect to what I propose as a model for intersubjective communication and embodied practices for transformational leaders, like Forrest Harris, who are on the run? I suggest it is possible for religious scholars, church leaders, and activists to become *runners/watchers* in order escape from the Great House Farm of academic protocols and churchly language and symbols that bind us to fixed paradigms, narratives, and performances that are antithetical to our liberative quests and yearnings for authenticity, wholeness, and human flourishing. This involves a threefold task of *congregating, conjuring, and conspiring in common(s) at crossing(s).*[16] Congregating, conjuring, and conspiring are tools of the spirit that are in our *runaway bags.*[17] Tools of the spirit refer to the different ways that deep spirituality and forms of cultural imagination (cultural narratives, myths, rituals, and aesthetic triggers) can be used to activate and inform experiential and reflective learning, critical thinking, and moral judgment. I suggest that after participating in a collective act of aesthetic creation and envisioning new futures, agents (*runners/watchers*) view the world differently.

Forrest Harris has provided us with such a model through his many interactions and productions of spaces where we can practice *congregating—gathering, binding, and coming together—*that involves *repenting* by rethinking, regretting, and running away from and running to new imagined futures. Black church leaders and scholars have excellent opportunities to begin this work of *repenting* (again, running away from and running to) by acknowledging and receiving the voices and visions of the new movements of the Spirit in our midst—*running to* by creating and appreciating spaces of *difference with empathy, respect, and justice:* different forms and styles of leadership where the socially and politically disrespected, dismissed, excluded, "impure," and "grotesque" can gather in our diasporic and exilic quests for *home.*[18] His invitation to, and defense

213

of, Bishop Yvette Flunder's iconoclastic participation at American Baptist College in 2015 is an example of this new way of *congregating*. According to Robin D. G. Kelley, the long and aggravating history of the Exodus metaphor is essentially a "freedom dream" of a new land composed of imaginative yearnings for return to a glorious past to Africa or an Afro-futurist intergalactic space-travel exposition to "anyplace but where we are now."[19]

Harris has taught us the inherited art of *conjuring*. *Conjuring* is a retelling and reliving of our many-layered and intertwined stories that garner a new sense of time—in and out of *epiphenomenal time*, *negotiating transcendence*—in search of a livable and flourishing future. As such, it signifies on modernist claims of knowledge and truth and revisits the quest for (Black) intersubjectivity that is unsequestered by linguistic-legal-aesthetic-moral forms of bondage that are "immune to deep egalitarian reimagining and restructuring."[20] Harris's performative ministry of preaching, teaching, and administration are done in real time while daring to return in narrative quest to a past that is already future and present simultaneously. This is the art of *conjuring par excellence* that he has done over the years without calling attention to himself. American Baptist College and Vanderbilt Divinity School are the sites of these performances and are better because of Forrest's run to the future!

Finally, Dr. Harris has taught us the practice of *conspiring*. *Conspiring* means to literally breathe together, to plot and to do together as one; only in its more modern sense does it connote something sinister or evil. *Conspiring* is used here to swear an oath against the ghosts of the Great House Farm and to literally breathe and run together (in Pentecostal-scattering diasporas) toward common goals and purposes that inspire and guide leaders, scholars, activists, and others to aspire toward new *commons*. This has been Forrest's *global* work in diasporas—*commons* that may well expire over time and new strategies for the moment will, of necessity, be constructed, but Forrest Harris's work has given us an example of this possibility in its own signature and testimony.

James Baldwin famously writes, "Nothing is fixed, forever and forever and forever, it is not fixed; the earth is always shifting, the light is always changing, the sea does not cease to grind the rock."[21] The challenges to Black life in the United States, and throughout the many diasporas of which we are a part, are so multitudinous that one could resign oneself to fatedness and despair, as many of our churches have done in this era of "Make America Great Again." We can also choose to congregate in Raphael Warnock's *fifth moment*[22] and begin again (for some, continue) the work of conjuring new narratives and new strategies that strengthen our struggle by building on legacies bequeathed to us from the past. These gifts and tools of the past are blessed sacraments that have been handed down to us from so many of our prophets and seers whose lives bear witness to the Broken One whose dangerous memory rests just above our heads and will lead us to new *crossing(s)*.[23]

Hallelujah, Dr. Harris! It is done! Well done!

Afterword

"The Fly Ain't in the Milk, It's on the Milk" Practical Theology, Homiletical Prophecy, and the Grassroots Hermeneutics of Forrest E. Harris

Michael Eric Dyson

It may be a cliché—I heard Toni Morrison say to a small group of students that clichés persist because they contain some truth – but when I met him Forrest E. Harris was tall, dark, and handsome. He was also the newly minted pastor of Oak Valley Baptist Church in Oak Ridge, Tennessee, a stone's throw away from Knoxville where I was attending Knoxville College. I arrived in Tennessee in 1979, the same year Harris took up his pastorate at Oak Valley. When I met him a short time later, I had been tapped to serve as interim pastor for a year of the Mother Love Baptist church in nearby Louisville, Tennessee.

Mother Love was helmed by an endearingly eccentric chocolate genius by the name of Riggins Renal Earl, Jr., who had taken leave from his church and his religious studies professorship at the University of Tennessee for postdoctoral study at Harvard. Earl pointed the way for Harris nearly a decade later to leave the pastorate and take up a prominent perch in the academy at Earl's alma mater Vanderbilt University, blazing a path there for me as well some forty years later.

What immediately struck me about Harris was his homiletical sophistication and his analytical acuity. He had already earned the sobriquet bestowed on him by ethicist Stacey Floyd-Thomas as "our watchman on the wall." He was unafraid in his erudite sermons to join the most probing queries about faith and humanity to cutting edge theological and philosophical arguments about God and culture.

He was H. Richard Niebuhr with a tan, Reinhold Niebuhr brimming with ebony brilliance. But he was even more indebted to the penetrating Black sacred rhetoric of Howard Thurman and the revolutionary Black Theology of James Cone. And the mother wit and vernacular speech of his Black native tongue and the urgent prophecy of Martin Luther King, Jr., permeated his pulpit proclamations and his published writings as well. In the nearly 45 years that I have known him, not much has changed. Harris's practical theology, homiletical prophecy and grassroots hermeneutics have grounded his vigorous public interventions.

Harris's efforts to mend the breach between theology in the academy, and the life and practice of the church in a vibrant practical theology, shine in his sermons and in books. In Harris's 2019 sermon, delivered at Charlotte, North Carolina's Friendship Missionary Baptist Church, "Hearing the Sound of the Genuine," Thurman haunts the homily like a character in a tale from Edgar Allen Poe. The very first words of the sermon, after he announces the text, are, "Howard Thurman was thought of throughout his life, foremost, as Black religious mystic and spiritual guide." Harris notes that Thurman mentored Martin Luther King, Jr., at Boston University, where King pursued his PhD. Harris cites Thurman's "enduring wisdom to speak to our need for authentic spirituality."

Thurman supplies the title of Harris's sermon. It is sampled from Thurman's 1980 Baccalaureate Address to Spelman College, "The Sound of the Genuine," where Thurman reminds the young ladies that there "is in you, something that waits and listens for the sound of the genuine in yourself. Nobody like you has ever been born." Thurman's spirit hovers over the homily as Harris confesses that he "stumbled upon him while doing graduate work at Vanderbilt University, a time when I was literally struggling with the complexities of life, and like many folk, void of knowing what should I do with the one life I have to live."

But, Harris doesn't simply quote Thurman; he enacts a Thurmanesque reading of the times and applies the master's philosophical approach to the contemporary moment. Harris highlights

Thurman's insistence on listening for signs of the authentic self that can only be heard when one ignores the siren calls of American success. Harris ponders aloud with his congregation how "to make life count...for a larger, purposeful narrative, something beyond what one might materially gain or possess." He argues that his listeners must use the "tools of the spirit that can help all of us stay on the track of authenticity and integrity of life." That message resonated in an audience of young folk perhaps hearing for the first time about a significant thinker on a Sunday dedicated to college graduates and others climbing the academic ladder.

In his 1993 book, *Ministry for Social Crisis: Theology and Praxis in the Black Church Tradition*,[1] Harris links Black Liberation Theology and the Black church in advocating an effective politic and a fruitful practical theology. Black theology is back on the agenda of the Black church as it seeks to give a theological and holistic ministry response to current social crises. Black church leaders and theologians are looking for a revival of dialogue among them that will help close the gap between Black theology and the ministry of Black churches. There is increased awareness that issues of Black poverty, unemployment, and political alienation are not separate matters from the theological concerns of the church.[2]

Harris's practical theology blends a Black theological worldview with the historic legacy of freedom fighting that marks the Black church at its best. Harris is concerned that the "objectives of the Black liberation theology have had relatively limited influence upon Black clergy and their congregations."[3] Harris argued that because "members of Black churches have little or no knowledge of Black liberation theology, they are not benefitting from its critical reflection on the nature and purpose of the Black church's social mission."[4] Although penned more than 30 years ago, that concern is just as true today.

Harris's heroic engagement with Black suffering and struggle bolsters his practical theology. In his 2023 essay, "Self-Amending Blackness and The Movement for Black Lives: Justice and Leadership in Liberatory Spaces,"[5] Harris offers nuance and depth to the interpretation of Black liberation traditions. He locates Black Lives Matter within a "self-amending" Blackness that insists on an ever-evolving transformation of Black identity.

This self-amending Blackness ranges from the struggle for equality for sanitation workers in the sixties to the affirmation of women and LGBTQIA folk in our own day. Harris's views the push for Black self-amendment, or a flexible, fluid, improvised Blackness, as a product of Black theology's interactions with Black womanism, Black religion, Black humanism and Black jeremiads. Harris's progressive view of gender motivates him to echo Black Lives Matter in centering Black female bodies in accounts of Black social resistance. Lamenting the relative anonymity of Black women who have waged warfare against racial oppression, Harris celebrates the courageous Black women who have helped shape the lives of Black folk.

From the anti-lynching journalism of Ida B. Wells, the "Ain't I A Woman" jeremiad of Sojourner Truth, the political activism of Fannie Lou Hamer, Barbara Jordan and Shirley Chisholm, [the] visionary organizing of Ella Baker and legal activism of Pauli Murray, [the] literary ethics of Alice Walker and Toni Morrison, civil rights icons Rosa Parks and Diane Nash to the Black feminist political leadership of BLM co-founders Patrisse Cullors, Alicia Garza, and Opal Tometi [these women all] are collective liberators of Blackness. As Black women, they embody the racial terror, the pain of executed children, husbands, and relatives. Their cry is symbolic of the genocidal pain of eighth-century Hebrew mothers for their children.[6]

Harris's practical theology endorses a just gender ethic at its core. Harris's practical theology has merged beautifully with his homiletical prophecy, a prophetic vision of justice that flows primarily from the pulpit and in public proclamation, and in his poignant essays. Harris's homiletical prophecy rests on a theological foundation and a philosophical premise that promotes three goals: to challenge patriarchy, sexism and homophobia in Black religious circles, to celebrate an emancipatory conception of Black

human agency, and to embrace a variety of religious experience in
its improvisational self-amending Blackness.

Harris's homiletical prophecy flows on both page and stage. In
"Self-Amending Blackness and The Movement for Black Lives,"
Harris writes about "the racist rhetoric and interlocking oppressive
systems of white supremacy aimed at dehumanizing Blackness" as
he theorizes how to "stitch love to liberation, Blackness to justice."[7]
In a 2021 talkback after a sermon at First Baptist Church of
Huntsville, Alabama, Harris lays bare the existential dilemmas his
homiletical prophecy addresses, especially the quest for a just self-
recognition and a healthy vision of Black self-worth in a society
that offers neither freely.

Harris says we can glimpse this quest in the struggles of a
prominent politician. "We are still trying to prove our worth to the
white world," Harris let on. "This is Kamala Harris's challenge…as
Vice President of the United States. And her edges get shown
around how she handles that." Forrest Harris seeks to counter the
dehumanizing force of white supremacy with what he terms "ontological dignity."

"As I said to my student," he recalls, "you can go as deep as
you can go until you can't go no more – that ontological… depth,
is your being." Harris argues that once that depth has been
plumbed, one might hear the voice of the Almighty. That is note-
worthy: Harris is arguing that the Black self is the warehouse for
the divine; he offers an implicit justification for the holiness of the
oppressed body while delivering an explicit rebuke to the white supremacist dehumanization of the Black body. In Harris's view,
there is at once a prophetic protection of the Black self-image and
support for a vital sense of destiny and a deep meaning of life.
"And once you get there, you'll hear the voice of God – your ontological sense of self. That rugged, ontological depth, and then you
have discernment about what's right for your life."

In "Transitions of Hope," a 2024 sermon he delivered at First
Baptist Church, Capitol Hill, in Nashville, Harris argued that life's
"greatest or most significant transition or challenge is to be a part

of something larger than yourself, holding on to what truly matters no matter what transition you're in."

Harris's homiletical prophecy has brilliantly targeted the vicious undercurrent of white supremacy, both at home in America and abroad, globally. In his 2015 essay "Pursuing American Racial Justice and a Politically and Theologically Informed Black Church Praxis,"[8] Harris tracks the run of racism in the United States and more broadly in North America. "Racism in the United States has reached outrageous levels of institutionalized hegemony that warrant serious investigation of its widespread impact on racial and gender identities at all levels of American life," Harris wrote. "Racism in North America has historical antecedents normalized in the political currency of race, class, and gender and in various modes of social arrangements of power."[9]

Harris pulled from theology, postcolonial theory, and race theory to make his case for "a revision of the Black church under a new ecclesial paradigm of theological and political literacy." Harris acknowledged the problems in fostering such a new paradigm – "the nature of imperialism in the globalization of racism, Western capitalism in sync with ecclesiology, and theology associated with North American Christianity" on one front, and on the other front, a "culture of privatization and public morality in American life, where matters of racial and gender justice are increasingly subject to the politics of denial." Harris argued that "the old colonial legacies of theological insight must be abandoned for new theological literacy that not only advocates for an egalitarian democracy, but substantively shifts the pedagogical aims and logic of North American Christianity and theology."[10]

Harris's courageous wrestling with the institutions and systems that pervade American Christianity and erode its ethical energy – undercut its moral power – is inspired by his homiletical prophecy. Harris has wielded a theology of justice and a philosophy of antiracist practice to argue the divine value of a Blackness that has been relentlessly degraded in the machinery of white supremacy, colonial captivity and gender oppression. His bold reimagining of Black church life with a new paradigm of theological and political literacy is a progressive dive into the deep waters of racial justice and radical democracy.

Harris's ecclesial revision, a central feature of his homiletical prophecy, has also urged the partnering of Black and Womanist Theologies. In his 2010 essay, "The Children Have Come to Birth: A Theological Response for Survival and Quality of Life,"[11] Harris argues that Black and Womanist theologians, "and the communities for whom they write are part of a prophetic dream and tradition that believes no place, or no time is beyond the reach of Divine presence, love, justice and power." Harris argues in an extended and powerful metaphor of birth for his feeling of a "communal pain for a new world to be born that changes the reality of a generation of Black and brown children whose reality today, as evidenced by disturbing systemic failures and global social crisis, is dying in the womb of human possibilities."[12]

His poetic prophesy argues that the quest for liberation must not overlook "the Black churches' historic role in the survival and quality of life for Black existence in America."

And yet, for Harris, the challenge remains of channeling "theological resources to nurture communal commitment in and beyond the Black church for the liberation of the Black poor." Harris argues that Black and Womanist theologies must reconnect Black churches to the forces of liberation and cultural heritage that birthed them even as they bring forth new forms of civic imagination and ideological and theological unity. If we are to make progress, Harris argues that the Black church must embrace rigorous self-criticism, writing that "racism in its many forms, classism and poverty, sexism and homophobia remain as the last leg of the Black struggle for holistic liberation."[13]

Harris wasn't merely speaking in theory. The year after the Vanderbilt University Divinity School professor's essay was published, Harris, who doubles as longtime president of American Baptist College (ABC) in Nashville, confronted the ugly specter of virulent homophobia in the Black church. In 2015 Harris invited a prominent clergywoman, Yvette A. Flunder, who happens to be a married, lesbian bishop, to speak at ABC about her work advocating for the rights of people who suffer from HIV and AIDS.

The National Baptist Fellowship of Concerned Pastors, who are affiliated with the National Baptist Convention, USA, Inc., the largest Black religious group in the nation, vehemently opposed her appearance. "For a Baptist college president to invite a lesbian bishop legally married to a woman, to be a guest speaker and worship leader on a Baptist college campus is irresponsible, scandalous, non-biblical, and certainly displeasing to God," the group proclaimed in a press release. They asked Harris to rescind Flunder's invitation, and if not, to move the event from ABC facilities. Dwight McKissick and Randy Vaughn, who coordinated the group of conservative pastors, claimed that Harris was a heretic who "trampled on the beliefs of the school's founders."[14]

Harris had merely upheld the principled homiletical prophecy he had been preaching and writing for more than 35 years. "It's sad that people use religion and idolatry of the Bible to demoralize same-gender-loving people," Harris maintained. "When people say (the Bible) is synonymous with God and the truth, [that's Biblical idolatry]. We can't be guided and dictated by a first-century world view."[15] Harris was deeply committed to a revision of the Black church that valued the humanity of each member and respected their worth as agents of their own destiny. He clearly believed that liberty and prophecy begin at home.

Harris was able to meet the preachers on their own turf because he had never surrendered the homiletical terrain despite being a distinguished professor and college president. He was able to code-switch and profession-flip, pivoting from pulpit to lecture podium with great ease. And his considerable verbal arsenal featured refined and sophisticated scholarly language and the rhetoric of the ordinary Black person. He is a past master of erudite and sometimes esoteric verbal displays while effortlessly receding into the chambers of gutbucket grammar and grassroots hermeneutics. We heard a bit of this when he was speaking in the talk back in

Alabama and spoke of going as "deep as you can go until you can't go no more."

In a telling, and defining, anecdote, Harris relays, perhaps, the origin of his brilliant verbal dexterity, his genius at toggling between learned language and homespun wisdom. Harris says his grandmother "taught me something one summer when I got back from college." A fly had landed on the milk she was churning.

"Grandma Charity, there's a fly in the milk," Harris insisted.

"There's no fly in this milk," she retorted.

"Grandma, there it is right there. There's a fly in the milk."

She chewed tobacco and spit it out. Harris says she saw how full of it he was.

"I told you boy, there's no fly in the milk."

She took a little cup, dipped it down just an inch, and got the fly that was on the milk and threw it out.

"The fly was *on* the milk, but it wasn't *in* the milk," Harris confessed. "Showed me how smart I was."

Harris has told this story time and again, reinforcing the value of folk wisdom and everyday rhetoric. It is not quite the literary art of using skepticism to expose hidden meanings in the hermeneutics of suspicion, as much as it is a hermeneutics of audition, of hearing the truth and gleaning wisdom in the idiom of the ordinary tongue.

Harris repeated the story in his sermon to the graduates in Charlotte. The function of grassroots hermeneutics is to render the complicated lucid, the complex plain, the dense clear. It is in such a story that Harris's practical theology, homiletical prophecy, and grassroots hermeneutics are knit together in a seamless narrative and flow.

"What I'm trying to say to you graduates…there is the mystery of the ingredients *in* the milk that God is trying to get you to listen to."

Harris encouraged his young charges to churn their own milk, their own lives, until they discovered what was inside of them. And when they did, they would discover that the milk would become the ingredients of their very souls.

"It's not outside of you, its inside of you."

"I don't know...what form it will take. It may take the form of a new planetary consciousness that you have a sense of the world's suffering." In whatever form it came, it would somehow be the sound of the genuine calling them.

"Thank God our ancestors have heard it.

Thank God Martin heard it.

Thank God Charles Drew heard it.

Thank God Fannie Lou Hamer heard it.

Thank God Mary McLeod Bethune heard it."

And thank God that Forrest E. Harris heard it too.

Appendix A

Eulogy for Representative John Lewis

James M. Lawson Jr.

Statement of Introduction

In his eulogy honoring the life of Representative John Lewis, Rev. James Lawson reminds us that the struggle for justice is not over and that the path, the spiritual path, requires determination and commitment. If we are paying attention, we will notice that the struggle for justice is not a struggle for individual rights and desires, but a very existential struggle for humankind by resisting and dismantling the structures that inflict economic deprivation, violence, racial inequities, heterosexism, gendered biases, and soul-shattering trauma.

Rev. Lawson invites us to notice that John Lewis began this work when he noticed, and because he experienced, the cruelty of Jim Crowism that shaped daily life in Alabama. He noticed and vowed to resist it and dismantle it. He was given this opportunity when Rev. Kelly Miller Smith invited him to a workshop with Rev. Lawson. Lawson understood that the Nashville Movement would be a student movement and set out to teach nonviolent, direct-action strategies. He also embodied the philosophical roots of these strategies as a way of life. The power of nonviolence is the force it carries; it is a nonaggressive force that disrupts the everyday violent practices of social injustice. The power of nonviolence is the way it reverberates between the societal, self, and relational: as it disrupts and dismantles oppressive structures, it forms practitioners by expanding their hearts, infusing their encounters with love, and inviting us all to be transformed away from the seduction of violence to become a beloved community.

We are still fighting for this beloved community in the United States and globally. We are on the cusp of either imploding and destroying the Earth or truly committing to a world made beautiful by a turn to deep justice and abiding love. Rev. Lawson, in this eulogy for John Lewis and by his own life, calls us to be driven by a courageous and unrelenting pursuit of justice.

Phillis Isabella Sheppard, Ph.D.
E. Rhodes and Leona B. Carpenter Chair
Professor of Religion, Psychology,
and Culture and Womanist Thought
Executive Director of the James Lawson
Institute for the Research and
Study of Nonviolent Movements
Vanderbilt University

Eulogy for John Lewis

Pastor, sisters, and brothers, members of this Lewis family that so wonderfully nurtured John in love, hope, courage faith, and the rest of it.

Czesław Miłosz, a Polish Catholic poet sets the tone, at least in part for me as John Lewis has journeyed from the eternity of this extraordinary, mysterious human race into the eternity that none of us know very much about when he wrote this poem called "Meaning."

> When I die, I will see the lining of the world.
> The other side beyond bird, mountain, sunset.
> The true meaning ready to be decoded.
> What never added up will add Up.
> What was incomprehensible will become comprehended.
> —And if there is no lining to the world?
> If a thrush on a branch is not a sign,
> But just a thrush on a branch, if night and day

227

Make no sense following each other?
And on this earth, there is nothing except this earth?
—Even if that is so, there will remain
A word awakened by the lips that perish,
A tireless messenger who runs and runs
Through interstellar places, through revolving galaxies,
And calls out, protests, screams.

And I submit that John and that other, the eternity will be heard by us again and again running through the galaxies, still proclaiming that we, the people of the USA can one day live up to the full meaning of we hold these truths live up to the full meaning we the people of the USA in order to perfect a more perfect union.

John Lewis practiced not the politics that we call bipartisan. John Lewis practiced the politics that we, the people of the US, need more desperately than ever before: the politics of the Declaration of Independence, the politics of the preamble to the Constitution of the United States. I've read many of the so-called Civil Rights books of the last 50 or 60 years about the period between 1953 and 1973. Most of the books are wrong about John Lewis. Most of the books are wrong about how John got engaged in the national campaign of 1959–60. This is the sixtieth year of the sit-in campaign, which swept into every state of the Union, largely manned by students because we recruited students. But put upon the map that the nonviolent struggle begun in Montgomery, Alabama, was not an accident, but as Martin King Jr. called it "Christian Love has power that we have never tapped. And if we use it, we can transform not only our own lives, but we will transform the earth in which we live."

I count it providential that as I moved to Nashville, Tennessee, dropping out of graduate school in Nashville came people like Kelly Miller Smith and Andrew White and JohnEtta Hayes and Helen Roberts and Delores Wilkerson and John Lewis, Diane Nash, CT Vivian, Marion Barry, Jim Bevel, Bernard Lafayette,

Pauline Knight, Angela Butler, how all of us gathered in 1958 and '59 and '60 and '61 and '62 in the same city at the same time. I count as being providential. We did not plan it. We were all led there. And when Kelly Miller Smith and the Nashville Christian Leadership Council met in the fall of 1958, we determined that if there's to be a second major campaign that will demonstrate the efficacy of *satyagraha*, of soul-force, of love-truth, that we would have to do it in Nashville. And so, I planned as the strategist and organizer, a four-point Gandhian strategic program to create the campaign. We decided, with great fear and anticipation, that we would desegregate downtown Nashville. No group of Black people or other people anywhere in the United States in the twentieth century against the rapaciousness of a segregated system, ever thought about desegregating downtown, tearing down the signs, renovating the waiting rooms, taking the immoral signs off of or off of drinking fountains.

But it was Black women who made that decision for us in Nashville. I was scared to death when we made that decision. I knew nothing about how we were going to do this. I had never done it before, but we planned the strategy. John Lewis did not stumble in on that campaign. Kelly Miller Smith, his teacher at ABC (American Baptist College), invited John to join the workshops in the fall of 1959 as we prepared ourselves to face violence and to do direct action and to put on the map the issue that the racism and the segregation of the nation had to end. And so, on the sixtieth anniversary of that sit-in campaign, which became the second major campaign of the Nonviolent Movement of America, those are not my words, John Lewis called what we did between 1953 and 1973, the nonviolent movement of America, not the CRM. I think we need to get the story straight because words are powerful. History must be written in such a fashion that it lifts up truly the spirit of the John Lewises of the world. And that's why I've chosen just to say a few words about it.

Kelly Miller Smith invited John Lewis. I met a Fisk student who told me about a student from Chicago who wanted to do

229

something about those vicious signs. I said, "Invite Diane Nash to the workshop in September because we're going to do something about those signs." I pushed this hard now. John Lewis had no choice in the matter. You should understand that because all the stories we've heard this morning of John becoming a preacher, preaching to the chickens, and other sorts of things becoming ordained as a Baptist minister, something else was happening to John. In those early years, John saw the malignancy of racism in Troy, Alabama. There formed in him a sensibility that he had to do something about it. He did not know what that was, but he was convinced that he was, indeed, called to do whatever he could do, get in good trouble, but stop the horror that so many folks lived through in this country in that part of the twentieth century.

John was not alone. Martin King had the same experience as a boy. I had the same experience from age four in the streets of Massillon, Ohio. Matthew McCullum, a pastor whose name you don't know, in South Carolina, had the same experience. CT Vivian had the same experience. I maintain that many of us had no choice to do, but we tried to do, primarily, because, at an early age, we recognized the wrong under which we were forced to live. And we swore to God that by God's grace, we would do whatever God called us to do in order to put on the table of the nation's agenda. This must end. Black lives matter.

And so, between 1953 and 1973, we had major campaigns year after year, thousands of demonstrations across the nation that supported it. We had folks in Congress, folks in the White House, and folks scattered across the United States who were beginning to formulate what the solutions are for change. The media makes a mistake when John is seen only in relationship to the Voting Rights Bill of 1965. However important that is, you must remember that in the sixties, Lyndon Johnson and the Congress of the United States passed the most advanced legislation on behalf of "we, the people" of the United States, that was ever passed. Head Start. Billions of dollars for housing. We would not be in the struggle we are today in housing if President Reagan hadn't cut those billions of dollars for housing. Where local churches and local nonprofits could build affordable housing in their own communities being sustained as financed by loans from the federal government. We passed Medicare.

We passed anti-poverty programs. Civil Rights Bill of 1964 and 1965, Voting Rights Bill, a whole array. John Lewis must be represented and must be understood as one of the leaders of the greatest advance of Congress and the White House. On behalf of "we, the people" of the USA. We do not need bipartisan politics if we're going to celebrate the life of John Lewis, we need the Constitution to come alive. We hold these truths to be self-evident. We need the Congress and the presidents to work unfalteringly on behalf of every boy and every girl so that every baby born under these shores will have access to the Tree of Life. That's the only way to honor John Robert Lewis. No other way.

Let all of us in this service today, let all the people of the USA determine that we will not be quiet. As long as any child dies in the first year of life in the United States, we will not be quiet. As long as the largest poverty group in our nation are women and children, we will not be quiet. As long as our nation continues to be the most violent culture in the history of humankind, we will not be quiet. As long as our economy is shaped, not by freedom, but by plantation capitalism that continues to cause domination and control rather than access and liberty in equality for all. The forces of spiritual wickedness are strong in our land; because of our history, we have not created them. John Lewis did not create them. We inherited them. But it's our task to see those spiritual forces. I've named them: Racism, sexism, violence, plantation capitalism. Those poisons still dominate far too many of us in many different ways. John's life was a singular journey from birth through the campaigns in the South and through Congress to get us to see that these forces of wickedness must be resisted.

Do not let our own hearts drink any of that poison. Instead, drink the truth of the life force. If we would honor and celebrate John Lewis's life, let us then recommit our souls, our minds, our hearts, our bodies, our strength to the continuing journey to dismantle the wrong in our midst and to allow a space for the new earth and new heaven to emerge.

I close with this poem from Langston Hughes, which is a kind of a sign and symbol of what John Lewis represents and what we too can represent in our continuing journey.

> I dream a world where no [human]
> No other [human] will scorn,
> Where love will bless the earth
> And peace its path adorned
> I dream a world where all
> Will know sweet freedom's way
> Where greed no longer saps the soul
> Nor avarice blights our day.
> A world I dream where black or white,
> [And yellow, and blue and green, and red and brown,]
> Whatever race you be,
> Will share the bounties of the earth
> And every [woman and] man [and boy and girl] is free,
> Where wretchedness will hang its head
> And joy, like a pearl,
> Attends the need of all humankind—
> Of such I dream, my world!

Of such a world I dream, celebrate life, dream, and labor for an Atlanta and Los Angeles and the United States, and a world that is to celebrate the spirit and the heart, and the mind and soul of John Lewis, and to walk with him through the galaxies seeking equality, liberty, justice in the beloved community.

Appendix B

"Worship that God Hates"

Julius Scruggs

This sermon, titled "The Worship that God Hates," is a powerful reminder of the prophetic leadership tradition in Black Christian theology. It was delivered at the 2009 annual session of the National Baptist Convention, USA, Inc. in Atlanta, Georgia by the Reverend Dr. Julius R. Scruggs, president of the Convention. The sermon emphasizes the disconnect between genuine worship and societal injustices like economic inequality that affect marginalized communities. Using scripture, Reverend Scruggs highlights the biblical mandate for justice and equity and emphasizes God's displeasure with worship that neglects the call to care for the oppressed and vulnerable.

Drawing upon the rich legacy of leaders like Martin Luther King Jr. and the civil rights movement, Reverend Scruggs underscores the imperative for Christians to actively engage in dismantling systems of oppression, particularly those perpetuating economic injustice. By challenging congregants to examine their worship practices considering societal realities, this sermon empowers Black Christian believers to become agents of change and advocates for economic equity in their communities.

Furthermore, given Reverend Scruggs's position as President of the National Baptist Convention, USA, Inc., his sermon carries significant weight and influence within the broader Black Christian community. Through his leadership and platform, Reverend Scruggs catalyzes a renewed commitment to the prophetic tradition of advocating for economic justice, inspiring congregations nationwide to embody worship that aligns with God's heart for justice and righteousness.

The sermon address focuses on the book of Amos in the Bible. Scruggs references specific verses that talk about God's disdain for insincere worship and emphasizes the importance of genuine justice and righteousness. Scruggs points out that God detested the worship of his people because it was not rooted in real justice and righteousness. The worshipers were exploitative and unjust, taking advantage of the poor and needy while publicly claiming to worship God. Scruggs draws parallels between the injustices in the time of Amos and modern economic issues, such as the housing crisis and unethical banking practices. He highlights the need for leaders and individuals to adopt a more selfless and responsible approach to economic matters, citing Warren Buffet's philanthropic efforts as an example.

Economic justice is a critical concern for Black people and Black Christianity due to historical and contemporary systemic inequalities that have disproportionately affected Black communities. These disparities have roots in centuries of slavery, segregation, discrimination, and economic exploitation, which have resulted in persistent poverty, limited access to resources, and unequal opportunities for economic advancement.

For Black Christianity, the connection between economic justice and God's justice is deeply rooted in biblical teachings and the prophetic tradition. Throughout the Old and New Testaments, numerous passages emphasize God's concern for the poor, marginalized, and oppressed. For instance, in Isaiah 1:17, believers are called to "seek justice, correct oppression; bring justice to the fatherless, plead the widow's cause." Similarly, Jesus' ministry prioritized uplifting the marginalized and challenging systems of injustice, as seen in his teachings on caring for the least of these (Matthew 25:31-46) and his actions of overturning tables in the temple (Matthew 21:12-13).

Economic justice is intricately tied to God's justice because it reflects the equitable distribution of resources and opportunities, ensuring that all individuals have the means to thrive and fulfill their God-given potential. When economic systems perpetuate inequality and marginalization, they stand in opposition to God's vision of a just and compassionate society.

Moreover, faith and Christian practice compel believers to embody the principles of economic justice in their actions and advocacy. The Apostle James emphasizes the importance of not showing favoritism to the wealthy while neglecting the poor (James 2:1-9), highlighting the inherent contradiction between faith and economic injustice. True Christian practice entails actively working towards the transformation of unjust systems and advocating for policies that promote economic equity, access to education, fair wages, affordable housing, and healthcare for all.

Economic justice is not only a concern for Black people and Black Christianity but a fundamental aspect of living out the principles of God's justice, faith, and Christian practice. It requires a commitment to challenging systemic injustices, addressing disparities, and advocating for policies that promote human flourishing and dignity for all individuals, particularly those who have been historically marginalized and oppressed. The Presidential Address of Rev. Dr. Julius Scruggs is an example of the prophetic proclamation of the Black Leadership Tradition in America. He highlights American Christianity's hypocrisy of worshipping God who demands justice but denies justice to flow. The Reverend Dr. Julius Scruggs passed away May 8, 2024.

The Worship that God Hates

I often draw inspiration from the book of Amos, particularly chapter five, verses 21, 23, and 24. In this passage, the prophet expresses God's disdain for his people's worship and gatherings. Despite the expectation that God would appreciate such acts of devotion, the book of Amos reveals that he detested their worship. Why? Because it lacked true justice and righteousness. Their public displays of worship did not align with their private actions, as they exploited the poor and needy.

God sent Amos to deliver this message, standing outside the king's palace in Bethel and proclaiming, "Let justice roll down like waters and righteousness like an ever-flowing stream." This call for justice was a response to the people's lack of economic fairness and righteousness. Amos accused the Israelites of selling the righteous for silver and exploiting the needy for minimal gains. This exploitation extended to their business practices, as the wealthy took advantage of the vulnerable during commercial transactions.

Listen to what Amos says in chapter eight verses four through six. "Hear this, you who trample upon the needed and bring the poor of the land to an end saying, when will the new moon be over that we may sell grain and the Sabbath that we may offer wheat for sale, that we may make the EFA small and the shekel great and deal deceitfully with false scales and sell the spoil of the wheat." These rich people in Israel were so economically corrupt that they were at worship meditating not on the goodness of God but meditating on how they could cheat the poor. They were thinking not how I could help but how I could wound. They were thinking; how can I decrease the amount of wheat while increasing the price of wheat?

How can I tip with the scales so that they would weigh the wheat in my favor, they were thinking, how can I sell the spoiled wheat sometimes called the shaft, the stuff you throw away? These folk were in worship not thinking about God and helping people, but they were thinking about how to cheat people and make a profit. Their minds were on the mighty dollar, the greedy were eating the lunch of the needy. When Amos, the Prophet saw God's people conducting themselves in such unethical and immoral ways he could not but help cry out, "let justice, economic justice, roll down like waters and righteousness like an ever-flowing stream."

Like Amos's Day, our day knows about the waters of economic justice being clogged, tampered with, and manipulated. We see it in the housing crisis. It was the greed of big bankers, mortgage companies, and mortgage managers, which has led to more homes being foreclosed than we have ever seen in our lifetime. In July 2009, the American people were informed that Countrywide Mortgage Company made a cut-rate loan to congresspersons and their staff while foreclosing mortgages on other people and small businesses. No wonder some Congresspersons voted against regulating the banking industry.

Additionally, unwise bankers have made risky and toxic loans, causing their banks to lose billions of dollars at the taxpayers' expense. This near failure of financial institutions almost led the country and others into depression. Yet, they try to blame President Barack Obama for the nation's economic hardships. It is due to their unbridled greed. These individuals have prioritized profit over people, which is both unethical and ungodly. From an economic standpoint, what we need are more leaders and individuals with unselfish spirits, like Warren Buffett. Mr. Warren Buffett generously donated $30 billion to the Bill and Melinda Gates Foundation to assist the needy, disenfranchised, and underprivileged, both domestically and internationally. Moreover, Mr. Buffett called a meeting of fellow billionaires a few months ago, urging them to consider the proposition of leaving half of their wealth for charitable and beneficial causes. This stands as a display of economic responsibility and accountability. We require more individuals like Warren Buffett. We need modern prophets and preachers to continue reminding America and other nations of the importance of economic accountability. We must strive for a level of the economic playing field, with equal access to opportunity in our schools and workforce. The soul-stirring lyrics of James Brown ring true when he sang years ago, "I do not need anybody to give me nothing. Just open the door, and I will get it from myself."

Moreover, it is just for everyone to pay their fair share of taxes. Governor Mitt Romney has been paying taxes in a bracket of 13 to 15%, while others have been paying taxes in a bracket of 20 to 30%. This is unfair and unjust. Once again, Mr. Warren Buffett addressed this inequity clearly, stating that it is not fair for his secretary to pay a higher tax rate than himself. He is a billionaire, not she. He suggested that he should be paying a higher tax rate than his secretary. Jesus said, "To whom much is given, much is required."

Let us consider that God detested the worship of his covenant people because it did not result in political justice. In Amos 5:12, Amos criticizes the judicial system by saying, "For I know how many your transgressions are and how great are your sins? You who afflict the righteous, take a bribe, and turn aside the needy at the gate." During that time, the gate was where the court was held. Amos stated that these elected judicial officials were not concerned with justice but were primarily profit oriented. They were manipulating the justice system to increase their wealth. Today, in certain places, our political actions do not result in fair and just behaviors. It is unfair and unethical for a Congress to block bills that could help the poor and middle class simply because they want to oppose an African American president. It is unfair and unethical for states to pass laws that aim to win elections by suppressing the voting rights of older Americans, minorities, and young people. This is diabolical. It is also unfair and unethical for congresspersons to have top-notch healthcare and then vote against affordable healthcare for others, especially the poor. In his 1961 inaugural address, President John F. Kennedy addressed this issue, saying, "If a free society cannot help the many who are poor, it cannot save the few who are rich."

Jesus spoke about it in a much better way. He emphasized the importance of feeding the hungry, clothing the naked, giving water to the thirsty, and welcoming strangers. Jesus was referring to those who are impoverished, those who have no water, food, clothing, or shelter. He advocated for affordable healthcare not only for the poor but for everyone. In our nation, we often discuss political justice eloquently but fail to put it into practice. We stand and recite the pledge of allegiance, but where is the justice for individuals like Trayvon Martin? Our political rhetoric often creates division. When figures like Sarah Palin and the Tea Party proclaim, "We must take our country back," whose country are they referring to?

238

Surely not the United States of America, a country that belongs to the Native Americans we refer to as Indians.

What is more, Sister Sarah Palin and the Tea Party need to be reminded that before they came, our ancestors were already here. Our ancestors helped build this nation with their sweat, tears, blood, and lives. They made cotton king in the South and never received fair compensation for their work. This is our country too. Haven't we blessed this nation? Have we not given this nation authentic music and creative dance? Have we not given this nation athletes and astronauts? Have we not given this nation doctors and nurses, statesmen and politicians, scientists and engineers, lawyers and judges, preachers, prophets, and a precedent? This is our country too, for people of all races. We should all respect our president. It is disrespectful, inconsiderate, and unethical to shake your finger in the president's face. We must remain vigilant and keep an eye on those who control economic and political justice.

Amos criticized the covenant people for their lack of economic and political justice despite their religious posture. He emphasized that God detested their worship because it did not prioritize spiritual justice and righteousness. In strong language, he conveyed God's displeasure with their feast days and solemn assemblies, indicating that their acts of worship held no meaning if justice and righteousness were not upheld.

Through Amos, God said to Israel, "I hate your worship" because it is a sham, it is phony, it is superficial, it is hollow. It is sick. When your religion is sick, the rest of your life is sick. Also, when your religion is sick, your politics is sick. When your religion is sick, your economics is sick. When your religion is sick, your social relations are sick. Israel's religion was sick because her heart was not in it. She was going through the motions. She had substituted ritual for righteousness, ceremony for conduct, rhetoric for reality, talk for the walk, hollowness for holiness, shallowness for substance, and showtime for sincerity. And so, Amos shouted. Listen to Israel. God said, take off your facades. Put away your phoniness. Pull off the veils of superficiality and let God's waters of justice flow. Let them flow everywhere to everyone. I joined Amos today and I say too, let them flow everywhere to everyone.

"Let them flow. Until every child in America and any other nation in the world, will have a nutritious meal for their stomach and a good education for their head. Let them flow until every child has sufficient clothes for their bodies and shoes to put on their feet, let them flow until everybody has a decent roof over their heads. Let them flow. Until everybody has affordable healthcare for their wellbeing. Let them flow until everyone has an opportunity to have a good religion for their lives and their souls. Let the water of justice flow until racism, classism, and sexism have been washed into complete obliteration. Let the waters of justice flow everywhere to everyone. Let them flow from the snow-covered plains of Maine to the sunny beaches of Florida. Let them flow from the lofty Adirondacks of New York to the rich deltas in Mississippi.

Let them flow from the blue lakes of the Midwest to the citrus fields of California. Let them flow from the ice lands of Alaska to the surge and surf waves of Hawaii. Let them flow from sea to shining sea and from continent to continent. Let them flow until the prophet's vision comes to fruition. Let them flow. Until every valley is exalted and every mountain brought low; crooked places made straight, and the rough places made smooth. Let them flow until the Glory of the Lord shall be revealed and all flesh shall see it. Let the waters flow until God's Glory is revealed to all flesh and when God's glory is revealed to all flesh, you are going to see Glory everywhere. When you turn to your left, you walk in the Glory. When you turn to your right, you will encounter thick Glory. When you go forward, it is Glory and when you back up, it is Glory. When you look up, it is Glory and when you look down, it is Glory. When God's Glory gets thick like that, what do you do? There is only one thing to do: just start shouting. Glory. Glory, Hallelujah."

Appendix C

Social Justice and the Black Church: Reframing Justice for Equity and Equality

Forrest E. Harris

"We must remember that liberation is costly. It needs unity. We must hold hands and refuse to be divided. We must be ready. Some of us will not see the day of liberation physically. But those people will have contributed to the struggle. Let us be united, let us be filled with hope, and let us be those who respect one another."[1]

—Desmond Tutu

"I dream of a church that welcomes the poor and combines prayer with social and political action to eliminate poverty.... I dream of a church where inclusive language about God is not considered too much to ask. I pray that others who share this dream will work together to make it a reality."[2]

—Annie Powell

"The American crisis, which is part of a global, historical crisis, [is not] likely to resolve itself soon. An old world is dying, and a new one, kicking in the belly of its mother, time, announces that it is ready to be born. This birth will not be easy; many of us are doomed to discover that we are exceedingly clumsy midwives. No matter, so long as we accept that our responsibility is to the newborn: accepting responsibility is the key to the necessarily evolving skill."[3]

—James Baldwin

I watched the historic election of November 4, 2008, on television with colleagues and friends at my neighbor's home. The highest euphoria I have ever experienced filled the room with overwhelming joy and shock that an African American had been elected by an electoral college landslide to the presidency of the United States of America. We were caught up in the historical belief that "the American crisis" of racial justice and equality would not likely yield this surprising result in our lifetime. We all felt a new era of change had been born. The mythic invocation Martin Luther King Jr. spoke to a crowd in Memphis, Tennessee, at Mason Temple just hours before his murder came to mind in the hours of this new social birth: "I just want to do God's will. And He's allowed me to go up to the mountain. And I've looked over. And I've seen the Promised Land. And I may not get there with you. But I want you to know tonight that we as a people will get to the Promised Land."[4]

This historic election was an eleventh-hour birth, "an old world is dying, and a new one is ready to be born" amidst a morass of racial identity politics and unprecedented systemic economic failures coupled with the moral crisis of two debilitating wars in Iraq and Afghanistan. Now, after delivering Obama's presidency, America's political institutions, Democrat and Republican parties, liberal and conservative religious ideologies, the public media, and church ecclesial bodies remain "exceedingly clumsy midwives" in the process of justice, equity, and equality for all the nation's citizens.

Historical memory will not let us forget the natal crisis through which this new era was born and has come to be. "Justice and liberation have been and remain costly."[5] The murders of civil rights workers in the South, the brutal violence freedom riders endured, and the many incarcerations and murders of ebony prophets are "dark symbols and obscure signs," reminding us of the greater cost of justice in America for people of color. We are now aware of the greater cost of justice. Eddie Glaude explains the battle that needs to be waged now "is a battle not only over the symbolic construction of America but political and economic as well...the larger view of the new Canaan" of human rights, justice, peace, and liberty for all Americans.

Whether it will ever be understood and appreciated by this nation, for some twenty years, a South Side Chicago prophetic Black church served as an incubator for the faith and represented the theological crystallization of justice and sociopolitical consciousness for Barack Obama. The understanding that a union between faith and freedom tempers prophetic radicalism, particularly when injustice stands in the way of human flourishing, has been the nature and character of the Black church. This represents the prophetic genius and yeast of the Black church acting as "a social midwife" calling for what this nation has yet to grant to all her citizens: "equal and exact justice to all."

What has become clear is that traditional *civil rights* have been cast through a narrow interpretive prism, a focus on preventing injuries and injustices from recurring white supremacist practices of economic control that have widened racial disparities and the suffering of the poor. I agree with John D. Carlson's article "The Justice We Need" that we would be wise to use this hour "to think creatively about justice and politics" or see this moment, as ethicist scholar Victor Anderson understands, as an opportunity for "creative exchange that keeps life open to the event of beloved community."

I propose that America's continuing need to rectify racial injustices calls for the reframing of justice as participatory parity denied marginal and poor communities. This has gone unaddressed as some assumed that all citizens were equal before the law with equality of opportunity. Others assumed that the post-Obama optimism of a color-blind society would increase access to people of color to resources needed to participate on par with others would materialize. But the current crisis is a crisis of reframing justice, a defining of justice that not only disputes the *what* of justice but demands focus on the *who* of justice. Responsible advocacy for the *who* of justice calls for the construction and innovative deployment of concepts such as race, gender, sexuality, God, and the world to do the work of interpretation, criticism, and directing possibilities toward openness for justice in the social world of poverty, racism, and sexism as well as in the social spheres of difference.[6]

The "eleventh-hour crisis" to affirm a new moral order, a process of reframing justice that rectifies past injustices, and to reclaim a prophetic role of the Black church is what Vincent Harding calls "social midwifery" for the recreation of public policies that bring the quality of life and human flourishing for the existence of children, women, and men whose reality today, as evidenced by disturbing systemic failures, is dying in the womb of human possibilities. This is a kairos opportunity to rethink race, justice, and political assumptions. The hour calls for political reformulation and the reframing of justice for equity and equality.[7]

Also, there is a concern for active alliances between civic entities, the academy, the church, and Black and womanist theologians in dialogue with agencies of hope in the Black community toward the survival and quality of life, empowerment, and liberation of the poor. I can think of no more urgent agenda than building the civic capacity and unity necessary for birthing alternative realities that connect Black churches to the liberation tradition that birthed them on American soil. If Black churches are to be viable instruments of justice and liberation, I argue that the way forward is to encourage honest self-critique of public agencies, the community, the Black churches, as well as the theologies that undergird them. Annie Powell's dream of a church that welcomes the poor and combines prayer with social action to eliminate poverty is a dream of theological and ethical "social midwifery" for the sake of children whose future we do not wish to see replicate America's past.[8]

In response to the urgent need for reframing justice, a biblical reference from a scene of crisis in the life of ancient Judah lifts rather poignantly and painfully the crisis economically and politically oppressed people of color face relative to who they are now and the liberated communities they are straining to become. The reference is found in 2 Kings 19:3: "This is what Hezekiah says: This day is a day of trouble and blasphemy and disgrace, as when children come to the point of birth and there is no strength to deliver them."

A brief exegesis of this text suggests that during the reign of King Hezekiah, Judah was rendered powerless by the threat of the Assyrian Empire and was threatened with defeat and enslavement. The metaphor Hezekiah uses to describe Judah's predicament is that of a child ready to be born, but there is no strength to bring it forth. This story of crisis is a post-exodus and pre-exilic crisis in Judah's life. Judah was trapped between the ages—one age of oppression and servitude that should have been dead and the other age of a peaceful reign of faithfulness and justice that Judah was too weak to birth. The age that Hezekiah and Judah were powerless to birth was the glorious age spoken of in Second Isaiah: "Every valley shall be exalted, and every mountain and hill shall be made low, and the crooked shall be made straight, and the rough places plain, and the glory of the Lord shall be revealed, and all flesh shall see it together, for the mouth of the Lord hath spoken it" (Isaiah 40:4). It was to be an age of a free people serving the purpose and celebrating the presence of a liberating God of love and justice in the ancient world. But within Judah, the power to birth it is not found.

Metaphorically, this story of crisis gives us access to language from the ancient biblical world that enables us to explore dimensions of unimaginable and systemic human suffering as it relates to the poor today. At this juncture of existence in America, the poor are trapped between two worlds—one that oppresses, hurts, and cripples life and another world that represents hopes and aspirations for a liberated future. Cornel West notes that "the lived experience of coping with a life of horrifying meaninglessness, hopelessness, and most importantly lovelessness (nihilism)" robs the community of the strength to bring it forth.

Children of color are at the point of birth, ready and ripe to name a new era of justice and wholeness. But it seems the unending pathology of the intersecting factors of racism, sexism, and white supremacy in America, coupled with Black middle-class complicity with classism and the saturation of what Cornel West describes as market forces of individualism and prosperity, have rendered Black solidarity weak and without the strength to birth it into reality.[9] Ripe and ready to be born also are multi-forms of justice—gender justice, economic justice, political justice, and civic justice in a nation whose Declaration of Independence promised unhindered access to "life, liberty, and the pursuit of happiness" to all its citizens. Yet centuries and decades of failure after failure, this dream has been deferred, or we might say conspired against its birth. Not only has this hope and dream been deferred but also events in the aftermath of Hurricane Katrina and post-Obama-era racism inform us that these matters of justice and equality have existed on the cutting edge of a sabotage agenda.

I applaud the reformation of the alliance between the Black church and the NAACP as it represents the strength of the Black community. For the first time in more than fifty years, Black Baptist denominations—the National Baptist Convention, USA, Inc.; Progressive National Baptist Convention, Inc.; National Baptist Convention of America, Inc.; and the National Missionary Baptist Convention of America—came together in January 2005. They gathered with an acute sense of the need to birth new realities for the transformation of Black life. Missing from that meeting were a significant number of Black and womanist theologians, social scientists, economists, and political and health care professionals with whom the Black churches must be in dialogue to deal with the deepest crises that threaten the future of Black life in America, and tragically for people of color globally: the quality of health and health care, education, the overpopulation of Black people in the industrial prison complex, and the reversal of poverty trends among people of color. These social conditions are theological matters as much as they are political matters. They need the urgent attention of economic analysis, theological and ethical conception for transformative praxis, and the reframing of justice. We need to ask ourselves these questions as we move forward:

- What is the proper frame within which to consider first-order questions of justice?

- Who are the relevant subjects entitled to a just distribution?

- How much economic inequality and inequity does justice permit?

- How much redistribution is required and according to whose principle of distributive justice?

It is not only the substance of justice but also the frame that needs to be considered.

New sociocultural-political forms and resurgent powers of racism, sexism, and classism in the Black community make self-critique imperative for birthing alternatives for liberation. As pastor-scholar Carlyle Fielding Stewart argues, "prophetic ministry involves not only confronting injustice in society, but equally witnessing against those forces, powers, and principalities which stifle the church from within, thus thwarting the full emergence of [liberation] in the Black community."[10]

The Black churches' historic role in the survival and quality of life in America cannot be overlooked in any effort to achieve liberation for the Black poor today. As Allison Calhoun-Brown notes, Black churches have been "free spaces—environments in which people are free to challenge racial inequality as an oppositional civic culture."[11] The concern is not only to unmask the destructive forces of white supremacy upon people of color but also to provide theological critique of Black churches as they struggle against dying in the spiritless materialism of what Pablo Richard refers to as "savage forms capitalism."[12] The formidable challenge Black churches face is how to bridge what Dale P. Andrews describes as "Black folk religion and practical theology" with the liberation goals of civic justice and the moral agency of Black churches.[13] In other words, how is healing to occur in light of the immeasurable human suffering and trauma Blacks have seen from the Atlantic Slave Trade and Middle Passage to the worst mass suicide of Black life in Jonestown, Ghana, to the highest poverty rates in the Ninth Ward of New Orleans, high incarcerations rates of Black people in America's prisons to the global traumas of African genocide and starvation and the pandemic of HIV and AIDS across Africa and among Black people in America?[14] In light of the legacy of such trauma and suffering, what knowledge(s) do Black churches need to unmask the demonic in public life and enhance theological and political literacy among Black churches, empowering them to speak publicly and prophetically for social justice change? How do we build an ecumenical, multicultural, multiethnic, and multiracial movement for economic justice?

Indeed, "the children have come to the point of birth," ripe and ready to be born to a quality of life, health, economics, and education, but where in American religious, educational, and social institutions can the strength be found to bring this forth? What should our political and theological response be for delivery? What is our moral assignment in this crisis? How do we do this with theological integrity and collective communal and political wisdom?

I propose that we employ a three-dimensional strategy to reframe justice, incorporating the political dimension of representation alongside the economic dimension of distribution and the cultural dimension of recognition. The most general meaning of justice is parity of participation that addresses the effects of past injustices and patterns of political powerlessness. Theologically and ethically, justice requires social arrangements and the ordering of the right relationships that permit all to participate as peers in social life. Overcoming injustice means dismantling institutional obstacles that prevent people from participating on par with others as full partners in social interaction. People can be impeded from full participation by economic structures that deny them the resources they need to interact with others as peers. Poor people of color suffer from the legacy of distributive injustice or maldistribution. People are also prevented from interacting on terms of parity by institutionalized hierarchies of cultural value that deny them requisite standing in the light of suffering from the status of inequality or misrecognition. Nancy Fraser argues that neither recognition theory nor distribution theory alone can provide an adequate understanding of justice in American capitalist society. Only an understanding of justice that encompasses both distribution and recognition can supply the necessary frame for the social, moral, and philosophical complexity of justice for the human flourishing of all citizens.

I return to what Hezekiah did in the face of Judah's national crisis not as a comprehensive strategy as a way forward but as a starting point for the theological and civic renewal of the Black churches, particularly in the light of the new era of economic change now occurring in America. Justice is a political and theological matter. First, I turn to justice as a theological matter. The chronicler of the story says when Hezekiah heard the defiant threat and insult of the Assyrian king against Judah and Judah's God, he resorted to Israel's ancient ritual of lament. He tore his clothes, put on sackcloth, and went into the temple of the Lord. Hezekiah's spiritual posture here is clearly one of deep lament. A theology for birthing a liberating future for the next generation of children must begin with the capacity for communal lament or, as Archie Smith Jr. puts it, "communal lament that is a personal and personal lament that is communal."[15] As womanist theologian Emilie M. Townes notes, "Without lament and institutional repentance, liberation will not follow."[16] There is a growing tendency among the upward and mobile middle class in the Black church movement to be complicit with and even tolerate the disgrace of poverty. Lamenting poverty's effect on life is distant from the religious sensibilities and emotional and spiritual concerns of many in the new Black megachurch movement. I agree with Dale P. Andrews's analysis that we have grossly underestimated "the hegemonic powers of racism and capitalism and the destructive element of individualism upon Black religious life" and the resulting chasm between the Black poor and the middle class.[17] Today, churches are turning in vast numbers "to market spirituality and gospels of prosperity" to avoid the pain of the labor room that leads to new birth and social transformation. As Cornel West notes, "We see many people, and the churches they attend, become eager upwardly mobile aspirants in the nihilistic American game of power and might where there is hardly a mumbling world heard about social justice, resistance to institutional evil, or courage to confront the powers that be." The political demands of justice must be played out on the public policy and decision-making stage where struggles over distribution and recognition can be examined. In other words, we must establish criteria for justice, social belonging, determining who counts, and who will be included and excluded from circles of power to share in a just distribution and reciprocal recognition.

Long-standing patterns of poverty and injustice create long-term trauma and, in some cases, irreparable hurt that becomes an integral part of everyday life for the poor. But prophetic churches with pastoral compassion and care must be resolved to stay in the labor room until justice is born. Black churches need a theology for birthing children ready to be born in communities of justice and wholeness that save them from what Howard Thurman scholar Walter Fluker describes as "natal alienation, eternal namelessness, and invisibility." Unfortunately, the identification of liberation with the material success of a few who, in a post-Obama presidency, think we have achieved a post-racial America and who themselves have become physically and mentally severed from the suffering masses trivializes the political unity essential for responding to our current crisis.

Black churches must become places where the prophetic commitment to justice is made real in what people need physically, socially, and spiritually for the wholeness of life. They must be inclusive places of love where God calls people to deepen relationships and tolerance for turning toward one's neighbor with all that love requires—justice, peace, and inner and outer liberation in the world. Black churches must become birthing stations of liberation and justice, places where moral imagination nurtures prophetic action. The question of "responsibility to the newborn" reality in this nation is the question of whether there is a liberating spiritual presence among churches and agencies of hope willing to resist the anxiety and threats of conformity to America's idolatry of capitalism, individualism, materialism, and the lust for power. A theological response for salvation depends upon healing love, liberating hope, and the power of faith, which, in the case of the Black churches, has worked in the past and can work through the human agency of any of us today. In brief, this is the enormous challenge of Black churches today: to recommit their resources to "social midwifery" of justice, peace, and liberty.

In conclusion, a career goal I have pursued as a former Black church pastor and current director of Vanderbilt's Kelly Miller Smith Institute on Black Church Studies and president of American Baptist College in Nashville has been to bring together Black preachers, social theorists, economists, ethicists, nonprofit organizations, political leaders, theologians, pastors, secondary educators, professors in higher education, church laity, and public health officials to clarify and define the parameters of justice for the liberating ministry for Black churches. In this regard, I propose a praxis agenda that examines what Colombia professor Manning Marable offers as a "social justice credo" to guide a reframing of justice and responsible praxis. Without a commitment to a social justice credo, we will be, at best, "clumsy midwives" falling short of doing the necessary theological and ethical research and work necessary for a new life. Black churches and the nation cannot afford to let this kairos opportunity of change pass, failing to fulfill our collective potential for birthing a new quality of life for children who have come to birth, ripe and ready to name a new existence and future for themselves. I offer modest revisions to Marable's credo for future dialogue.[18]

Social Justice Credo

We must strive for theological education that makes essential the God-human relationship in the world to reveal and sustain a movement of liberation.

We should strive to do theological education in Black churches to decolonize Christianity and show how people of faith can change the world for a communal sharing of gifts and resources given to humanity by God and show how the teaching of Islam, Christianity, and other religions are commensurate with the goal of liberation and justice.

We must strive for quality education for all.

We must develop a civic capacity within the Black community to build and maintain effective alliances among a broad cross section of stakeholders that will work toward a collective goal for reform of public education. We should demand greater funding for our public schools, investment in Black teacher development and higher teacher salaries, classroom construction, computers, and other materials that make learning possible. We should support antiracist curriculum and educational programs and reinforce Black history and culture. We should support the preservation and enrichment of historically Black colleges and universities.

We must strive to enhance the emotional, physical, spiritual, and intellectual health of Black people.
The quality of life, health, and health care involves more than the absence of disease. Black churches should establish educational programs of health awareness that include not only physical well-being but also spiritual, emotional, and intellectual health. More attention must be paid to the political education and literacy of Black clergy in the area of public health and poverty. We must be committed to a society that allows for the healthy and positive development of children. We must demand quality education, health care, housing, and safety for every child.

We must be committed to a social policy agenda that invests in human beings. We must strive for a society in which all people have the resources to develop their fullest potential.

This can only occur when the basic needs of all people are met. At minimum, this includes free and universal health care, childcare, quality education, lifelong access to retraining and vocational learning, and low-cost quality public housing. We must strive for a comprehensive national economic policy that places the interests of people above profits. We should replace minimum wage with a mandated living wage for the poor. We should demand emergency action by the government, especially in areas of concentrated high unemployment, to create real jobs at living wages.

We must strive for justice in the legal system.
The US prison-industrial complex has become a vast warehouse for millions of the Black poor and unemployed. We should be in the forefront of a campaign to call for the abolition of the death penalty, this twentieth-first century's version of lynching.

We must strive for civil and human rights, affirmative action, and compensation for centuries of institutional racism.
In a post-Obama election, we should defend the policies of affirmative action and all equal opportunity legislation to create equal conditions as essential in attacking racial inequality and inequity.

We must strive for gender justice and women's rights.
We must support full pay equity and the abolition of job discrimination for Black women. We must support strong measures to protect Black women's lives from domestic violence, sexism, sexual abuse, and harassment in Black churches and the wider society.

We must strive for an end to homophobia and discrimination against people of different sexual orientations.
We should oppose and reject any arguments or constitutional amendments that exclude or marginalize the contributions of people of different sexual orientations toward the goal of freedom in American society at large and particularly in the African American community.

We must strive for liberation for all oppressed people throughout the world.

The struggles of people of African descent are inextricably linked to the many diverse struggles of oppressed people and nations across the globe.

Finally, we must commit ourselves to striving for a liberated future against the false premise of a democracy that has not manifested justice in the United States for all citizens.

Contributors

Dr. Emilie M. Townes is a prominent American Baptist clergy-woman, ethicist, and theologian. She is the Martin Luther King, Jr., Professor of Religion and Black Studies at Boston University's School of Theology. Before this role, she was the dean and Distinguished Professor of Womanist Ethics and Society at Vanderbilt University Divinity School, where she was the first African American woman to serve as dean.

Born on August 1, 1955, in Durham, North Carolina, Townes has an impressive academic background. She holds a Doctor of Ministry degree from the University of Chicago Divinity School and a PhD in Religion in Society and Personality from Northwestern University. Her extensive career includes positions at Yale University Divinity School, Union Theological Seminary, and Saint Paul School of Theology.

Dr. Townes has authored and edited several influential works in womanist ethics and theology, including *Womanist Ethics and the Cultural Production of Evil* and *Breaking the Fine Rain of Death: African American Health Issues and a Womanist Ethic of Care*. Her scholarship focuses on Christian ethics, cultural theory, and African American religious studies, among other areas.

In addition to her academic contributions, Dr. Townes has led several scholarly organizations, serving as the first African American woman president of the American Academy of Religion and as a fellow of the American Academy of Arts and Sciences. Her work continues to influence and shape discussions on ethics, society, and theology within and beyond the academy.

Dr. Victor Anderson is the John Frederick Oberlin Theological School Professor of Ethics and Society at Vanderbilt Divinity School. He is also a professor in the African American and Diaspora Studies and Religious Studies program at the College of Arts and Sciences at Vanderbilt University. Dr. Anderson holds a Master of Divinity and Master of Theology from Calvin Theological Seminary and an MA and PhD in religion from Princeton University.

Dr. Anderson's scholarly work focuses on philosophy and ethics, Black studies, American philosophy, religious thought, and African American religious and cultural studies. He has published several influential books, including *Beyond Ontological Blackness: An Essay on African American Religious and Cultural Criticism*, *Pragmatic Theology: Negotiating the Intersections of an American Philosophy of Religion and Public Theology*, and *Creative Exchange: A Constructive Theology of African American Religious Experience*.

Dr. Anderson has served on the editorial boards of prestigious journals such as the *Journal of the American Academy of Religion* and *The Journal of Religion*. His current projects include two collections of essays: *And Then His Son Cried: Grotesque Masculinities and Sexualities* and *Creative Conflict and Creative Exchange: A Christian's Social Witness to the Public and Its Problems*.

Dr. Lewis V. Baldwin is a distinguished scholar and professor emeritus of religious studies at Vanderbilt University. Born in 1949 in Camden, Alabama, Baldwin's early experiences in the heart of the Civil Rights Movement deeply influenced his academic and professional trajectory. He participated in student demonstrations and other civil rights activities during high school, and he was inspired by Martin Luther King Jr., whom he heard speak at Antioch Baptist Church in his hometown in 1966.

Baldwin pursued higher education at Talladega College, where he earned a BA in history in 1971. He furthered his studies at Colgate Rochester Divinity School/Bexley Hall/Crozer Theological Seminaries, earning an MA in Black church studies in 1973 and an MDiv in theology in 1975. In 1980, he received a PhD in American Christianity from Northwestern University.

Baldwin, an ordained Baptist minister, has had a prolific academic career, teaching at several institutions, including the College of Wooster, Colgate University, and Colgate Rochester Divinity School, before joining Vanderbilt University. He is widely recognized for his extensive work on African American religious history and the legacy of Martin Luther King Jr. Baldwin has authored numerous influential books, including *There Is a Balm in Gilead: The Cultural Roots of Martin Luther King, Jr.*, *To Make the Wounded Whole: The Cultural Legacy of Martin Luther King, Jr.*, and *Never to Leave Us Alone: The Prayer Life of Martin Luther King, Jr.*

Baldwin's scholarship has significantly contributed to the understanding of African American religious traditions and the cultural and political impact of the Black church.

Dr. Karen Brown Dunlap is a highly respected figure in the field of journalism, having devoted more than thirty years to educating journalists and aspiring media professionals. She was president of the Poynter Institute in St. Petersburg, Florida, a prestigious school dedicated to training journalists and media leaders. Dr. Dunlap has also held teaching positions at Tennessee State University and the University of South Florida and continues to teach at Poynter.

Dr. Dunlap's career began as a reporter for *The Nashville Banner* and later as a staff writer for *The Macon News*. She joined the Poynter Institute in 1985, initially participating in a seminar for university educators. She eventually became the dean of the faculty in 1994 before being appointed president in 2003. During her tenure, Dr. Dunlap significantly expanded Poynter's programs and faculty, emphasizing the importance of practical newsroom experience for journalism educators.

Dr. Dunlap has coauthored two influential books, *The Effective Editor* and *The Editorial Eye*, and has served as editor for the Best Newspaper Writing series. Her contributions to journalism have been recognized with numerous awards, including the Gerald M. Sass Distinguished Award from the Association of Schools of Journalism and Mass Communication and an honorary doctorate from Eckerd College.

Dr. Dunlap's influence extends beyond her educational roles. She has served on several boards, including the Newspaper Association of America Foundation and the Florida Education Fund. Her leadership and dedication to the field have left a lasting impact on journalism education and practice.

Dr. Michael Eric Dyson is a renowned academic, author, and public intellectual known for his extensive work on race, religion, and cultural criticism. Born on October 23, 1958, in Detroit, Michigan, Dyson has held teaching positions at several prestigious institutions, including Princeton, Brown, Georgetown, and currently, Vanderbilt University, where he serves as the Centennial Chair and University Distinguished Professor of African American and Diaspora Studies, and University Distinguished Professor of Ethics and Society.

Dr. Dyson has authored more than twenty-five books, seven of which reached New York Times bestseller status. His notable works include *Making Malcolm: The Myth and Meaning of Malcolm X, Holler If You Hear Me: Searching for Tupac Shakur, The Black Presidency: Barack Obama and the Politics of Race in America,* and *Tears We Cannot Stop: A Sermon to White America.* His writing often addresses critical issues of race and justice in America, blending scholarly rigor with accessible prose.

In addition to his academic pursuits, Dr. Dyson is an ordained Baptist minister and a frequent media commentator. He has appeared on numerous radio and television programs to discuss social justice and cultural issues. His contributions have been recognized with several awards, including the Langston Hughes Medal and two NAACP Image Awards.

Dr. Riggins R. Earl Jr. is a Distinguished Professor of Ethics and Theology at the Interdenominational Theological Center (ITC) in Atlanta, Georgia, where he has been a significant faculty member for more than thirty years. Dr. Earl earned his PhD in social ethics from Vanderbilt University and pursued postdoctoral studies at both Harvard and Boston universities.

Dr. Earl's career began at the University of Tennessee, Knoxville, where he served as an assistant professor of religious studies from 1974 to 1982. Dr. Earl is known for his extensive contributions to discussions on ethics, theology, and social justice, particularly within the African American religious context. He has also served as a consultant and teacher at urban youth academies. He has been a guest lecturer at various institutions, including Berea College, where he held the Martin Luther King, Jr., Lectureship.

Dr. Earl's work has profoundly impacted intellectual conversations about civil rights and ethical leadership. His engagement with these topics extends beyond the classroom into public discourse and community involvement, making him a respected voice in academic and religious circles

Dr. Walter Earl Fluker is a prominent figure in ethical leadership and spirituality. Born on August 26, 1951, in Vaiden, Mississippi, Dr. Fluker has had a distinguished career in academia and ministry. He is the Dean's Professor of Spirituality, Ethics, and Leadership at Emory University's Candler School of Theology and Professor Emeritus of Ethical Leadership at Boston University, where he previously held the Martin Luther King, Jr., Chair.

Fluker completed his PhD in social ethics at Boston University in 1988. His early career included serving as pastor at St. John's Congregational Church in Springfield, Massachusetts, and as a university chaplain and assistant professor of religion at Dillard University. He held teaching and leadership roles at several institutions, including Colgate Rochester Crozer Divinity School and Morehouse College, where he was the founding executive director of the Leadership Center, now known as the Andrew Young Center for Global Leadership.

Dr. Fluker is also known for his work on the Howard Thurman Papers Project and extensive publications on ethical leadership and the Black church. His notable works include *The Ground*

Has Shifted: The Future of the Black Church in Post-Racial America, which received an honorable mention from the Theology and Religious Studies PROSE Award.

Dr. Fluker has been a consultant and speaker throughout his career, providing ethical leadership training for various organizations. He has also been a distinguished lecturer internationally, contributing to programs in South Africa, China, and India. Dr. Fluker and his wife, Sharon Watson Fluker, have four children and six grandchildren.

Reverend Dr. Yvette A. Flunder is the founder and senior pastor of the City of Refuge United Church of Christ in Oakland, California, and the presiding bishop of the Fellowship of Affirming Ministries (TFAM), a multidenominational coalition of primarily African American Christian leaders and laity.

In 1991, Dr. Flunder founded the City of Refuge UCC to merge gospel ministry with social outreach. She particularly focused on marginalized communities, including those affected by HIV/AIDS and the LGBTQ+ community. Under her leadership, the church has grown into a vibrant congregation known for its radical inclusivity and social activism.

In 2003, Dr. Flunder was consecrated as the presiding bishop of TFAM, which supports churches and faith-based organizations in promoting a theology of radical inclusivity and social justice across the United States and internationally.

Dr. Flunder founded Ark of Refuge, Inc., a nonprofit that provides housing, direct services, and education for individuals affected by HIV/AIDS. She has also served on boards such as the National Sexuality Resource Center and the Human Rights Campaign's Religion Council and has been a vocal advocate for marriage equality and other civil rights issues.

Dr. Flunder's dedication to justice and inclusivity have earned her numerous accolades, including the Heritage OUTMUSIC Award from the LGBT Academy of Recording Arts and recognition from the White House for her contributions to the fight against AIDS.

Dr. Marvin A. McMickle is a distinguished scholar, author, and pastor who has had a significant impact on theological education and the church community. He earned a BA in philosophy from Aurora University, an MDiv from Union Theological Seminary in New York City, and a Doctor of Ministry degree from Princeton Theological Seminary. He completed his PhD in 1998 at Case Western Reserve University.

Dr. McMickle served as the twelfth president of Colgate Rochester Crozer Divinity School from 2011 to 2019. Before this role, he was the senior pastor of Antioch Baptist Church in Cleveland, Ohio, for fourteen years, where he led groundbreaking initiatives such as a ministry for individuals affected by HIV/AIDS and a community tithing program. He has also held academic positions, including professor of homiletics at Ashland Theological Seminary and visiting professor of preaching at Yale University Divinity School.

An accomplished author, Dr. McMickle has written eighteen books and numerous articles. His work often addresses social justice, church leadership, and the intersection of religion and public life. He is a Martin Luther King, Jr., International Board of Preachers member at Morehouse College. He has been recognized for his leadership and contributions to academia and the church community.

Dr. McMickle continues influencing theological discourse and practice through his writing, teaching, and leadership roles. He joined the First Baptist Church of Greater Cleveland as interim senior pastor in January 2024.

Dr. Herbert Marbury is an associate professor of the Hebrew Bible and Ancient Near East at Vanderbilt Divinity School. He is a renowned scholar whose research focuses on the textuality of the Bible—how biblical texts come to mean both in their ancient contexts and in contemporary US communities. His academic journey includes a BA from Emory University, an MDiv from the Interdenominational Theological Center, and a PhD in religion from Vanderbilt University.

Marbury's scholarly work includes exploring the implications of biblical texts in the context of imperial domination and resistance. His first book, *Imperial Dominion and Priestly Genius: Coercion, Accommodation, and Resistance in the Divorce Rhetoric of Ezra-Nehemiah*, investigates the meanings of these texts for ancient Israel under Persian rule. His subsequent work, *Pillars of Cloud and Fire: The Politics of Exodus in African American Biblical Interpretation*, examines the story of the Exodus's significance for African American communities from the antebellum period through the Black Power Movement.

In addition to his academic pursuits, Dr. Marbury has served in various pastoral and educational roles, including as pastor of Old National United Methodist Church in Atlanta and university chaplain at Clark Atlanta University. His contributions to theological education and the church community have been recognized with numerous accolades, including the Vanderbilt University Chancellor's Award for his work on African American biblical interpretation.

Dr. Marbury's commitment to academia and ministry exemplifies his dedication to exploring and teaching the intersections of faith, history, and social justice.

Dr. Peter J. Paris is a distinguished scholar in Christian social ethics. He is the Elmer G. Homrighausen Professor Emeritus of Christian Social Ethics at Princeton Theological Seminary. Throughout his esteemed career, Dr. Paris has also held faculty positions at Vanderbilt University Divinity School, Howard University School of Divinity, and Union Theological Seminary in New York.

Dr. Paris has contributed extensively to ethics, as well as African, Caribbean, and African American studies. His notable works include *The Spirituality of African Peoples: The Search for a Common Moral Discourse, Virtues and Values: The African and African American Experience*, and *Religion and Poverty: Pan-African Perspectives*. He has also served as the general editor of a religion, race, and ethnicity series with New York University Press.

A native of Nova Scotia, Canada, Dr. Paris completed his undergraduate education at Acadia University and earned his MA and PhD from the University of Chicago. He has received numerous accolades, including honorary doctorates from Lafayette College, Lehigh University, Acadia University, and McGill University. Dr. Paris has been actively involved in various academic and religious organizations, serving as president of the American Theological Society, the Society for the Study of Black Religion, the American Academy of Religion, and the Society of Christian Ethics.

Dr. Paris's influence extends globally through his lectures and teachings across the United States, Canada, Jamaica, Nigeria, Ghana, South Africa, India, and Brazil.

Dr. DeWayne R. Stallworth is an assistant professor of religion and counseling at American Baptist College. He is known for his work on the shared experiences of African Americans and the impact of systemic structures on Black and white privilege. His book *Existential Togetherness: Toward a Common Black Religious Heritage* explores these themes in depth. Dr. Stallworth contributes significantly to race, religion, and social justice discussions through his teaching, writing, and public speaking engagements.

Dr. R. Drew Smith is a highly esteemed professor and scholar at Pittsburgh Theological Seminary, where he holds the position of Henry L. Hillman Professor of Urban Ministry. He is also the former director of the Metro-Urban Institute at the seminary. Dr. Smith's academic background is robust and includes a Bachelor of Science degree from Indiana University and both a Master of Divinity and a PhD in political science from Yale University.

Before his tenure at Pittsburgh Theological Seminary, Dr. Smith was a scholar-in-residence and director of religion and public life projects at Morehouse College. He has also served on the faculties of Indiana University and Butler University and has held visiting faculty positions at Emory University and Case Western Reserve University. Dr. Smith served as director of the Center for Church and the Black Experience at Garrett-Evangelical Theological Seminary and has been involved internationally as a Fulbright professor at the University of Pretoria in South Africa and as a Fulbright senior specialist in Cameroon.

Dr. Smith's research and publications focus on religion and public life, particularly urban ministry and Black churches. He has edited or coedited ten books and authored more than eighty articles, chapters, and essays. His notable works include *Urban Ministry Reconsidered: Contexts and Approaches* and *Racialized Health, COVID-19, and Religious Responses: Black Atlantic Contexts and Perspectives*. He is a co-convener of the Transatlantic Roundtable on Religion and Race, a network that addresses racial issues through scholarly and community engagement.

Dr. Stacey M. Floyd-Thomas is the E. Rhodes and Leona B. Carpenter Professor of Ethics and Society at Vanderbilt University Divinity School and College of Arts and Sciences. She is a nationally recognized scholar in social ethics with extensive contributions to the fields of liberation theology, womanist thought, Black church studies, critical race theory, and postcolonial studies.

Dr. Floyd-Thomas holds multiple advanced degrees, including a BA from Vassar College, an MTS from Emory University's Candler School of Theology, an MA and PhD in religion and ethics from Temple University, and an MBA from Tennessee State University. Her academic work explores the intersections of race, gender, and class, and she is deeply committed to issues of social justice, ethical responsibility, and moral agency.

In addition to her role at Vanderbilt, Dr. Floyd-Thomas serves as the executive director of the Society of Christian Ethics and the Black Religious Scholars Group and is a cofounder of the Society for the Study of Race, Ethnicity, and Religion. Her extensive publication record includes seven books, numerous articles, and book chapters. Her notable works include *Mining the Motherlode: Methods in Womanist Ethics*, *Deeper Shades of Purple: Womanism in Religion and Society*, and *Black Church Studies: An Introduction*.

Dr. Floyd-Thomas has received numerous awards for her scholarship and teaching, including the American Academy of Religion Excellence in Teaching Award and the Womanist Legend Award.

Dr. William H. Myers is a distinguished scholar and professor of New Testament and Black church studies at Ashland Theological Seminary in Ashland, Ohio. He is also the president and CEO of the McCreary Center for African American Religious Studies. Dr. Myers was born in Stonewall, Mississippi, and completed his PhD in religious studies in 1991 at the University of Pittsburgh.

Dr. Myers has made significant contributions to the study of African American religious experiences, particularly through his focus on the narratives of "call" stories within the African American clergy. His notable publications include *The Irresistible Urge to Preach: A Collection of African American "Call" Stories* and *God's Yes Was Louder Than My No: Rethinking the African American Call to Ministry*, both of which provide deep insights into the spiritual and cultural dimensions of the African American religious call to ministry.

In addition to his scholarly work, Dr. Myers is known for his role in developing and promoting Black church studies programs, exemplified by his leadership at the McCreary Center and his academic influence at Ashland Theological Seminary.

Reverend Dr. Wallace Charles Smith is the senior minister of Shiloh Baptist Church in Washington, DC, one of the oldest African American churches in the nation's capital. A native of Philadelphia, Dr. Smith graduated from Villanova University in 1970. He holds a Master of Divinity degree and a Doctor of Ministry degree from Andover Newton Theological School.

Before his tenure at Shiloh Baptist Church, Dr. Smith served as president of Palmer Theological Seminary of Eastern University from 2005 to 2010 and was the dean of the Wallace Charles Smith School of Christian Ministries at the same institution. His pastoral career includes leadership roles at the First Baptist Church, Capitol Hill, in Nashville, Tennessee, and Calvary Baptist Church in Chester, Pennsylvania.

Dr. Smith is deeply involved in various community and educational initiatives. He has served in outreach programs, including AIDS education and youth employment, and has been active in the Baptist World Alliance Youth Ministry. Additionally, he has played a significant role in the Lott Carey Baptist Foreign Mission Convention.

Dr. Smith's leadership extends to his role with the Ministers and Missionaries Benefit Board (MMBB), where he has served since 2007. His contributions to theological education and the church community are widely recognized, making him a respected figure in both academic and religious circles.

Reverend Dr. Julius Richard Scruggs was a highly esteemed pastor and leader within the Baptist community. Born in Elkton, Tennessee, and raised in Toney, Alabama, he graduated from Council Training High School in Huntsville. Dr. Scruggs pursued higher education at American Baptist College in Nashville, Tennessee, earning a Bachelor of Arts. He furthered his theological studies at Vanderbilt University School of Divinity, obtaining both a Master of Divinity and a Doctor of Ministry. He was also awarded an honorary doctor of humane letters from Alabama Agricultural and Mechanical University.

In 1977, Dr. Scruggs became the senior pastor of First Missionary Baptist Church in Huntsville, Alabama, a position he held for more than forty-two years. Under his leadership, the church grew significantly in membership and community impact, including the development of partnerships with Habitat for Humanity to build homes and the establishment of numerous outreach programs.

Dr. Scruggs held prominent roles in various religious and civic organizations. He was the nineteenth president of the Alabama State Missionary Baptist Convention and later served as president of the National Baptist Convention, USA, Inc. His leadership extended to the NAACP and American Baptist College's board of trustees.

Dr. Scruggs was widely recognized for his contributions to the church and community. He received accolades such as the Dr. Martin Luther King, Jr., Award and was listed in "Who's Who in Religion" and "Outstanding Young Men in America." He authored four books and was known for his biblically based and life-centered preaching and teaching.

Dr. Scruggs passed away on May 8, 2024, leaving behind a legacy of faith, service, and leadership.

Reverend James Lawson. A supporter of the Gandhian philosophy of nonviolent protest, the Reverend James M. Lawson, Jr., was one of the Civil Rights Movement's leading theoreticians and tacticians in the African American struggle for freedom and equality in the 1950s and 1960s. Raised in a household of ten children, Lawson was born in Uniontown, Pennsylvania, to the Reverend James Morris and Philane May Cover Lawson, Sr. Lawson grew up in Massillon, Ohio.

After high school, Lawson entered Baldwin-Wallace College in Berea, Ohio, in 1947. Consistent with his beliefs toward nonviolence, Lawson became a conscientious objector during the Korean War. In April 1951, Lawson was found guilty of violating the draft laws of the United States and sentenced to three years in a federal prison. Upon his release from prison, Lawson returned to Baldwin-Wallace and earned his bachelor's degree. Afterward, Lawson traveled to India to work the Methodist Board of Missionaries and he studied the Gandhian principles of *satyagraha*, the strategy of passive political resistance.

Lawson entered Oberlin College's Graduate School of Theology, and in 1957, one of Lawson's professors introduced him to the Reverend Dr. Martin Luther King, Jr., who urged him to move south and aid in the Civil Rights Movement. Lawson moved to Nashville, Tennessee, and enrolled at the Divinity School of Vanderbilt University, where he served as the southern director for Fellowship of Reconciliation (FOR) and began hosting nonviolence training workshops for the Southern Christian Leadership Conference (SCLC). There Lawson trained many of the future leaders of the Civil Rights Movement, including James Bevel, Diane Nash, John Lewis, Bernard Lafayette, and Marion Barry.

In 1960, Lawson was expelled from Vanderbilt for organizing the Nashville student sit-ins. Lawson moved to Memphis in June 1962, where he became pastor of Centenary Methodist Church. Throughout the decade, he led various community movements for racial justice in Memphis. In 1968, while involved in the sanitation workers strike, he invited Dr. Martin Luther King, Jr., to Memphis to speak. Fifteen thousand people heard King's famous "I've Been to the Mountaintop Speech." King was assassinated in Memphis the following day on April 4, 1968.

In 1974, James Lawson moved to Los Angeles, California, where he became pastor of Holman United Methodist Church and continued his social activism, advocating for Palestinian and immigrant rights; gay and lesbian issues; the poor; and an end to war in Iraq. Rev. Lawson retired from Holman United Methodist Church in 1999 but continues to live in Los Angeles. (Hasan Tesfa, *James Lawson*. African American History Timeline, BlackPast.org.)

Bibliography

Agang, Sunday Bobai. "The Need for Public Theology in Africa." In *African Public Theology*. Edited by Sunday Bobai Agang et. al. Lakewood, WA: Hippo Books, 2020.

———. "Work."

Allen, Richard. *The Life, Experience, and Gospel Labors of the Rt. Rev. Richard Allen*. Philadelphia: Martin and Boden, [1833] 1880.

Anderson, Victor. *Creative Exchange: A Constructive Theology of African American Religious Experience*. Minneapolis: Fortress Press, 2008.

Andrews, Dale P. *Practical Black Theology for Black Churches: Bridging Black Theology and African American Folk Religion*. Louisville, KY: John Knox Press, 2002.

Aptheker, Herbert, ed. *A Documentary History of Negro People in the United States*. Toronto: Citadel Press, 1968.

Baldwin, James. *No Name in the Street*. New York: Dial Press, 1972.

———. Nothing Personal." In *The Price of the Ticket: Collected Non-fiction 1948–1945*. New York: St. Martin's/Marek, 1985.

———. *The Voice of Conscience: The Church in the Mind of Martin Luther King, Jr.* New York: Oxford University Press, 2010.

Baldwin, Lewis V. "Black Church Studies as an Academic Interest and Initiative: A Historical Perspective." In *In the Black Church Studies Reader*. Edited by Alton B. Pollard III and Carol B. Duncan. New York: Palgrave Macmillan, 2016.

Barber, William J., II. "An Open Letter to Clergy Who Prayed with Donald Trump." *ThinkProgress* (July 19, 2017). https://archive.thinkprogress.org/an-open-letter-to-clergy-who-prayed-with-trump-7876ee87dbc2/

Barr, Anthony and Andre Perry. "To Restore North Nashville's Black Middle Class, Local Policymakers Should Pursue Reparations." Brookings Institute, 2021. https://www.brookings.edu/articles/to-restore-north-nashvilles-black-middle-class-local-policymakers-should-pursue-reparations/

Berlin, Ira et al., eds. *The Wartime Genesis of Free Labor: The Lower South*. Cambridge: Cambridge University Press, 1991.

Berlin, Ira, Barbara J. Fields, et al. *Free At Last: A Documentary History of Slavery, Freedom, and the Civil War*. New York: New Press, 1993.

Berlin, Ira, Joseph Patrick Reidy, and Leslie S. Rowland. *Freedom's Soldiers: The Black Military Experience in the Civil War*. Cambridge: Cambridge University Press, 1998.

Blake, John. "Modern Black Church Shuns King's Message," CNN, April 6, 2008. https://www.com/2008/US/04/06mlk.role.church/index.html.

Blount, Brian K. *Go Preach! Mark's Kingdom Message and the Black Church Today*. New York: Orbis Press, 1998.

Bond, Adam L. *The Imposing Preacher: Samuel DeWitt Proctor and Black Public Faith*. Minneapolis: Fortress Press, 2013.

Brown, Douglas Kelly. *Sexuality and the Black Church: A Womanist Perspective*. Orbis Books. Kindle.

Bruggeman, Walter. *The Prophetic Imagination*. 2nd ed. Minneapolis: Fortress Press, 2001.

Bryce, James. *Studies in History and Jurisprudence*. New York: Macmillan, 1901.

Burge, Ryan P. "The Nones: Where They Came From, Who They Are, and Where They Are Going." Religious News Service (RNS). http://religionnews.com/2021/03/24/the-nones-are-growing-and-growing-more-diverse/.

Burrow, Rufus. Jr. "Martin Luther King, Jr., and Ethical Leadership." *Telos* 182 (Spring 2018).

Butler, Anthea. *White Evangelical Racism: The Politics of Morality in America*. Chapel Hill: University of North Carolina Press, 2021.

Butler, Olivia. *The Parable of the Sower*. Reprint, New York: Grand Central Publishing, 2019.

Buttrick, David. *A Captive Voice: The Liberation of Preaching*. Louisville, KY: John Knox Press, 1994.

Caldwell, Christopher. "The Browning of America: A Review of Diversity Explosion: How New Racial Demographics are Remaking America, by William H. Frey." *Claremont Review of Books* 15/1 (Winter 2014–2015). https://claremontreviewofbooks.com/the-browning-of-america/.

Calhoun-Brown, Alison. "What a Fellowsip: Civil Society, African American Churches and Public Life." In *New Day Begun: African American Churches and Civic Culture in Post-Civil Rights America*. Vol. 1. Edited by R. Drew Smith. Durham, NC: Duke University Press, 2003.

Camp, Ken. "Denominational Leader Jimmy Allen Dies at Age 91," *Baptist Standard* (January 9, 2019). https://www.baptiststandard.com/news/baptists/denominational-leader-jimmy-allen-dies-at-age-91/#:~:text=He%20was%2091.,and%20the%20New%20Baptist%20Covenant.

Cannon, Katie. *Black Womanist Ethics*. Oxford: Oxford University Press, 1988.

Carruthers, Iva E., Fredrick D. Haynes, and Jeremiah A. Wright, eds. "The Black Church in the Age of False Prophets: An Interview with Gayraud Wilmore." In *Blow the Trumpet in Zion! Global Vision and Action for the 21st-Century Black Church*. Minneapolis: Fortress Press, 2004.

Carson, Clayborne and Peter Holloran, eds. *A Knock at Midnight: Inspiration from the Great Sermons of Reverend Martin Luther King, Jr.* New York: Warner Books, 1998.

Cassidy, John, "Donald Trump's Alternative Reality Press Conference." *The New Yorker* (February 16, 2017). https://www.newyorker.com/news/john-cassidy/donald-trumps-alternate-reality-press-conference/.

"College President Demographics and Staistics in the US." Zippia (2019). https://www.zippia.com/college-president-jobs/demographics/.

Cone, James H. *A Black Theology of Liberation: Twentieth Anniversary Edition.* Maryknoll, NY: Orbis, 1990.

———. "The Story Context of Black Theology." *Theology Today* (July 1976).

Cone, James H. and Gayraud S. Wilmore. "Black Theology and African Theology: Considerations for Dialogue, Critique, and Integration." In *Black Theology: A Documentary History, 1966–1979.* Maryknoll, NY: Orbis, 1979.

Connick, Jasmyn. "Pimpin Ain't Easy: The New Face of Today's Black Church." *Jacksonville Free Press* 19/40 (October 20–26, 2005).

Craddock, Fred B. *Preaching.* Nashville, TN: Abingdon Press, 1985.

Culp, Daniel Wallace. "Twentieth Century Negro Literature: Or, Cyclopedia of Thought on Vital Topics Relating to the American Negro." Issue 71 of *Black Biographical Dictionaries, 1790–1950.* Napierville, IL.: J. L. Nichols & Company, [1902] Ann Arbor: University of Michigan, 2008.

Davis, Mary Kemp. *Nat Turner Before the Bar of Judgement: Fictional Treatments of the Southhampton Slave Insurrection.* Southern Literacy Studies. Baton Rouge: Louisianna University Press, 1999.

Du Bois, W. E. B. *The Gift of Black Folk.* New York: Oxford University Press, 2014.

———. "A Litany of Atlanta." *The Book of American Negro Poetry.* Edited by James Weldon Johnson. New York: Harcourt, Brace, 1922.

———. *The Souls of Black Folk.* New York: Cosimo Publishing, 2007.

Edwards, Haley Sweelands. "How Christine Blasey Ford's Testimony Changed America." *Time* (October 4, 2018). https://time.com/5415027/christine-blasey-ford-testimony/.

Empowering Congregations Executive Summary.

Erskine, Noel Leo. *King Among the Theologians.* Cleveland: Pilgrim Press, 1994.

Fair, Bryan. "SPLC Fights White Supremacy, Threats to Democracy in 2020." *SPLC Report* 49/4 (Winter 2019).

Falconer, Rebecca. "Trump Meets with African American Pastors Amid Accusations of Racism." *Axios* (July 30, 2019). https://www.axios.com/trump-black-pastors-meeting-amid-racism-claims/.

Fiedler, R. N. and J. W. Hofmeyr. "The Conception of the Circle of Concerned African Women Theologians: Is it African or Western?" *Acta Theologica* 31/1 (2011).

"The 15 Greatest Black Preachers." *Ebony* 49/1 (1993).

"Florida Slave Narratives: Scott, Anna." Federal Writers' Project, 1937. Exploring Florida: Social Study Resources for Students and Teachers website. Floripedia, https://fcit.usf.edu/florida/docs/s/slave/slave33.htm.

Fluker, Walter E. *The Ground Has Shifted: The Future of the Black Church in Post-Racial America*. New York: New York University Press, 2016.

Franklin, John Hope, ed. *The Souls of Black Folk in Three Negro Classics*. New York: Avon Books, 1965.

Frazier, E. Franklin. *The Negro Church in America*. New York: Schocken Books, 1963.

Freund, David M. P. *State Policy and White Racial Politics in Suburban America*. Chicago: University of Chicago Press, 2010.

Frey, William H. *Diversity Explosion: How New Racial Demographics Are Remaking America*. Washington, DC: Brookings Institution Press, 2018.

Gajanan, Mahita. "Kellyanne Conway Defends White House's Falsehoods as 'Alternative Facts.'" *Time* (January 22, 2017) https://time.com/4642689/kellyanne-conway-sean-spicer-donald-trump-alternative-facts/.

Gannon, Kathy. "Afghanistan's Taliban Order Women to Cover Up Head to Toe." AP News. May 7, 2022. https://apnews.com/article/afghanistan-taliban-49b17d77d03022ad4817eeecf4f5da93.

Garvey, Marcus. *The Philosophy and Opinions of Marcus Garvey, Or Africa for Africans*. New York: Open Road Integrated Media.

Gates, Henry Louis Jr. *Lincoln on Race & Slavery*. Princeton, NJ: Princeton University Press, 2009.

Glaude, Eddie Jr. "Updated with Response: The Black Church Is Dead—Long Live the Black Church." *Religion Dispatches* (March 15, 2011). https://religiondispatches.org/bupdated-with-responseb-the-black-church-is-dead-long-live-the-black-church/.

Gore, Bob. *We've Come This Far: The Abyssinian Baptist Church—A Photographic Journal*. New York: Stewart, Tabori & Chang, 2001.

Gorski, Phillip and Samuel L. Perry. *The Flag and the Cross: White Christian Nationalism and the Threat to America*. New York: Oxford, 2022.

Hamilton, Clarles. *The Black Preacher in America*. New York: Morrow, 1972.

Harriet Ross Tubman (1819–1913) Timeline. University of Buffalo. http://www.math.buffalo.edu/~sww/0history/hwny-tubman.html.

Harris, Forrest E., Sr. "American Baptist College: The Official Report of the President 2020," 11. https://abcnash.edu/wp-content/uploads/2021/06/Presidents-Report-2021_FE.pdf.

———. "Forward." *The Black Church Studies Reader*. Edited by Alton B. Pollard III and Carol B. Duncan. New York: Palgrave Macmillan, 2016.

———. *Ministry for Social Crisis: Theology and Praxis in the Black Church Tradition*. Macon, GA: Mercer University Press, 1993.

———. "Pursuing American Racial Justice and a Politically and Theologically Informed Black Church Praxis." *Contesting Post-Racialism: Conflicted Churches in the United States and South Africa*. Edited by R. Drew Smith et. al. Oxford: University Press of Mississippi, 2015.

Harris, Forrest E., Sr., James T. Robertson, and Larry Darnell George, eds. *What Does It Mean to Be Black and Christian? Pulpit, Pew, and Academy in Dialogue*. Nashville, TN: Townsend Press, 1995.

Hayes, John. *Hard, Hard, Religion: Interracial in the Poor South*. Chapel Hill: University of North Carolina Press, 2017.

Haynes, Arthur Vertreae. *Scar of Segregation*. New York: Vantage Press, 1974.

Haynes, Campbell. "One Mile North." *Belmont Law Review* 8/1 (2020).

Higginbotham, Evelyn Brooks. *Righteous Discontent: The Women's Movement in the Black Baptist Church, 1880–1920*. Cambridge, MA: Harvard University Press, 1994.

Houston, Benjamin and Project Muse. *The Nashville Way: Racial Etiquette and the Struggle for Social Justice in a Southern City*. Athens: University of Georgia Press, 2012.

Hudson, Winthrop S. *Religion in America*. New York: Charles Scribner's Sons, 1965.

Hurston, Zora Neale. *Dust Tracks on the Road: An Autobiography*. Urbana: University of Illinois, (1942) 1984.

Iton, Richard. *In Search of the Black Fantastic: Politics and Popular Culture in the Post-Civil Rights Era*. New York and London: Oxford University Press, 2010.

Jim Crow Museum Timeline, Part 4 (1877–1964). https://jimcrowmuseum.ferris.edu/timeline/jimcrow.htm.

Johnson, Bishop Joseph. *The Soul of the Black Preacher*. Cleveland: Pilgrim Press, 1971.

Johnson, Dale A., ed. *Vanderbilt Divinity School: Education, Contest, and Change*. Nashville, TN: Vanderbilt University Press, 2001.

Jones, Isabelle, Paula Jimeno Lara, and Augustin Tornabene. "Housing Segregation in Nashville: Exploring the Legacy of De Jure Segregation in Nashville" (2020). https://storymaps.arcgis.com/stories/050e09fabed0474b9687525fbc4e4c9a.

Kahne, J. and J. Westheimer. "Teaching Democracy: What Schools Need to Do." *Phi Delta Kappan* 85/1 (2003): 34–66.

Kelly, Robin D. G. *Freedom Dreams: The Black Radical Imagination*. Boston: Beacon Press, 2002.

King, Martin Luther, Jr. "A Challenge to the Churches and Synagogues." In *Race: A Challenge to Religion—Original Essays and an Appeal to the Conscience from the National Conference on Religion and Race.* Edited by Ahmann, Mathew. Chicago: Henry Regnery Company, 1963.

———. "The Negro Gains in Rights—1965," unpublished and typed version of a speech, Atlanta. November 10, 1965.

———. "Strength to Love." 30. In *The Papers of Martin Luther King, Jr.: Advocate of the Social Gospel, September 1948–March 1963.* 7 vols. Edited by Clayborne Carson et al. Berkeley: University of California Press, 2007.

———. *Strength to Love.* Philadelphia: Fortress Press, 1981; originally published in 1963.

———. *Stride toward Freedom: The Montgomery Story.* New York: Harper & Row, 1958.

———. "Transformed Nonconformist." Unpublished and typed version of a sermon, Ebenezer Baptist Church, Atlanta, January 16, 1966.

———. *The Trumpet of Conscience.* San Francisco: Harper & Row, 1968.

———. *Where Do We Go from Here: Chaos or Community.* Boston: Beacon Press, 1967.

———. *Why We Can't Wait.* New York: New American Library, 1963.

———."People to People." Unpublished version of an essay prepared for *New York Amsterdam News.* September 17, 1964.

The King Papers, Library and Archives of the Martin Luther King, Jr., Center for Nonviolent Social Change, Inc. (KCLA). Atlanta.

Klein, Ezra. "White Threat in a Browning America: How the Demographic Change Is Fracturing Our Politics." *Vox* (July 30, 2018). https://www.vox.com/policy-and-politics/2018/7/30/17505406/trump-obama-race-politics-immigration/.

Kuhardt Film Foundation. "King in the Wilderness." Diane Nash Interview (August 1, 2018) 9:59.

Labeodan, Helen A. "Revisiting the Legacy of the Circle of Concerned African Women Theologians Today: A Lesson in Strength and Perseverance." *Verbum et Ecclesia* 37/2 (2016).

Lipsitz, George. *The Possessive Investment in Whiteness: How White People Profit from Identity Politics.* Revised and expanded ed. Philadelphia: Temple University Press, 2009.

Lovett, Bobby L. *The African-American History of Nashville, Tennessee, 1780–1930: Elites and Dilemmas.* Black Community Studies. Fayetteville: University of Arkansas Press, 1999.

Lucas, Fred. "Trump 'Most Pro-Black President,' Pastor Says in White House Meeting." *Daily Signal.* August 2, 2018. https://www.dailysignal.com/2018/08/02/trump-most-pro-black-president-pastor-says-in-white-house-meeting/.

Lui, Meizhu, Barbara Robles, Betsy Leondar-Wright, Rose Brewer, and
Rebecca Adamson. *The Color of Wealth: The Story Behind the U.S. Racial
Wealth Divide*. New York: New Press, 2006.

Marable, Manning. "Black Leadership, Faith, and the Struggle for Freedom." In
Black Faith, and Public Talk. Edited by Dwight Hopkins. Waco, TX:
Baylor University Press, 2007.

Marbury, Herbert Robinson. "Exogamy and Divorce in Ezra and Nehemiah." In
The Oxford Handbook of the Historical Books of the Bile. Edited by Brad E.
Kelle and Brent Strawn. New York: Oxford, 2020.

———. "Ezra-Nehemiah. " In *The Africana Bible: Reading Israel's Scriptures from
Africa and the African Diaspora*. Edited by Hugh R., Randall C. Bailey,
Valerie Bridgeman, Stacy Davis, Cheryl Kirk-Duggan, Madipoane
Masenya, N. Samuel Murrell, and Rodney Steven Sadler. Minneapolis:
Fortress Press, 2010.

———. *Imperial Dominion and Priestly Genius: Coercion, Accomodation, and
Resistance in the Divorce Rhetoric of Ezra-Nehemiah*. Upland, CA: Sopher
Press, 2012.

———. "Nehemiah: Caught between Court and Cult with Lessons for Church
and State." In *Focusing Biblical Studies: The Crucial Nature of the Persian and
Hellenistic Periods*. Edited by Alice W. Hunt and Jon L. Berquist. New
York: Bloomsbury Press, 2012.

Mays, Benjamin E. *Born to Rebel*. Athens: University of Georgia Press, 2003.

Mays, Benjamin E. and Joseph William Nicholson. *The Negro Church as
Reflected in His Literature*. Reprint. Eugene, OR: Wipf & Stock, 2010.

McClusky, Aubrey Thomas and Elaine M. Smith, eds. *Mary McLeod Bethune:
Building a Better World, Essays and Selected Documents*. Reprint.
Bloomington: Indiana University Press, 2002.

McFalls, Laurence. *Max Weber's Objectivity Reconsidered*. Toronto: University of
Toronto Press [2016] 2007.

McIntyre, Lee. *Post Truth*. Cambridge, MA: MIT Press, 2018.

McKinney, Richard I. *Mordecai, The Man and His Message: The Story of Mordecai
Johnson*. Washington, DC: Howard University, 1997.

McMickle, Marvin A. *An Encyclopedia of African American Christian Heritage*.
Valley Forge, PA: Judson Press, 2002.

Miller, Keith. "Martin Luther King, Jr., and the Black Folk Pulpit." *The Journal
of American History* 78/1 (June 1991): 120–23.

Miller, Keith. *Voice of Deliverance: The Language of Martin Luther King, Jr., and
Its Sources*. New York: Free Press, 1992.

Mitchell, Henry H. "Black Church Studies: Some of the Roots." In *The Black
Church Studies Reader*. Edited by Alton B. Pollard III and Carol B.
Duncan. New York: Palgrave Macmillan, 2016.

Mitchell, Henry H. and Emil M Thomas. *Preaching for Black Self-Esteem.* Nashville, TN: Abingdon Press, 1994.

Mitchell, T. D., D. M. Donahue, and C. Young-Law, "Service Learning as a Pedagogy of Whitness." *Equity & Excellence in Education* 45/4 (2012): 612–29.

Montanaro, Domenico. "How the Browning of America Is Upending Both Political Parties.", NPR. October 12, 2016. https://www.npr.org/2016/10/12/497529936/how-the-browning-of-america-is-upending-both-political-parties/.

Morgan-Smith, Kai. "Black Pastors Meet with Trump and Get Blasted by Social Media for Accomplishing Nothing." *The Grio* (August 2, 2018). https://thegrio.com/2018/08/02/black-pastors-meet-with-trump-and-get-blasted-by-social-media-for-accomplishing-nothing/.

Moujaes, Anthony. "UCC Minister Yvette Flunder Won't 'Bow to Threats' over Baptist College Appearance." https://ucc.org/yvette_flunder_baptist_college_03182015/.

Mugambi, J. N. K. *Christian Theology and Social Reconstruction.* Nairobi: Acton Press, 2003.

Myers, William H. "The Hermeneutical Dilemma of the African American Biblical Student." *Stony the Road We Trod: African American Biblical Interpretation.* Edited by Cain Hope Felder. Minneapolis: Fortress Press, 1991.

Nancy, Jean-Luc. *The Experience of Freedom.* Redwood City, CA: Stanford University Press, 1994.

Nittle, Nadra Kareen. "The Short-Lived Promise of '40 Acres and a Mule.'" History. https:www.history.com/news/40-acres-mule-promise.

Noll, Mark A. *The Civil War as a Theological Crisis.* Chapel Hill: University of North Carolina Press, 2006.

Onishi, Bradley. *Preparing for War: The Extremist History of White Christian Nationalism—and What Comes Next.* Minneapolis: Broadleaf Publishing, 2023.

Osunsami, Steve and Sarah Netter. "4th Man Accuses Bishop Long." ABCNews.com. September 24, 2010.

Paris, Peter. *The Social Teaching of the Black Churches.* Minneapolis: Fortress Press, 1985.

Payne, Daniel A. *Recollections of Seventy Years.* New York: Arno Press, 1966; Scotts Valley, CA: Create Space Independent Publisher, reprint 1991.

Powell, Annie. "Hold On to Your Dream: African American Protestant Worship." In *Women at Worship: Interpretations of North American Diversity.* Edited by Marjorie Proctor-Smith and Janet R. Watson. Louisville, KY: Westminster/John Knox Press, 1993.

Powers, Bernard. *Charleston and Black Reconstruction: A Social History, 1822–1885*. Fayetteville: University of Arkansas Press, 1994.

Proctor, Samuel DeWitt. *The Substance of Things Hoped For*. Valley Forge, PA: Judson Press, 1995.

Raboteau, Albert J. *Slave Religion: The "Invisible Institution" in the Antebellum South*. New York: Oxford University Press, 2004.

Radford, Phyllis I. and Bob Brown, eds. *Alternative Truths*. Benton City, WA: B Cubed Press, 2017.

Rancière, Jacques. *Disagreement: Politics and Philosophy*. Translated by Julie Rose. Minneapolis and London: University of Minnesota Press, 1999.

Rawick, George, ed. *The American Slave: A Composite Autobiography*. Westport, CT: Greenwood, 1972.

Richard, Pablo. "A Theology of Life: Rebuilding Hope." In *Spirituality of the Third World*. Edited by K. C. Abraham and Bernadette Mbuy-Beya. New York: Orbis, 1994.

Robinson, G. D. "Paul Ricouer 'The Hermeneutic of Suspicion': A Brief Overview and Critique." *Premise* 2/8 (September 27, 1995): 12.

Rosenfeld, Sophia. *Democracy and Truth: A Short History*. Philadelphia: University of Pennsylvania Press, 2019.

Ross, Lawrence. "Donald Trump's Factory of Ignorant Black Surrogates." *The Root* (August 31, 2016). https://www.theroot.com/donald-trump-s-factory-of-ignorant-black-surrogates/

Rothstein, Richard. *The Color of Law: A Forgotten History of How Our Government Segregated America*. New York: Liveright Publishers, 2017.

Schaberg, Christopher. *The Work of Literature in an Age of Post-Truth*. New York: Bloomsburg Publishing, 2018.

Schaeffer, Cathrine. "6 Facts about Economic Inequality in the U.S." Pew Research Center. February 7, 2020. https://www.pewresearch.org/short-reads/2020/02/07/6-facts-about-economic-inequality-in-the-u-s/

Scott, Charles E. "The Betrayal of Democratic Space." In *Journal of Speculative Philosophy*. University Park: Pennsylvania State University, 2009.

Shellnutt, Kate. "J. D. Grear Elected Youngest Southern Baptist President in Decades." *Christianity Today* (June 12, 2018). https://www.christianitytoday.com/news/2018/june/jd-greear-elected-southern-baptist-president-sbc-2018.html

Smith, Archie Jr. "Death and the Maiden—The Complexity of Trauma and Ways of Healing: A Challenge for Pastoral Care and Counseling." Edited by K. H. Federschmidt and D. J. Louw. *Intercultural and Interreligious Caregiving*. Dusseldorf: Society for Intercultural Pastoral Care and Counselling, 2015.

———. "We Need to Press Forward: Black Religion and Jonestown Twenty Years Later." Alternative Considerations of Jonestown and Peoples Temple website. 1998. https://jonestown.sdsu.edu/?page_id=16595.

"SPLC Fights Back against Bigotry in White House." *SPLC Report* 47/1 (Spring 2017).

"SPLC Launches New Initiatives to Fight Online Extremism." *SPLC Report* 51/4 (Winter 2021).

"SPLC Steps Forward to Protect the Human Rights of Immigrants." *SPLC Report* Special Edition (2012).

Stallworth, DeWayne R. *Existential Togetherness: Toward a Common Black Religious Heritage.* Eugene, OR: Pickwick Publications, 2019.

Stewart, Carlyle Fielding, III. *African American Church Growth: Twelve Prophetic Principles for Prophetic Ministry.* Nashville, TN: Abingdon Press, 1994.

Stinton, Diane B. *Jesus of Africa: Voices of Contemporary African Christology.* Maryknoll, NY: Orbis Books, 2004.

Thomas, Frank A. *They Like to Never Quit Praising God: The Role of Celebration in Preaching.* Cleveland: United Church Press, 1997.

Thurman, Howard. "Exposition of the Book of Habakkuk." *The Interpreter Bible* (November 19, 1956). Reprinted in *The Papers of Howard Washington Thurman, Vol. 4.* Edited by Walter E. Fluker. 2016.

Tisdale, Leonora Tubbs. *Preaching as Local Theology and Folk Art.* Minneapolis: Fortress Press, 1997.

Toalston, Art. "Southern Baptist Leader Frank Page Resigns Over 'Morally Inappropriate Relationship,'" March 22, 2018. https://www.christianitytoday.com/news/2018/march/frank-page-resigns-southern-baptist-executive-committee-sbc.html

Turner, Victor. "Liminality and Communitas." http://faculty.trinity.edu/mbrown/whatisreligion/PDF%20readings/Turner Victor-%20Liminality%20and%20Communitas.pdf.

———. "Betwixt and Between: The Liminal Period in *Rites de Passage.*" In *The Forrest of Symbols, Aspects of Ndembu Ritual.* Ithaca, NY: Cornell University Press, 1967.

Tutu, Desmond. "Liberation Is Costly." In *Singing the Living Tradition* (Boston: Unitarian Universalist Association, 1993).

"2021 State of Black America." The Hamilton Project of the Brookings Institute. National Urban League. https://nul.org/sites/default/files/2021-07/NUL-SOBA2021-ES-web.pdf.

Van Gennep, Arnold. *The Rites of Passage.* Chicago: University of Chicago Press, 2019.

Vellem, Vuyani S. "Black Theology of Liberation and the Economy of Life." *The Ecumenical Review* 67/2 (July 2015).

Wahneema, Lubiano, ed. *The House That Race Built: Black Americans, U.S. Terrain.* New York: Pantheon, 1997.

Ward, Richard. *Speaking from the Heart: Preaching with Passion.* Nashville, TN: Abingdon Press, 1992.

Washington, James. M., ed. *A Testament of Hope: The Essential Writings and Speeches of Martin Luther King, Jr.* San Francisco and New York: HarperCollins Publishers, 1991.

Washington, Jesse. "Why Trump's Tiny Band of Black Supporters Stick with Him." *Andscape* (October 17, 2016). https://andscape.com/features/why-trump's-tiny-band-of-black-supporters-stick-with-him/.

Washington, Joseph R. *Black Religion: The Negro and Christianity in the United States.* Boston: Beacon Press, 1966.

Websdale, Neil. *Policing the Poor: From Slave Plantation to Public Housing.* Boston: Northeastern University Press, 2001.

Wells, Ida B. *Crusade for Justice: The Autobiography of Ida B. Wells.* Edited by Alfreda M. Duster. Chicago: University of Chicago Press, 1970.

West, Cornel. "Black Theology of Liberation as Critique of Capitalist Civilization." In *Black Theology: A Documentary History, 1980–1992.* Edited by James H. Cone and Gayraud S Wilmore. Maryknoll, NY: Orbis Books, 1993.

———. *Democracy Matters: Winning the Fight Against Imperialism.* New York: Penguin Press, 2004.

Williams, Jamye Coleman. *The Negro Speaks: The Rhetoric of Contemporary Black Leaders.* Noble and Noble, 1970.

Williams, Jesse, dir. *The Undefeated.* "Bearing Witness: A Profile of Darnella Frazier." ESPN.

Williamson-Lott, Joy Ann, Linda Darling-Hammond, and Maria E. Hyler. "Emancipation and Reconstruction: African American Education 1865–1919." In *African American Education Citizenship, 1865–Present.* Edited by Lawrence D. Bobo et al. New York: Oxford University Press, 2012.

Wilmore, Gayraud S. "Black Church Studies as Advocate and Critic of Black Christian Ecclesial Communities." In *The Black Church Reader.* Edited by Alton B. Pollard III and Carol B. Duncan. New York: Palgrave Macmillan, 2016.

———. *Black Religion and Black Radicalism: An Examination of the Black Experience in Relgion.* New York: Doubleday, 1972.

———. *Black Religion and Black Radicalism: An Interpretation of the Religious History of African Americans.* Maryknoll, NY: Orbis Books, 1998.

Wimbush, Vincent L. "Interpreters—Enslaving/Enslaved/Runagate." *Journal of Biblical Literature* 130/1 (2011).

Winfrey, Oprah and Bruce D. Perry. *What Happened to You? Conversations on Trauma, Resilience and Healing.* New York: Flatiron Books, 2021.

Wise, Tim. *Between Barack and a Hard Place: Racism and White Denial in the Age of Obama.* San Francisco: City Lights Books/Open Media Series, 2009.

Woodson, Carter G. "The Negro Church, an All-Comprehending Institution." *The Negro History Bulletin* 3/1 (October 1939).

———. *The Rural Negro.* Washington, DC: Association for the Study of the Negro, Inc.

Wynn, Linda T. "Interstate 40 and the Decimation of Jefferson Street." Paper presented at the Nashville Conference on African American History and Culture, Tennessee State University, 2019.

NOTES

INTRODUCTION
[1] Edited by Dale A. Johnson, Vanderbilt University Press: Nashville, 2001.

[2] Joseph C. Hough, "Theological Studies in the Context of the University," in *Vanderbilt Divinity School: Education, Contest, and Change*, 3-21.

[3] Peter Paris, "The African American Presence in the Divinity School," in *Vanderbilt Divinity School: Education, Contest, and Change*, 234–51.

[4] Ibid., 20.

[5] Paris, "African American Presence," 250.

[6] Ibid., 251.

[7] A. W. Martin Jr., "The Lawson Affair, The Sit-Ins, and Beyond: Observations of an Eyewitness," *Tennessee Historical Society* 75/2 (2016): 142–65.

[8] Forrest Harris, *Ministry for Social Crisis: Theology and Praxis in the Black Church Tradition* (Macon, GA: Mercer University Press, 1997).

[9] W. E. B. DuBois, *The Negro Church: With an Introduction by Alton B. Pollard III* (Eugene, OR: Wipf and Stock Publishers, 2011).

[10] Richard C. Goode, "A School of Prophets of the New South," in *Vanderbilt Divinity School: Education, Contest, and Change*, 113.

[11] "Hill's Island: Stewarding an Island in the Cumberland," *Cumberland River Compact*, accessed May 31, 2024, https://cumberlandrivercompact.org/explore/explore-hills-island.

CHAPTER 1
[1] In early summer of 2019, Dr. Donald E. Greene and I met for breakfast at the Bennett Hotel in the iconic city of Charleston, South Carolina. Here, we planned, along with a film crew led by Santana Hayes, a documentary on the genesis of the black Baptist church in South Carolina. Greene is a prominent Baptist pastor of Orangeburg and president of its Education and Missionary Baptist Convention of South Carolina. We mutually agreed to start the project in Charleston for several reasons: (a) it is known as the premier port city for having brought millions of enslaved Africans into

North America; (b) it was known economically, during enslavement, as the premiere rice-producing city of the Western world; and (c) it is still known as the Protestant Vatican of North America because of its plethora of Protestant churches, which were built with enslaved labor during and after the colonial era. These huge sacred edifices, along with the ghostly spirit of slavery that lingers in Charleston, attract hundreds of thousands of tourists annually. All of this makes Charleston a queen city of religious and moral contradiction on the American landscape. Attempts to answer the question of the genesis and making of black Baptists and their organizational development must start with Charleston's enslavement history.

What did the enslaved learn and reappropriate from their enslavers' interpretations of the Gospel of Jesus Christ from the balcony sections of the latter's churches? For an answer, we must start with the genesis and making of the black preacher in the enslavers' churches. In the white church, the enslaver created the segregated ethos for the making of the black preacher and its complex phenomenon. We started with the question, How did the enslaved become Christian Baptist ministers under the canopy of the white Baptist enslavers' church? The literature for exploring an answer to the question is scarce. Scholars of religion have yet to show interest in addressing the problem critically in the literature of that era.

Charles Hamilton, a black political scientist, writing on the black preacher during the civil rights era, noted that from Nat Turner to Jesse Jackson, the black minister has always been a leader of his people. This has been the case in every epoch of the American experience. See *The Black Preacher in America* (New York: Morrow, 1972). Bishop Joseph Johnson, a black scholar with a PhD in New Testament studies, wrote *The Soul of the Black Preacher* (Cleveland: The Pilgrim Press, 1971). He addressed the phenomenon of the black preacher as the proclaimer of the Word of God to the oppressed. Johnson's read of the black preacher as a religious messenger was critical for understanding his role in the Civil Rights Movement of the 1960s.

Teaching thousands of black students during my professional career as a seminary professor has brought me face-to-face with the question, What is the genesis and the making of the black preacher? We sought to answer this question by starting the study at the First Baptist Church of Charleston. This iconic church was built with slave labor in 1683. Until the Civil War, it had a large membership of enslaved Africans.

[2] The *prophetic-preacher type* must be seen as antithetically evolving out of the *parrot-preacher type* in the enslaved community. This evolvement created such leaders as Demark Vesey and Harriet Tubman. The s/he must be seen as having been initiated into the enslaver's view of ministry under the parrot-preacher type. The prophetic-preacher type would have had to hear the voice of the enslavement community's Jesus of the wilderness. The *educator-preacher* type must be seen as the result of the work of the white Northern missionaries and the formerly enslaved community.

Here, I am using the ideal-type introduced by the famous social theorist Max Weber. The ideal-type for Weber is partial and perspectival in all of its aspects. It is dependent on cultural values in the selection of its object and on practical values in its construction, and it is a subjectively constructive distillation of relevant facts about a social tendency or activity and, therefore, cannot be a representation of historical or social reality. It is, as Weber says, a utopia. (See Peter Breiner, "Ideal-Types as 'Utopias' and Impartial Political Clarification: Weber and Mannheim on Sociological Prudence," in Laurence McFalls's *Max Weber's Objectivity Reconsidered* (Toronto: University of Toronto Press [2007] 2016.)

Understandably, the prophetic black preacher type, such as Nat Turner, Denmark Vesey, Sojourner Truth, and Harriet Tubman, is mentioned more often in the literary sources. It is clear in these sources that the white church had no intention of creating a prophetic-preacher type. The educator-preacher type was a collaborative creation of benevolent whites and those of the progressive black community following the Civil War.

[3] I intend the use of polarization to engender an understanding of these prototypes as observable depending on one's position in space/place and time while the thing/being itself remains a singular entity. See W. E. B. Du Bois, "Of the Faith of the Fathers," in *The Souls of Black Folk* (New York: Cosimo Publishing, 2007). W. E. B. Du Bois, *The Gift of Black Folk* (New York: Oxford University Press, 2014). Walter Bruggeman's interpretation of the interface of "prophetic" and "imagination" has greatly influenced my reading of the tension between the black prophetic preacher and the black parrot preacher types. Black prophetic preacher types "tell truth in a way and at an angle that assures it will not be readily co-opted or domesticated by hegemonic interpretive power." The black parrot preacher must be seen as having been robbed of his imagination by the white preacher he is parroting. See

Walter Bruggeman, *The Prophetic Imagination* (Minneapolis: Fortress Press, 2001, 2nd ed.).

[4] By *black consciousness*, I mean an "attitude of mind" that transcends the oppressor. See for an example the writings Mubarak Aliyu, "Steve Biko and the philosophy of Black consciousness," Africa at LSE (blog) August 19, 2021. https://blogs.lse.ac.uk/africaatlse/2021/08/19/steve-biko-philosophy-of-black-consciousness-theology-south-africa-bio/.

[5] The black preacher is probably one of the most artistic creations of the Western world, a complex religious and moral phenomenon. W. E. B. Du Bois, the eminent black sociologist, spoke to this fact in *The Souls of Black Folk* and *The Gifts of Black Folk*.

[6] The historical sources I have used for this body of work indicate that both females and males functioned in the role of religious/spiritual leaders during and following the period of chattel slavery in America. I acknowledge the absence of gender-inclusive language in many sources and for this reason will from this point in the text use both gendered pronouns interchangeably unless there are instances where the gendered pronoun is specific to the historical account. Mary Kemp Davis, *Nat Turner Before the Bar of Judgment: Fictional Treatments of the Southampton Slave Insurrection*, Southern Literacy Studies (Baton Rouge: Louisiana State University Press, 1999). University at Buffalo, *Harriet Ross Tubman (1819–1913) Timeline*. http://www.math.buffalo.edu/~sww/0history/hwny-tubman.html.

[7] We rely here upon biographical accounts of leaders such as Nat Turner and Harriet Tubman.

[8] See Arnold van Gennep, *The Rites of Passage* (Chicago: University of Chicago Press, 2019). See Victor Turner, "Liminality and Communitas." http://faculty.trinity.edu/mbrown/whatisreligion/PDF%20readings/Turner Victor-%20Liminality%20and%20Communitas.pdf.

[9] The use of the possessive pronoun *his* is intended to reflect the black preacher's and other enslaved people's connectivity through a reciprocal spiritual and communal kinship rather than *ownership* in similitude of the enslaver's ownership.

[10] Excerpt from "Florida Slave Narratives: Scott, Anna," Federal Writers' Project, 1937. Floripedia, https://fcit.usf.edu/florida/docs/s/slave/slave33.htm.

[11] Diane B. Stinton, *Jesus of Africa: Voices of Contemporary African Christology* (Maryknoll, New York: Orbis, 2004).

[12] Ibid.

[13] Ibid.

[14] Joseph R. Washington, *Black Religion: The Negro and Christianity in the United States* (Boston: Beacon Press, 1966).

[15] Gayraud S. Wilmore, *Black Religion and Black Radicalism: An Interpretation of the Religious History of Afro American History* (New York: Doubleday, 1972).

[16] Due to the length limitations of this essay, this idea is not further developed here. However, I make a nuanced use of the term *space* to suggest an extension of the perceived and actual reality for the enslaved in the condition of enslavement as well as a created moveable space in the collective imagination/consciousness of the enslaved as being in and surrounded by an unbounded spiritual freedom. Bruggeman.

[17] See "The Centennial Encyclopedia of the Bishops of the A.M.E Church." AME Bishop Stock Photos, https://www.gettyimages.com/ photos/african-methodist-episcopal-bishops. Starting with bishops, mulattos heavily dominated the church or roster.

[18] Van Gennep, *Rites of Passage*; Turner, "Liminality and Communitas."

[19] See G. D. Robinson, "Paul Ricoeur and the Hermeneutics of Suspicion: A Brief Overview and Critique," *Premise* 2/8 (September 27, 1995): 12.

[20] See Joy Ann Williamson-Lott, Linda Darling-Hammond, and Maria E. Hyler, "Emancipation and Reconstruction: African American Education 1865–1919," in *African American Education Citizenship, 1865–Present*, ed. Lawrence D. Bobo et al. (New York: Oxford University Press, 2012).

[21] Mark A. Noll, *The Civil War as a Theological Crisis* (Chapel Hill: University of North Carolina Press, 2006). Mark Noll's research illuminates how the Civil War as a theological crisis influenced the development of black religious leadership.

[22] Noll, *Theological Crisis*.

[23] Nadra Kareem Nittle, "The Short-Lived Promise of '40 Acres and a Mule'" at https:www.history.com/news/40-acres-mule-promise.

[24] These were the twenty black preachers of Savannah, Georgia, who met with General Sherman following the ending of the Civil War in 1865. "Sherman's Meeting with the Black Preachers of Savannah," in *The Wartime Genesis of Free Labor: The Lower South*, eds. Ira Berlin et al. (Cambridge: Cambridge University Press, 1991) 331–38. Ira Berlin, Barbara J. Fields, et al., *Free at Last: A Documentary History of Slavery, Freedom, and the Civil War* (New York: The New Press, 1993) 310–18, and in Ira Berlin, Joseph Patrick Reidy, and Leslie S. Rowland, eds., *Freedom's Soldiers: The Black Military Experience in the Civil War* (Cambridge: Cambridge University Press, 1998) 149–53.

[25] John Hayes, *Hard, Hard, Religion: Interracial Faith in the Poor South* (Chapel Hill: University of North Carolina Press, 2017) 116–17.

[26] See Gates's introductory chapter, "African American Citizenship," in the coedited volume *The Oxford Handbook of African American Black Citizenship, 1865–Present*. See Carla Peterson, "A Black Preacher Addresses Congress," *New York Times*, February 11, 2015. See also Herbert Aptheker, ed., *A Documentary History of Negro People in the United States* (Toronto: Citadel Press, 1968). Henry Highland Garnet, minister of the Fifteenth Street Presbyterian Church, Washington, DC, delivered a sermon in the US House of Representatives.

[27] Benjamin E. Mays and Joseph William Nicholson, *The Negro Church as Reflected in His Literature* (Eugene, Oregon: Wipf & Stock Publishers, reprint, 2010). Victor Turner, "Betwixt and Between: The Liminal Period in *Rites de Passage*," in *The Forest of Symbols: Aspects of Ndembu Ritual* (Ithaca, NY: Cornell University Press, 1967) 93–111. Van Gennep, *Rites of Passage*.

[28] See Keith Miller, "Martin Luther King, Jr., and the Black Folk Pulpit," *Journal of American History* 78/1 (June 1991): 120–23, Oxford University Press.

[29] Carter G. Woodson, *The Rural Negro* (Washington, DC: The Association for the Study of Negro Life and History), chapter 8, "Things of the Spirit."

[30] Bernard Powers, *Charleston and Black Reconstruction: A Social History, 1822–1885* (Fayetteville: University of Arkansas Press, 1994).

[31] See Daniel Wallace Culp, *Twentieth Century Negro Literature, or a Cyclopedia of Thought on the Vital Topics Relating to the American Negro*. Issue

71 of *Black Biographical Dictionaries, 1790–1950* (Naperville, IL: J. L. Nichols & Company, 1902; Ann Arbor: University of Michigan Press, 2008).

[32] Ibid.

[33] See Evelyn Brooks Higginbotham, *Righteous Discontent: The Women's Movement in the Black Baptist Church, 1880–1920* (Cambridge: Harvard University Press, 1994).

[34] Richard Allen, *The Life, Experience, and Gospel Labors of the Rt. Rev. Richard Allen* (Philadelphia: Martin and Boden, 1833): Archive org [1880]. On Daniel Payne, see *Recollections of Seventy Years* (Scotts Valley, CA.: Create Space Independent Publisher, reprint, 1991). Hayes, *Hard, Hard, Religion*, 116–17.

[35] Aubrey Thomas McClusky and Elaine M. Smith, eds., *Mary McLeod Bethune: Building a Better World, Essays and Selected Documents* (Bloomington: Indiana University Press, reprint, 2002).

[36] See the Darlington County Historical Commission, museum historian, Brian E. Gandy, African American Heritage sources on Brockenton, https://dchclbog.net/ip-brockenton/. See https:www.bucknell.du/meetbucknell/history-traditions/Edward-mcknight-brawley on Edward Brawley.

[37] Higginbotham, *Righteous Discontent*.

[38] Benjamin Elijah Mays, *Born to Rebel: An Autobiography* (Athens: University of Georgia Press, 2003).

[39] Richard I. McKinney, *Mordecai: The Man and His Message: The Story of Mordecai Johnson* (Washington, DC: Howard University, 1997).

[40] For more information on Jim Crow and Jim Crowism, see "Jim Crow Era" on the Jim Crow Museum of Racist Imagery website: https://jimcrowmuseum.ferris.edu/timeline/jimcrow.htm.

CHAPTER 2

[1] Early versions of this essay were first published as "Contour of an African American Public Theology" in the *Journal of Theology* (Summer 2000) and again as a paper entitled "Contour of an American Theology," collected by the Project in Lived Theology (www.livedtheology.org [2001]). It is here significantly, substantively, and specially revised for this collection in honor of Dr. Forrest E. Harris Sr.

[2] Victor Anderson, "The Search for Public Theology in the United States," in *Preaching as a Theological Task: World, Gospel, Scripture, In Honor*

of David Buttrick, ed. Thomas G. Long and Edward Farley (Louisville, KY: Westminster John Knox Press, 1996) 20–21.

[3] Victor Anderson, *Beyond Ontological Blackness: An Essay on African American Religious and Cultural Criticism* (London: Bloomsbury, 2016) 38.

[4] Cornel West, *Democracy Matters: Winning the Fight Against Imperialism* (New York: Penguin Press, 2004) 7–8; full explanation, "Democracy Matters Are Frightening in Our Time," chapter 1, 1–23.

[5] Paul Tillich, *The Religious Situation* (New York: Meridian Books, 1956) 5–6.

[6] Ibid.

[7] Anderson, *Beyond Ontological Blackness*, 38.

[8] Ibid.

[9] This distinction acknowledges that beyond the professional, academic, and theological community, many critical religious voices are addressing America's public crises from many sites, communities, and interests inclusive of Catholic churches, congregations, synagogues, temples, mosques, social media, nonprofits, and ordinary believers. This essay is restricted to the contour of an *academic public theology*. For a discussion of Catholic and Protestant public theology, see my essay, "The Search for Public Theology in the United States," in *Preaching as a Theological Task*, pp. 20–31, footnote 2.

[10] Victor Anderson, "Contour of an American Public Theology," *Project in Lived Theology*, www.livedtheology.org, 2001, 2; also, "Contour of an African American Public Theology," *Journal of Theology* (Summer 2000): 53.

[11] Anderson, "Contour of an American Public Theology," *Project in Lived Theology*, 2.

[12] Victor Anderson, "Pragmatic Naturalism and Public Theology," in *Pragmatic Theology: Negotiating the Intersections of an American Philosophy of Religion and Public Theology* (Albany: State University of New York Press, 1998) 110–32.

[13] Ibid., 53–92.

[14] Henry Nelson Wieman, "Theistic Religion," in *The Chicago School of Theology: Pioneers in Religious Inquiry*, ed. Jerome A. Stone and Peden Creighton (Lewiston, NY: Edwin Mellen Press, 1996) 66.

[15] Howard Thurman, *The Search for Common Ground* (Richmond, IN: Friends United Press: 1986) 74.

[16] Nancy Frankenberry, *Religion and Radical Empiricism* (Albany: State University of New York, 1987) 191.

[17] Ibid.

[18] James M. Gustafson, "God in Relation to Man and the World," in *Ethics from a Theocentric Perspective* (Chicago: University of Chicago Press, 1981) 236–51.

[19] Ibid., 246.

[20] Ibid., 246.

[21] Robert Corrington, *Nature & Spirit* (New York: Fordham University Press, 1992) 81.

[22] Howard Thurman, "Knowledge...Shall Vanish Away," in *For the Inward Journey: The Writings of Howard Thurman*, ed. Anne Spencer Thurman (Richmond, IN: Friends United Meeting, 1984) 11.

[23] Howard Thurman, *Jesus and the Disinherited* (Richmond, IN: Friends United Meeting, 1981) 108–109.

[24] Anderson, *Pragmatic Theology*, 119–20.

CHAPTER 3

[1] Several recent works bear this assertion out. Three works that have recently shaped my thinking include Anthea Butler, *White Evangelical Racism: The Politics of Morality in America* (Chapel Hill: University of North Carolina Press, 2021); Philip Gorski and Samuel L. Perry, *The Flag and the Cross: White Christian Nationalism and the Threat to American Democracy* (New York: Oxford, 2022); Bradley Onishi, *Preparing for War: The Extremist History of White Christian Nationalism—and What Comes Next* (Minneapolis: Broadleaf Publishing, 2023).

[2] Charity is as old as the ancient world; it offers immediate relief to those who need resources. However, several studies show charity's more insidious consequences in late capitalist societies. T. D. Mitchell, D. M. Donahue, and C. Young-Law, "Service Learning as a Pedagogy of Whiteness," *Equity & Excellence in Education* 45/4 (2012); J. Kahne and J. Westheimer, "Teaching Democracy: What Schools Need to Do," *Phi Delta Kappan* 85/1 (2003).

[3] Charity focuses on immediate relief from suffering. It does not interrogate the structures that create social suffering in the first place. Charitable giving raises the benefactor's psychological and social esteem but often shames the beneficiary for needing relief. Because charity offers such power-

ful inducements for those who give, there is little incentive to change the social arrangements that create inequity. Justice work that intends to flatten the social and economic hierarchy removes the social and psychological good experienced by the benefactor and may, in fact, shame the benefactor for enjoying social arrangements that are unjust.

[4] Empowering Congregations executive summary.

[5] "We will utilize, as an interactive narrative for the three areas of our focus, the Old Testament story of Nehemiah, a Jewish exile who became a 'cup bearer' or administrator to the king of Babylon and whose communal care was prime inspiration for a movement to rebuild the ruins back home in Jerusalem." *Thriving Congregations Executive Summary.*

[6] Herbert Robinson Marbury, *Imperial Dominion and Priestly Genius: Coercion, Accommodation, and Resistance in the Divorce Rhetoric of Ezra-Nehemiah* (Upland, CA: Sopher Press, 2012) 86–87.

[7] Herbert Robinson Marbury, "Nehemiah: Caught Between Court and Cult with Lessons for Church and State," in *Focusing Biblical Studies: The Crucial Nature of the Persian and Hellenistic Periods*, ed. Alice W. Hunt and Jon L. Berquist (New York: Bloomsbury Press, 2012).

[8] Bobby L. Lovett, *The African-American History of Nashville, Tennessee, 1780–1930: Elites and Dilemmas*, Black Community Studies (Fayetteville, AK: University of Arkansas Press, 1999) 221.

[9] Neil Websdale, *Policing the Poor: From Slave Plantation to Public Housing* (Boston: Northeastern University Press, 2001) 23.

[10] Lovett, *African-American History of Nashville*, 225–26.

[11] The same fears prompted a similar maneuver by the city in 1961. As the Civil Rights Movement ramped up and greater black political participation became imminent, it reconstituted itself as Metropolitan Davidson County to prevent a black voting majority in its capital city. "Historians: Metro Nashville's creation was rooted in race-related compromise" (tennessean.com).

[12] Lovett, *African-American History of Nashville*, 120.

[13] "Golden Age of Jefferson Street," https://www.jeffersonstreetsound.com/our-story

[14] Lovett, *African-American History of Nashville*, 249.

[15] David M. P. Freund, *State Policy and White Racial Politics in Suburban America* (Chicago: University of Chicago Press, 2010) 110.

[16] Richard Rothstein, *The Color of Law: A Forgotten History of How Our Government Segregated America* (New York: Liveright Publishing, 2017) 30.

[17] George Lipsitz, *The Possessive Investment in Whiteness: How White People Profit from Identity Politics,* rev. ed. (Philadelphia: Temple University Press, 2009) 6.

[18] Meizhu Lui, Barbara J. Robles, Betsy Leondar, Lara, Paula Jimeno, Augustin Torabene, *The Color of Wealth: The Story Behind the U.S. Racial Wealth Divide* (New York: New Press, distributed by W. W. Norton, 2006) 98.

[19] Isabelle Jones, Paula Jimeno Lara, and Agustin Tornabene, "Housing Segregation in Nashville: Exploring the Legacy of De Jure Segregation in Nashville" (2020) https://storymaps.arcgis.com/stories/050e09fabed0474b9687525fbc4e4c9a.

[20] Linda T. Wynn, "Interstate 40 and the Decimation of Jefferson Street." Paper presented at the Nashville Conference on African American History and Culture, Tennessee State University, 2019.

[21] Ibid.

[22] Campbell Haynes, "One Mile North," *Belmont Law Review* 8/1 (2020): 16–17.

[23] Ibid., 21–22.

[24] Wynn, "Interstate 40." See also Ibid., 23.

[25] See Haynes, "One Mile North," who devotes two sections of his article to chronicling the legal battle.

[26] Benjamin Houston and Project MUSE, *The Nashville Way: Racial Etiquette and the Struggle for Social Justice in a Southern City* (Athens: University of Georgia Press, 2012). https://yale.idm.oclc.org/login?URL=http://muse.jhu.edu/books/9780820343280/. 206.

[27] Houston, *The Nashville Way,* 207.

[28] Wynn, "Interstate 40."

[29] I refer to Raboteau's concept of the black church serving black life outside of white strategies of surveillance. Albert J. Raboteau, *Slave Religion: The "Invisible Institution" in the Antebellum South* (New York: Oxford University Press, 2004).

[30] Vision statement for Called to Lives of Meaning and Purpose.

[31] James H. Cone, *A Black Theology of Liberation: Twentieth Anniversary Edition* (Maryknoll, NY: Orbis, 1990) 1.

[32] Obery M. Hendricks Jr., *The Politics of Jesus: Rediscovering the True Revolutionary Nature of Jesus' Teachings and How They Have Been Corrupted* (New York: Crown Publishing Group, 2007).

[33] Empowering Congregations executive summary.

[34] Ibid.

[35] Ibid.

[36] See particularly, Marcus Garvey, *The Philosophy and Opinions of Marcus Garvey, Or, Africa for the Africans* (New York: Open Road Integrated Media). 32.

[37] Zora Neale Hurston, *Dust Tracks on the Road: An Autobiography* (Urbana: University of Illinois, 1984) 266–67.

[38] Empowering Congregations executive summary.

[39] Ibid.

[40] Anthony Barr and Andre M. Perry, "To Restore North Nashville's Black Middle Class, Local Policymakers Should Pursue Reparations" (Brookings Institute, 2021).

[41] To read the style of leadership taken by Nehemiah in his reforms as a warrant for the black church, reproduces the unjust structures that church is called to dismantle.

[42] Herbert Robinson Marbury, "Exogamy and Divorce in Ezra and Nehemiah," *The Oxford Handbook of the Historical Books of the Hebrew Bible*, ed. Brad E. Kelle and Brent Strawn (New York: Oxford University Press, 2020).

[43] This scene eerily and painfully conjures images of thousands of same-gender relationships that have been rent asunder for the sake of the church.

[44] Empowering Congregations executive summary.

[45] Ibid.

[46] Herbert Robinson Marbury, "Ezra-Nehemiah," in *The Africana Bible: Reading Israel's Scriptures from Africa and the African Diaspora*, ed. Hugh R. Page et al. (Minneapolis: Fortress Press, 2010).

CHAPTER 4

[1] Daniel A. Payne, *Recollections of Seventy Years* (New York: Arno Press, 1966) 154.

[2] Marvin A. McMickle, *An Encyclopedia of African American Christian Heritage* (Valley Forge: Judson Press, 2002) 22.

[3] Ibid., 76–78.

[4] Cornel West, in a back-page endorsement of Samuel DeWitt Proctor, *The Substance of Things Hoped For* (Valley Forge: Judson Press, 1995).

[5] Proctor, *Things Hoped For*, 113–15; Adam L. Bond, *The Imposing Preacher: Samuel DeWitt Proctor and Black Public Faith* (Minneapolis: Fortress Press, 2013) 56–59.

[6] "The 15 Greatest Black Preachers," *Ebony*, 49/1 (November 1993).

[7] McMickle, *African American Christian Heritage*, 114–15, and Proctor, *Things Hoped For*, 240.

[8] Bond, *Imposing Preacher*, 1.

[9] Bob Gore, *We've Come This Far: The Abyssinian Baptist Church–A Photographic Journal* (New York: Stewart, Tabori & Chang, 2001) 70–71.

[10] McMickle, *African American Christian Heritage*, 91–92.

[11] Jordan Buie, "Pastors Oppose Lesbian Bishop Speaker at Baptist College," March 10, 2015, https://www.tennessean.com/story/news/2015/03/10/pastors-oppose-lesbian-bishop-at-baptist-college/24727465/.

[12] Anthony Moujaes, "UCC Minister Yvette Flunder Won't 'Bow to Threats' Over Baptist College Appearance," March 18, 2015, https://ucc.org/yvette_flunder_baptist_college_03182015/.

[13] Abraham Lincoln in a temperance address, in Henry Louis Gates Jr., ed., *Lincoln on Race & Slavery* (Princeton: Princeton University Press, 2009) 14.

[14] Ibid.

[15] Haley Sweetland Edwards, "How Christine Blasey Ford's Testimony Changed America," *Time* (October 4, 2018). https://time.com/5415027/christine-blasey-ford-testimony/

[16] Elizabeth Dias, "The Evangelical Fight to Win Back California," *New York Times*, May 27, 2018, 1.

[17] David Crary, "Placing Their Faith in Gender Equality," *Newark Star Ledger*, January 15, 2019, A1.

18 Steve Osunsami and Sarah Netter, "4th Man Accuses Bishop Long," ABCNews.com, September 24, 2010.

19 Ida B. Wells, *Crusade for Justice: The Autobiography of Ida B. Wells*, ed. Alfreda M. Duster (Chicago: University of Chicago Press, 1970) 40.

20 Ibid.

21 Liam Stack, "Pastor Who Praised Pulse Nightclub Gunman Resigns After Allegedly Paying for Sex," January 9, 2019. https://www.nytimes.com/2019/01/09/us/donnie-romero-orlando-shooting-prostitutes.html#:~:text=A%20Baptist%20minister%20in%20Texas,paying%20for%20sex%20with%20prostitutes.

22 Ken Camp, "Denominational Leader Jimmy Allen Dies at Age 91," January 9, 2019. https://www.baptiststandard.com/news/baptists/denominational-leader-jimmy-allen-dies-at-age-91/

23 Kate Shellnutt, "J.D. Greear Elected Youngest Southern Baptist President in Decades," June 12, 2018. https://www.christianitytoday.com/news/2018/june/jd-greear-elected-southern-baptist-president-sbc-2018.html

24 Art Toalston, "Southern Baptist Leader Frank Page Resigns Over 'Morally Inappropriate Relationship,'" March 27, 2018. https://www.christianitytoday.com/news/2018/march/frank-page-resigns-southern-baptist-executive-committee-sbc.html

25 Amy Harmon, "Southern Baptist Leader Removed as Seminary President for Remarks on Women," May 23, 2018. https://www.nytimes.com/2018/05/23/us/southern-baptist-seminary-leader-removed.html

26 Walter Fluker, *The Ground Has Shifted: The Future of the Black Church in Post-Racial America* (New York: NYU Press, 2016).

27 Kathy Gannon, "Afghanistan's Taliban Order Women to Cover Up Head to Toe," AP News (May 7, 2022). https://apnews.com/article/afghanistan-taliban-49b17d77d03022ad4817eeecf4f5da93

28 Marvin A. McMickle, "Minority Rule Is Upon Us, as Draft of *Roe v. Wade* Opinion Reveals," *PlainDealer.com*, May 6, 2022.

CHAPTER 5
1 Henry H. Mitchell and Emil M. Thomas, *Preaching for Black Self-Esteem* (Nashville, TN: Abingdon Press, 1994) 133.

[2] Fred B. Craddock, *Preaching* (Nashville, TN: Abingdon Press, 1985) 27.

[3] David Buttrick, *A Captive Voice: The Liberation of Preaching* (Louisville, KY: John Knox Press, 1994) 30.

[4] Lenora Tubbs Tisdale, *Preaching as Local Theology and Folk Art* (Minneapolis: Fortress Press, 1997) 57.

[5] Craddock, *Preaching*, 164.

[6] Frank A. Thomas, *They Like to Never Quit Praisin' God: The Role of Celebration in Preaching* (Cleveland: United Church Press, 1997) 5.

[7] Richard Ward, *Speaking from the Heart: Preaching with Passion* (Nashville, TN: Abingdon Press, 1992) 48–49.

[8] Ibid.

[9] James Bryce, *Studies in History and Jurisprudence, Volume I* (New York: Macmillan Company, 1901), chapter 6.

[10] Noel Leo Erskine, *King Among the Theologians* (Cleveland: Pilgrim Press, 1994) 173.

[11] George Rawick, ed., *The American Slave: A Composite Autobiography, 1936–1938, Volume 8* (Westport, CT: Greenwood, 1972), Arkansas Pt. 1, 35.

[12] Peter J. Paris, *The Social Teaching of the Black Churches* (Minneapolis: Fortress Press, 1985) 117.

[13] Ibid.

CHAPTER 6

[1] See Forrest E. Harris Sr., *Ministry for Social Crisis: Theology and Praxis in the Black Church Tradition* (Macon, GA: Mercer University Press, 1993) 1–7.

[2] Forrest E. Harris Sr., James T. Robertson, and Larry Darnell George, eds., *What Does It Mean to Be Black and Christian? Pulpit, Pew, and Academy in Dialogue* (Nashville, TN: Townsend Press, 1995) ix–xvi, 1–190; Forrest E. Harris Sr., ed., *What Does It Mean to Be Black and Christian? The Survival of a Whole People–The Meaning of the African American Church* (Nashville, TN: Townsend Press, 1998) vii–x, 1–168.

[3] Harris et. al. eds., *Pulpit, Pew, and Academy*, ix–xvi.

4? Ibid.; *Meaning of the African American Church*, vii–x, 49–67, 73–81, and 113–22.

5 *Meaning of the African American Church*, 1–12.

6 See William H. Frey, *Diversity Explosion: How New Racial Demographics Are Remaking America* (Washington, DC: Brookings Institution Press, 2018) 1–20, 131–48, 167–90, 213–44; Christopher Caldwell, "The Browning of America: A Review of Diversity Explosion: How Racial Demographics Are Remaking America, by William H. Frey," *Claremont Review of Books* 15/1 (Winter 2014–2015).

7 Frey, *Diversity Explosion*, 1–20; Caldwell, "The Browning of America"; Domenico Montanaro, "How the Browning of America Is Upending Both Political Parties," National Public Radio, October 12, 2016. https://www.npr.org/2016/10/12/497529936/how-the-browning-of-america-is-upending-both-political-parties/.

8 Montanaro, "Browning of America"; Ezra Klein, "White Threat in a Browning America: How Demographic Change Is Fracturing Our Politics," *Vox* (July 30, 2018). https://www.vox.com/policy-and-politics/2018/7/30/17505406/trump-obama-race-politics-immigration/.

9 "SPLC Fights Back Against Bigotry in White House," *SPLC Report* 47/1 (Spring 2017): 1, 3.

10 Frederick Wine, "The Rev. King's Dream Has Finally Come True: Letters to the Editor," *The Tennessean*, November 6, 2008, 15A; Tim Wise, *Between Barack and a Hard Place: Racism and White Denial in the Age of Obama* (San Francisco: City Lights Books/Open Media Series, 2009) 17–149. The newspaper columnist Charles Blow rightly questions the premise that the changing demographics potentially benefit blacks in their struggle against white supremacy and oppression. This trend is already reinforcing and, indeed, increasing white racial fears and resentment. White Americans' determination to maintain their institutions and structures of privilege should never be underestimated. The United States could possibly become a carbon copy of the old apartheid South Africa, in which a white minority maintains white supremacy and oppression through violence; voter intimidation and suppression; divide-and-conquer tactics aimed at communities of color; and other devious means. See Charles M. Blow, "The Impact of the Browning of America on Anti-Blackness," *Austin American Statesman*, November 16, 2021,

https://www.statesman.com/story/opinion/2021/11/16/blow-impact-browning-america-anti-blackness/8622659002/.

[11] "Immigration Fervor Fuels Racist Extremism," *SPLC Report* 36/2 (June 2006): 1, 3; "SPLC Helps Nation Combat Hate after Charlottesville," *SPLC Report* 47/3 (Fall 2017): 1, 3.

[12] "SPLC Launches New Initiatives to Fight Online Extremism," *SPLC Report* 51/4 (Winter 2021): 1, 3.

[13] For a sense of the SPLC's range of activities in recent years, see "SPLC Steps Forward to Protect the Human Rights of Immigrants," *SPLC Report, Special Edition* (2012) 1–2; "SPLC Sues to Restore Miss. Citizens' Voting Rights," *SPLC Report* 48/2 (Summer 2018): 1; Bryan Fair, "SPLC Fights White Supremacy, Threats to Democracy in 2020," *SPLC Report* 49/4 (Winter 2019): 1, 3.

[14] Martha Waggoner, "'Poor People's Campaign' Readies Its Effort for Nationwide Mobilization: Activists Say Government Ignoring Poverty in the US," *The Tennessean*, February 5, 2018, 14A.

[15] This topic is explored at some length in Lewis V. Baldwin, *The Voice of Conscience: The Church in the Mind of Martin Luther King, Jr.* (New York: Oxford University Press, 2010) 101–40, 219.

[16] Quoted in Baldwin, *Voice of Conscience*, 219.

[17] See Cleve R. Wootson Jr., "Rev. William Barber Builds a Moral Movement," *The Washington Post*, June 29, 2017; Waggoner, "'Poor People's Campaign.'"

[18] Baldwin, *Voice of Conscience*, 242–43.

[19] Martin Luther King Jr. held and consistently expressed this viewpoint. See Martin Luther King Jr., *Stride Toward Freedom: The Montgomery Story* (New York: Harper & Row, 1958) 224; Martin Luther King Jr., "The Negro Gains in Rights–1965," unpublished and typed version of a speech, Atlanta, November 10, 1965, the King Papers, Library and Archives of the Martin Luther King Jr. Center for Nonviolent Social Change (henceforth abbreviated as KCLA for King Center Library Archives) Atlanta, 18–19. At other points, King described the Negro as "the conscience of the Western World." See Martin Luther King Jr., "People to People," unpublished version of an essay prepared for *New York Amsterdam News*, September 17, 1964, KCLA, 2; Baldwin, *Voice of Conscience*, 189, 242–43.

[20] Phyllis I. Radford and Bob Brown, eds., *Alternative Truths* (Benton City, WA: B Cubed Press, 2017) iv–vi; Mahita Gajanan, "Kellyanne Conway Defends White House's Falsehoods as 'Alternative Facts,'" *Time*, January 22, 2017, https://time.com/4642689/kellyanne-conway-sean-spicer-donald-trump-alternative-facts/; John Cassidy, "Donald Trump's Alternative Reality Press Conference," *The New Yorker*, February 16, 2017. https://www.newyorker.com/news/john-cassidy/donald-trumps-alternative-reality-press-conference.

[21] Rufus Burrow treats Martin Luther King Jr. as a striking example of such a figure in the nation's history. See Rufus Burrow Jr., "Martin Luther King, Jr., and Ethical Leadership," *Telos* 182 (Spring 2018): 11–28.

[22] Christopher Schaberg, *The Work of Literature in an Age of Post-Truth* (New York: Bloomsbury Publishing, 2018) 1–2; Lee McIntyre, *Post-Truth* (Cambridge, MA: MIT Press, 2018) 1–34; Radford and Brown, *Alternative Truths*, iv–vi; Sophia Rosenfeld, *Democracy and Truth: A Short History* (Philadelphia: University of Pennsylvania Press, 2019) 2, 15, 20.

[23] Eddie Glaude Jr., "The Black Church Is Dead," *HuffPost* (blog), April 26, 2010, updated August 23, 2012, https://www.huffpost.com/ entry/the-black-church-is-dead_b_473815.

[24] Du Bois declared in 1903 that "the Negro church today is the social center of negro life in the United States, and the most characteristic expression of African character." Woodson observed in 1939, some thirty-six years later, that "the Negro church touches every ramification of the life of the Negro" and that "a definitive history of the Negro church, therefore, would leave practically no phase of the history of the Negro in America untouched." See W. E. B. Du Bois, *The Souls of Black Folk*, in *Three Negro Classics*, ed. John Hope Franklin (New York: Avon Books, 1965) 340; Carter G. Woodson, "The Negro Church, an All-Comprehending Institution," *The Negro History Bulletin*, 3/1 (October 1939):7.

[25] Eddie S. Glaude Jr., "Updated with Response: The Black Church Is Dead—Long Live the Black Church," *Religion Dispatches* (March 15, 2010), https://religiondispatches.org/bupdated-with-responseb-the-black-church-is-dead-long-live-the-black-church/.

[26] Ibid.

[27] Ibid.

[28] Ibid.

[29] Ibid.

[30] Ibid.

[31] E. Franklin Frazier's image of the Negro church as "a refuge in a hostile white world" in the late nineteenth and early twentieth centuries still holds true to some degree today. See E. Franklin Frazier, *The Negro Church in America* (New York: Schocken Books, 1963) 44–46.

[32] Winthrop Hudson acknowledged these positive dimensions of black church life decades ago, and his analysis is still very relevant to any discussion of the roles of black churches today. See Winthrop S. Hudson, *Religion in America* (New York: Charles Scribner's Sons, 1965) 225, 351.

[33] See King, *Why We Can't Wait*, 91–92.

[34] David Weigel, "What Makes a Black Cleveland Pastor Back Donald Trump?," *The Washington Post*, July 17, 2016; Lawrence Ross, "Donald Trump's Factory of Ignorant Black Surrogates," *The Root*, August 31, 2016, https://www.theroot.com/donald-trump-s-factory-of-ignorant-black-surrogates-1790856566; Kia Morgan-Smith, "Black Pastors Meet with Trump and Get Blasted by Social Media for Accomplishing Nothing," *The Grio*, August 2, 2018, https://thegrio.com/2018/08/02/black-pastors-meet-with-trump-and-get-blasted-by-social-media-for-accomplishing-nothing/; Fred Lucas, "Trump 'Most Pro-Black President,' Pastor Says in White House Meeting," *Daily Signal*, August 2, 2018, https://www.dailysignal.com/2018/08/02/trump-most-pro-black-president-pastor-says-in-white-house-meeting/; Dave Boyer, "Black Pastor Calls Trump More 'Pro-Black' Than Barack Obama," *The Washington Times*, August 2, 2018, https://www.washingtontimes.com/news/2018/aug/2/black-pastor-calls-donald-trump-more-pro-black-bar/; Jesse Washington, "Why Trump's Tiny Band of Black Supporters Stick with Him," *Andscape*, October 17, 2016, https://andscape.com/features/why-trumps-tiny-band-of-black-supporters-stick-with-him/; and Rebecca Falconer, "Trump Meets with African American Pastors Amid Accusations of Racism," *Axios*, July 30, 2019, https://www.axios.com/2019/07/30/trump-black-pastors-meeting-amid-racism-claims.

[35] See, for example, Sabrina Tavernise, "In Trump's Remarks, Black Churches See a Nation Backsliding," *The New York Times*, January 14, 2018; "AME Church Responds to Trump's Racist Rhetoric," *Los Angeles Sentinel*, January 17, 2018, https://lasentinel.net/ame-church-responds-to-trumps-

racist-rhetoric.html; and William J. Barber II, "Rev. Barber: An Open Letter to Clergy Who Prayed with Donald Trump," *ThinkProgress*, July 19, 2017, https://archive.thinkprogress.org/an-open-letter-to-clergy-who-prayed-with-trump-7876ee87dbc2/.

[36] See Gayraud S. Wilmore, *Black Religion and Black Radicalism: An Interpretation of the Religious History of African Americans* (Maryknoll, NY: Orbis, 1998) 190.

[37] Baldwin, *Voice of Conscience*, 222.

[38] John Blake, "Pastors Choose Sides Over Direction of Black Church," *Atlanta Journal-Constitution*, February 15, 2005, 1A; and Ibid., 223.

[39] John Blake, "Modern Black Church Shuns King's Message," CNN, April 6, 2008, https://www.cnn.com/2008/US/04/06/mlk.role.church/index.html; Baldwin, *Voice of Conscience*, 223.

[40] Ibid.

[41] Baldwin, *Voice of Conscience*, 223–24; Wilmore, *Black Religion and Black Radicalism*, 190.

[42] Baldwin, *Voice of Conscience*, 224.

[43] King further elaborated this point in a brilliant sermon outline prepared during the early days of his pastorate at Dexter Avenue Baptist Church in Montgomery. Entitled "The One-Sided Approach of the Good Samaritan," this piece celebrated what the Good Samaritan did for the wounded Jew on the Jericho road, but it criticized the Good Samaritan for not investigating "the lack of police protection on the Jericho road" and for not appealing to "public officials to set out after the robbers and clean up the Jericho road." "Here was the weakness of the Good Samaritan," King declared. See Martin Luther King Jr., *Strength to Love* (Philadelphia: Fortress Press, 1981; originally published in 1963) 30; ed. Clayborne Carson et al., *The Papers of Martin Luther King, Jr., Volume VI: Advocate of the Social Gospel, September 1948–March 1963*, 7 vols. (Berkeley: University of California Press, 2007) 239–40; Baldwin, *Voice of Conscience*, 233.

[44] King, *Strength to Love*, 30; Carson et al., King Papers, 239–40; Baldwin, *Voice of Conscience*, 233.

[45] "The Black Church in the Age of False Prophets: An Interview with Gayraud Wilmore," in Iva E. Carruthers, Frederick D. Haynes III, and Jeremiah A. Wright Jr., eds., *Blow the Trumpet in Zion!: Global Vision and Ac-

tion for the 21st-century Black Church (Minneapolis: Fortress Press, 2004) 171–72.

[46] Martin Luther King Jr., *The Trumpet of Conscience*, 68; Washington, *A Testament of Hope*, 280–81.

[47] Baldwin, *Voice of Conscience*, 227.

[48] Martin Luther King Jr., "Transformed Nonconformist," unpublished and typed version of a sermon, Ebenezer Baptist Church, Atlanta, January 16, 1966, King Papers, KCLA, 4–5; King, *Strength to Love*, 59; Baldwin, *Voice of Conscience*, 227.

[49] See DeWayne R. Stallworth, *Existential Togetherness: Toward a Common Black Religious Heritage* (Eugene, OR: Pickwick Publications, 2019) 137, 140–41. King was very critical of the kinds of attitudes and actions that lead to structures of privilege in certain black Christian communities. He identified the historical thread of elitism and classism within the black church and also the deficiency in the area of social activism due in large part to what he called morbid class consciousness. This is clear from a close reading of his sermons "A Knock at Midnight" and "The Drum Major Instinct." See King, *Strength to Love*, 63; and Clayborne Carson and Peter Holloran, eds., *A Knock at Midnight: Inspiration from the Great Sermons of Reverend Martin Luther King, Jr.* (New York: Warner Books, 1998) 169–86.

[50] Blake, "Pastors Choose," 1A.

[51] This is the point coursing through parts of Baldwin, *Voice of Conscience*, 222–49.

[52] The late Eddie Long, who pastored the massive New Birth Missionary Baptist Church in Dekalb County, Georgia, for many years, reflected much of this attitude. He declared, "We're not just a church, we're an international corporation. We're not just a bumbling bunch of preachers who can't talk and all we're doing is baptizing babies. I deal with the White House. I deal with Tony Blair. I deal with presidents around the world. I pastor a multimillion-dollar congregation." See Baldwin, *Voice of Conscience*, 227–28, 350, n5; Jasmyn Connick, "Pimpin Ain't Easy: The New Face of Today's Black Church," *Jacksonville Free Press* 19/40 (October 20–26, 2005): 4.

[53] Baldwin, *Voice of Conscience*, 228.

CHAPTER 7

[1] Martin Luther King Jr., *Where Do We Go from Here: Chaos or Community?*, (Boston: Beacon Press, 1967) 177.

[2] Forrest E. Harris Sr., "American Baptist College: The Official Report of the President 2020," 11, https://abcnash.edu/wp-content/uploads/2021/06/Presidents-Report-2021_FE.pdf.

[3] James H. Cone and Gayraud S. Wilmore, "Black Theology and African Theology: Considerations for Dialogue, Critique, and Integration," in Gayraud S. Wilmore and James H. Cone, *Black Theology: A Documentary History, 1966–1979* (Maryknoll, NY; Orbis, 1979) 1:463–76; introduction, 445.

[4] R. N. Fiedler and J. W. Hofmeyr, "The Conception of the Circle of Concerned African Women Theologians: Is It African or Western?" *Acta Theologica* 31/1 (2011): 40–41, 53–56; and Helen A. Labeodan, "Revisiting the Legacy of the Circle of Concerned African Women Theologians Today: A Lesson in Strength and Perseverance," *Verbum et Ecclesia* 37/2 (2016).

[5] Cornel West, "Black Theology of Liberation as Critique of Capitalist Civilization," ed. James H. Cone; and Gayraud S Wilmore, *Black Theology: A Documentary History, Volume 2: 1980–1992* (Maryknoll, NY: Orbis, 1993) 2:410–16.

[6] See, for example, Katie Cannon, *Black Womanist Ethics* (Oxford: Oxford University Press, 1988); J. N. K. Mugambi, *Christian Theology and Social Reconstruction* (Nairobi: Acton Press, 2003); Sunday Bobai Agang, "Work," ed. Sunday Bobai Agang et. al., *African Public Theology* (Lakewood, WA: Hippo Books, 2020); Vuyani S. Vellem, "Black Theology of Liberation and the Economy of Life," *The Ecumenical Review* 67/2 (July 2015).

[7] Quoted in West, "Black Theology of Liberation," 414.

[8] Sunday Bobai Agang, "The Need for Public Theology in Africa," in Agang et. al., *African Public Theology*, 8.

[9] Forrest E. Harris Sr., "A Theological Reading of Liberation and Spirituality: Mapping Justice for the Poor," (n.d., unpublished paper on file with author).

[10] See the National African-American Reparations Commission website for details on these objectives, https://reparationscomm.org/reparations-plan/.

[11] Forrest E. Harris Sr., "Pursuing American Racial Justice and a Politically and Theologically Informed Black Church Praxis," ed. R. Drew Smith et. al., *Contesting Post-Racialism: Conflicted Churches in the United States and South Africa* (Oxford: University Press of Mississippi, 2015).

CHAPTER 8

[1] Brian K. Blount, *Go Preach! Mark's Kingdom Message and the Black Church Today* (New York: Orbis, 1998) 234.

[2] See Dale A. Johnson, ed., *Vanderbilt Divinity School: Education, Contest, and Change,* (Nashville, TN: Vanderbilt University Press, 2001) 134–35; 238–39; 396, n.9.

[3] See Forrest E. Harris Sr., *Ministry for Social Crisis: Theology and Praxis in the Black Church Tradition* (Macon: Mercer University Press, 1993) 3–5.

CHAPTER 9

[1] Forrest E. Harris Sr., "Forward," *The Black Church Studies Reader*, ed. Alton B. Pollard III and Carol B. Duncan (New York: Palgrave Macmillan, 2016) ix–xi.

[2] Lewis V. Baldwin, "Black Church Studies as an Academic Interest and Initiative: A Historical Perspective," in *In the Black Church Studies Reader*, ed. Alton B. Pollard III and Carol B. Duncan (New York: Palgrave Macmillan, 2016) 31–55.

[3] Ibid., 32.

[4] Ibid.

[5] Henry H. Mitchell, "Black Church Studies: Some of the Roots," *The Black Church Studies Reader*, ed. Alton B. Pollard III and Carol B. Duncan (New York: Palgrave Macmillan, 2016) 15–21.

[6] Gayraud S. Wilmore, "Black Church Studies as Advocate and Critic of Black Christian Ecclesial Communities" *The Black Church Reader*, ed. Alton B. Pollard III and Carol B. Duncan (New York: Palgrave Macmillan, 2016) 23–30.

[7] William H. Myers, "The Hermeneutical Dilemma of the African American Biblical Student," in *Stony the Road We Trod: African American Biblical Interpretation,* ed. Cain Hope Fielder (Minneapolis: Fortress Press, 1991) 40–50. William H. Myers, "Zoom-ing in on a Watershed Moment in Biblical Interpretation," in *Bitter the Chastening Rod: Africana Interpretation*

after Stony the Road We Trod *in the Age of BLM, SayHerName, and MeToo*, ed. Mitzi J. Smith, Angela N. Parker, and Ericka S. Dunbar Hill (New York: Lexington Books/Fortress Academic, 2022) 25–35.

CHAPTER 10

[1] Quinester Knox Calloway compiled much of this history of William Haynes for the Haynes School alumni group. See "Reverend William Haynes, 1850–1933," http://www.haynesalumni.yolasite.com/resources/Rev%20William%20Haynes.pdf. Calloway graduated from and later taught at the school. She was also an elementary school principal and wife of an ABC alumnus Rev. Paul Calloway. Her research on Reverend Haynes was confirmed by his grandson Joe Herrod, a 1944 Haynes graduate.

[2] Rev. William Haynes is listed as founder or pastor of Spruce Street, Sylvan Street, Roger Heights, and Pleasant Green Baptist churches in Nashville.

[3] Calloway, "Reverend William Haynes."

[4] Ibid.

[5] Arthur Vertrease Haynes, *Scars of Segregation* (New York: Vantage Press, 1974).

[6] Ibid.

[7] College President: Demographics and Statistics in the US, https://www.zippia.com/college-president-jobs/demographics/ (2019).

[8] "2021 State of Black America," 11, National Urban League; https://nul.org/sites/default/files/2021-07/NUL-SOBA2021-ES-web.pdf. The report was taken from a study by the Hamilton Project of the Brookings Institute.

[9] Teammates were Sydney McLaughlin, Allyson Felix, Dalilah Muhammad, and Athing Mu.

[10] Catherine Schaffer, "6 Facts About Economic Inequality in the U.S.," Pew Center, February 7, 2020.

[11] Ryan P. Burge, "The Nones: Where They Came From, Who They Are, and Where They Are Going," 2021. African Americans' numbers are increasing in this group. http://religionnews.com/2021/03/24/the-nones-are-growing-and-growing-more-diverse/.

[12] David Brooks, "The Dissenters Trying to Save Evangelicalism from Itself," *New York Times*, February 4, 2022.

[13] Oprah Winfrey and Bruce D. Perry, *What Happened to You? Conversations on Trauma, Resilience, and Healing* (New York: Flatiron Books, 2021) 129.

[14] Jamiles Lartey, "Diane Nash: 'Non-violent Protest Was the Most Important Invention of the 20th Century," *The Guardian*, April 6, 2017.

[15] Kuhardt Film Foundation, Diane Nash Full Interview: King in the Wilderness, August 1, 2018, 9:59.

[16] Hanna Rosin, "AME Church Elects Its First Female Bishop," http://www.washingtonpost.com/archive/politics/2000/07/12/ame-church-elects-its-first-female-bishop/8d825ccf-5817-43f3-9780-bd445ac66900/?tid=ss_mail.

[17] "A.M.E. Church May Elect Its First Woman as Bishop." https://www.nytimes.com/2000/07/09/us/ame-church-may-elect-its-first-woman-as-bishop.html?referringSource=articleShare.

[18] Bishop E. Anne Henning-Byfield, funeral of Dr. Jamye Coleman Williams, January 28, 2022, Big Bethel AME Church, Atlanta.

[19] Jamye Coleman Williams and McDonald Williams, eds. *The Negro Speaks: The Rhetoric of Contemporary Black Leaders* (Noble and Noble, 1970).

[20] Henning-Byfield, 1:51:5. You Tube Video is "01-28-22 Celebration of the Life – Dr. Jamye C. Williams. You Tube. Big Bethel AME Church"

[21] Jesse Williams, director, *Bearing Witness: A Profile of Darnella Frazier*, ESPN, The Undefeated.

[22] Ibid.

[23] Winfrey and Perry, *What Happened to You*, 203.

[24] Longtime residents assume the familiar last names represent these and other outstanding figures.

CHAPTER 11

[1] Peter J. Paris, *The Social Teaching of the Black Churches* (Minneapolis: Fortress Press, 1985).

[2] Kelly Brown Douglas, *Sexuality and the Black Church: A Womanist Perspective*. Orbis, Kindle edition.

CHAPTER 12

[1] Eddie S. Glaude, Jr., "The Black Church is Dead," HuffPost: The Blog (August 23, 2012), https://www.huffpost.com/entry/the-black-church-is-dead_b_473815.

[2] See the Gloria T. Hull, Patricia Bell-Scott, and Barbara Smith, eds.s, *All the Women Are White, All the Blacks Are Men, But Some of Us Are Brave: Black Women's Studies*, (New York: Feminist Press, 1982).

[3] Forrest E. Harris, Sr. et al. eds. *What Does It Mean to Be Black and Christian: The Meaning of the African American Church*, Vols. 1 & 2 (Nashville, TN: Townsend Press; 1995).

[4] Howard Thurman, *Jesus and the Disinherited* (Nashville: Abingdon Press, 1949), 7.

[5] Martin King, "Letter from the Birmingham City Jail," Philosophical Thought, August 12, 2022, https://open.library.okstate.edu/introphilosophy/chapter/letter-from-the-birmingham-city-jail/.

[6] Vincent Harding, Hope and History, *Why We Must Share the Story of the Movement*, (Maryknoll, NY: Orbis, 1990), 10.

[7] Sluggite Zone, Jeremiah Wright's Sermon, "Confusing God and Government," (http://www.sluggy.net/forum/viewtopic.php?p=315691&sid=4b3e97ace4ee8cee02bd6850e52f50b7).

CHAPTER 13

[1] Walter E. Fluker, *The Ground Has Shifted: The Future of the Black Church in Post-Racial America* (New York: New York University Press, 2016).

[2] Unless noted otherwise, the King James Version of the Bible was used for biblical references herein.

[3] Howard Thurman, "Exposition of the Book of Habakkuk," November 19, 1956, *The Interpreter Bible*; reprinted in *The Papers of Howard Washington Thurman*, ed. Walter E. Fluker, 4 (2016): 136–49.

[4] In his sermon of the same title, one first notices King's improvisational play with great ideas, borrowed from the critique of social conformity by Henry Emerson Fosdick, Eugene Austin, and other sources. See Keith D. Miller, *Voice of Deliverance: The Language of Martin Luther King, Jr., and Its Sources* (New York: Free Press, 1992) 105–108, 110–11, 164.

[5] Vincent L. Wimbush, "Interpreters—Enslaving/Enslaved/Runagate," *JBL* 130/1 (2011): 5–24.

[6] According to Vincent Wimbush, the term *runagate* is an alternate form of *renegate*, from Middle Latin *renegatus*, meaning "fugitive" or "runaway." It has come to carry the meaning of a more transgressive act than mere flight. It is marronage, running away with an attitude and a plan, a taking flight—in body, but even more importantly in terms of consciousness.

[7] Phrase used by Jürgen Moltmann in *Theology of Hope*, trans. W. Leitch (New York: SCM Press, 1967) and Moltmann, *God in Creation: A New Theology of Creation and the Spirit of God*, trans. Margaret Kohl (Minneapolis: Fortress Press, 1993) 92.

[8] Wahneema Lubiano, ed., *The House That Race Built: Black Americans, U.S. Terrain* (New York: Pantheon, 1997).

[9] Here, I am entertaining the notion of "democratic space." Creating democratic space signifies the ongoing struggle against the reconfiguration of space and the reordering of time for subjugated bodies that deny their inherent worth and dignity and, therefore, their freedom and equality, both before the law and in practice. This idea is represented in political philosopher Jacques Rancière's notion of "*policing* as the rule that governs the body's appearing, a configuration of *occupations* and the properties of the spaces where these *occupations* are distributed." Here, the concern is with the *demos* that are not accounted for in the configuration of power, those relegated to animal life with sound (*phônê*) but cannot speak. Nonetheless, these bodies dare to speak, break, shift, and redefine the spaces they have been assigned. Because they dare to use speech (*logos*), they reveal the process of equality, because only a free human can speak. *Politics*, on the other hand, is "an extremely determined activity antagonistic to *policing*; whatever breaks with the tangible configurations whereby parties or the lack of them are defined by a presupposition that by definition, has no place in that configuration—that of the part of those who have no part." Jacques Rancière, *Disagreement: Politics and Philosophy*, trans. Julie Rose (Minneapolis and London: University of Minnesota Press, 1999) 29–30. Beyond the facility of speech as a mark of rationality (rational communication), I am also interested in this brief discussion in the human capacity for "affective experiences, occurrences in the world, or aesthetic events" that cannot be thought but are *embodied* and *experienced* in the sense of freedom and equality as profoundly imaginative and creative potentialities that point to newness, openness, expectation, and

boundary-less-ness. Unlike Rancière's definition of politics, my imaginary theological project seeks something akin to *paraousia* (παρουσία), i.e., the coming presence that denotes expectation, advent, and celebration that extends into the political. For quote, see Charles. E. Scott, "The Betrayal of Democratic Space," *Journal of Speculative Philosophy* (University Park: Pennsylvania State University, 2009) 22/4 (2008): 304. See Jean-Luc Nancy, *The Experience of Freedom* (Redwood City, CA: Stanford University Press, 1994).

[10] James H. Cone, "The Story Context of Black Theology" *Theology Today* (July 1976).

[11] The Book of Habakkuk, unlike most prophetic books, provides no biographical information about its author. Because of its mention of the Babylonians, also known as the Chaldeans, who came to prominence around 612 BCE, we know that it was written after that date. Scholars have disagreed on whether it was written before or after the destruction of the Judean kingdom in 586 BCE by the Babylonian armies under King Nebuchadnezzar, but this debate is not a primary concern for us in this presentation.

[12] W. E. B. Du Bois, "A Litany of Atlanta," in James Weldon Johnson, ed., *The Book of American Negro Poetry* (New York: Harcourt, Brace, and Company, 1922).

[13] Thurman, "Exposition of the Book of Habakkuk," November 19, 1956, *The Interpreter Bible*; reprinted in *The Papers of Howard Washington Thurman*, ed. Walter Earl Fluker, 4 (2016) 136–49.

[14] Ibid., 142.

[15] Howard Thurman, *With Head and Heart* (New York: Harcourt, Brace Jovanovich, 1979) 193.

[16] See Fluker, *The Ground Has Shifted*, "Returning to the Little House Where We Lived and Made Do," 165–96.

[17] Octavia Butler, *The Parable of the Sower* (New York: Grand Central Publishing, reprint, 2019); see also theologian Monica Coleman's and Afrofuturist author Tananarive Due's monthly webinars called "Octavia Tried to Tell Us."

[18] As Stuart Hall suggests, "The future belongs to the impure. The future belongs to those who are ready to take in a bit of the other, as well as being what they themselves are. After all, it is because their history and ours is so deeply and profoundly and inextricably intertwined that racism exists. For otherwise how could they keep us apart?" Hall, "Subjects in History:

Making Diasporic Identities," in Wahneema Lubiano, *The House That Race Built: Black Americans, U.S. Terrain* (New York: Pantheon Books, 1997) 299. For use of "grotesque," see Victor Anderson, *Creative Exchange: A Constructive Theology of African American Religious Experience* (Minneapolis: Fortress, 2008). I have also made the same arguments in Fluker, *The Ground Has Shifted*.

[19] Robin D. G. Kelley, *Freedom Dreams: The Black Radical Imagination* (Boston: Beacon Press, 2002) 35. For a fuller exposition of the Exodus narrative in the African American cultural imaginary see chapter 1, "Dreams of a New Land," 13–35.

[20] To use the language of the late Richard Iton, this is the "search of the black fantastic," "a genre that destabilizes, at least momentarily, our understandings of the distinctions between the reasonable and the unreasonable, and reason itself, the proper and the improper, and propriety itself, by bringing into the field of play those potentials we have forgotten or did not believe accessible or feasible." Iton, *In Search of the Black Fantastic: Politics and Popular Culture in the Post-Civil Rights Era (Transgressing Boundaries: Studies in Black Politics and Black Communities)* (New York and London: Oxford University Press, 2010) 290.

[21] James Baldwin, "Nothing Personal," *The Price of the Ticket: Collected Non-fiction 1948–1985* (New York: St. Martin's/Marek, 1985) 393.

[22] Raphael G. Warnock, *The Divided Mind of the Black Church: Theology, Piety, and Public Witness* (New York: New York University Press, 2014) 185–89.

[23] "The Broken One" represents both the broken body of Christ and the many bodies that are broken at *crossing(s)*. The source of hope for African American church traditions has and continues to be in theological constructions of the Cross. See Fluker, *The Ground Has Shifted*, 41; 142–61.

AFTERWORD
[1] Forrest Harris, *Ministry for Social Crisis: Theology and Praxis in the Black Church Tradition* (Macon, GA: Mercer University Press, 1993).

[2] Ibid., p. 48.

[3] Ibid., p. 49.

[4] Ibid.

[5] Forrest Harris, "Self-Amending Blackness and The Movement for Black Lives: Justice and Leadership in Liberatory Spaces," in *Moved by the*

Spirit: Religion and the Movement for Black Lives, ed. Christophe D. Ringer, Teresa L. Smallwood, and Emilie M. Townes (Lanham, Maryland: Lexington Books, 2023).

[6] Ibid.

[7] Ibid.

[8] Forrest Harris, "Pursuing American Racial Justice and a Politically and Theologically Informed Black Church Praxis," in *Contesting Post-Racialism: Conflicted Churches in the United States and South Africa*, ed. R. Drew Smith, William Ackah, Anthony G. Reddie, and Rothney S. Tshaka (Jackson: University Press of Mississippi, 2015).

[9] Ibid.

[10] Ibid.

[11] Forrest Harris, "The Children Have Come to Birth: A Theological Response for Survival and Quality of Life," in *Walk Together Children: Black and Womanist Theologies, Church, and Theological Education*, ed. Dwight N. Hopkins and Linda E. Thomas (Eugene, Oregon: Wipf and Stock Publishers, 2010).

[12] Ibid.

[13] Ibid.

[14] Jordan Buie, "Pastors Oppose Lesbian Bishop Speaker at College," *USA Today Network – Tennessee*, March 10, 2015.

[15] Ibid.

APPENDIX B

[1] See Desmond Tutu, "Liberation Is Costly," in *Singing the Living Tradition* (Boston: Unitarian Universalist Association, 1993) 593.

[2] See Annie Powell, "Hold on to Your Dream: African American Protestant Worship," in *Women at Worship: Interpretations of North American Diversity*, ed. Marjorie Procter-Smith and Janet R. Watson (Louisville, KY: Westminster/John Knox Press, 1993) 43–53.

[3] James Baldwin, *No Name in the Street* (New York: Dial Press, 1972) 196.

[4] See James M. Washington, ed., *A Testament of Hope: The Essential Writings and Speeches of Martin Luther King, Jr.* (San Francisco: Harper and Row, 1986) 286.

[5] Tutu, *Singing the Living Tradition*, 593.

⁶ Victor Anderson, *Creative Exchange: A Constructive Theology of African American Religious Experience* (Minneapolis: Fortress Press, 2008) 3.

⁷ See John D. Carlson, "The Justice We Need," *The Immanent Frame* (website), November 13, 2008,
https://tif.ssrc.org/2008/11/13/the-justice-we-need/.

⁸ Powell, "African American Protestant Worship," 43–53.

⁹ Cornel West's book *Democracy Matters: Winning the Fight against Imperialism* (New York: Penguin Press, 2004) is a must-read for black churches who take seriously a democratic and prophetic vision of liberation in America.

¹⁰ See Carlyle Fielding Stewart III, *African American Church Growth: 12 Prophetic Principles for Prophetic Ministry* (Nashville: Abingdon Press, 1994).

¹¹ Allison Calhoun-Brown, "What a Fellowship: Civil Society, African American Churches, and Public Life" in R. Drew Smith, ed., *New Day Begun: African American Churches and Civic Culture in Post-Civil Rights America, Volume I* (Durham: Duke University Press, 2003).

¹² Pablo Richard, "A Theology of Life: Rebuilding Hope," in *Spirituality of the Third World*, ed. K. C. Abraham and Bernadette Mbuy-Beya (New York: Orbis, 1994).

¹³ See Dale P. Andrews, *Practical Black Theology for Black Churches: Bridging Black Theology and African American Folk Religion* (Louisville, KY: John Knox Press, 2002), in which he argues that black theology's otherworldly critique of black churches is misdiagnosis of the folk tradition of black religious culture and praxis.

¹⁴ See Archie Smith Jr.'s article "We Need to Press Forward: Black Religion and Jonestown, Twenty Years Later," Alternative Considerations of Jonestown and Peoples Temple website, 1998, Accessed from https://jonestown.sdsu.edu/?page_id=16595] in which Smith gives an important analysis of the kind of trauma faced by victims of the Jonestown, Guyana, crisis. The reference to the high rates of poverty in the Ninth Ward in New Orleans is taken from media releases regarding the hardest hit areas of Hurricane Katrina.

¹⁵ See Smith's and U Riedel-Pfafflin's article "Death and the Maiden: The Complexity of Trauma and Ways of Healing—A Challenge for Pastoral Care and Counseling," in K. H. Federschmidt and D. J. Louw, eds. *In-*

tercultural and Interreligious Pastoral Caregiving. Dusseldorf: Society for Intercultural Pastoral Care and Counselling, 2015.

[16] Emilie M. Townes, *Breaking the Fine Rain of Death: African American Health Issues and a Womanist Ethic of Care* (New York: Continuum, 1998) 23–25.

[17] See Andrews, *Practical Black Theology*, 10.

[18] Manning Marable, "Black Leadership, Faith, and the Struggle for Freedom," in *Black Faith, and Public Talk*, ed. Dwight Hopkins (Waco, TX: Baylor University Press, 2007).

Indexes

Colleges, Seminaries, and Universities

People

315

Topics